LOOKING BEYOND THE MIRROR

Twelve Steps to Overcoming Self-doubt

TRICIA BRENNAN

NEW
HOLLAND

First published in Australia in 2005 by
New Holland Publishers (Australia) Pty Ltd
Sydney • Auckland • London • Cape Town

14 Aquatic Drive Frenchs Forest NSW 2086 Australia
218 Lake Road Northcote Auckland New Zealand
86 Edgware Road London W2 2EA United Kingdom
80 McKenzie Street Cape Town 8001 South Africa

10 9 8 7 6 5 4 3 2 1

National Library of Australia Cataloguing-in-Publication Data:

Brennan, Patricia, 1957– .
Looking beyond the mirror: twelve steps to overcoming self-doubt

ISBN 1 74110 254 5.

1. Self-actualisation (Psychology). 2. Motivation
(Psychology). 3. Compulsive behavior—Anecdotes.
4. Inspiration—Anecdotes. 5. Conduct of life—Anecdotes.
I. Title.

158.1

Publisher: Fiona Schultz
Managing editor: Angela Handley
Project editor: Monica Berton
Printer: Griffin Press, Adelaide
Cover image: Getty Images
Back cover photograph: Clinton Gaughran

Although every effort has been made to verify the accuracy of the information contained in this book, it is not a substitute for medical or professional opinion. Neither the author nor the publishers can be held responsible for any loss, injury or inconvenience sustained by any person using this book. The names of people mentioned in this book have been changed to protect their privacy.

CONTENTS

ACKNOWLEDGMENTS

I relish this opportunity to express my gratitude to each and every one of my cherished friends, both seen and unseen, who are a constant source of love and inspiration. You bring magic to my world, awaken my spirit and nourish my soul.

During the course of writing this book I was prompted to overcome a few specific areas of my own self-doubt. My progress was steady and swift thanks to the generous contribution of Fleur Brown, who stood on the sidelines with a watchful eye, ready to offer her support. I am truly grateful for the time she spent proofing each chapter and making positive suggestions. Above all else, she helped me realise I have the power to go beyond my limits by reminding me to trust my creative resources.

I am also grateful to Russell for being there to lend a helping hand and encourage me to hold the vision.

I would also like to thank Theresa Miller for her invaluable contribution in editing the manuscript. It was a pleasure to work with someone I absolutely trust.

A special note of thanks to Selwa Anthony, a woman I greatly admire and respect. Her guidance, insight and wisdom have proven invaluable. I feel truly blessed to have met her in the remarkable way that I did. Her presence serves as a reminder that the journey towards success can be a happy, graceful one.

To Tania, who is an angel in my world—thanks for always believing in me and lifting my spirits during our 'conversations in the car'.

I would also like to acknowledge David for his unceasing generosity—I am sincerely grateful to you for helping me discover more of my heart. Thank you for the countless dozens of roses and for inviting me into your world.

INTRODUCTION

Of all the cities in the world, Los Angeles is surely a monument to how we artfully create 'illusion' within the limits of our physical reality. It's a city that offers makeovers to bring out your full potential with one swift swipe of the credit card. Where else can a girl have her breasts enlarged, hair extended, wrinkles removed, marriage terminated and palm read all on one street? A mecca for the rich and famous, LA is a beacon for what is possible. This is where looks, glamour and power are ranked highest on the priority list.

I've spent a lot of time in this city as well as other cities during the past fifteen years, helping many wealthy, powerful and attractive people unravel the mystery of why, despite their vast achievements, they are still not happy. Have power and money made them feel secure? Do a 'perfect body' and a high profile satisfy their hearts? Unfortunately, in many cases the answer is no.

While you may be tempted to disregard these celebrities as superficial or even arrogant, how many of us 'simple folk' have fallen prey to the same antics of the ego? We may downplay the influence of the media, yet how many of us fully accept ourselves in a world where 'performance and appearance' are celebrated more often than a person's essence and the quality of their heart?

The title of this book, *Looking Beyond the Mirror*, came about from the observation that so many of us walk around in a trance with no idea of who we really are. We fall asleep under the ego's spell and become far too attached to our external self-image. Many of us become addicted to upholding that image at any cost, believing that it alone will get us what we want. Yet we are challenged when it comes to connecting with our soul—or our deeper essence—which is where the source of true happiness lies.

So how do we break the spell? When we realise we have the power to transform our lives by acknowledging the importance of our feelings and changing the way we see ourselves.

As an intuitive counsellor, my capacity to 'read' people is based on my clairaudient, clairsentient and clairvoyant abilities. My perceptive nature allows me to go beyond the identity of an individual and uncover their deepest fears, aspirations and fundamental beliefs. Working with people in this way over many years has taught me one specific lesson—no matter who we are, where we live, or what we do, we all struggle with self-doubt.

I am about to give you an insider's view of what goes on beneath the facade of a select group of people who have risen above mediocrity to create extraordinary lives. I have chosen to write about individuals who by 'worldly standards' may appear to have everything. I have done so to accentuate the fact that, despite appearances, they are still challenged by the same issues we all face.

There are twelve diverse individuals portrayed in this book. As I disclose their personal profiles, I go way beyond what most people see to expose their strengths and challenges. By presenting the 'inside story', we can all learn by observing their emotional issues and repetitive patterns. Each of the twelve tales conveys a message on the pitfalls of addictive behaviour and offers a remedy for self-doubt.

Those baffling questions about finding love and peace are finally put to rest. By getting to the heart of the matter, some of the answers that normally elude us are easily revealed. The masks are dismantled and the illusion is shattered to finally disclose the truth.

At the end of each chapter, I pose a series of questions to help you evaluate the relationship you have with yourself and discover your strengths and your weaknesses. If you are willing to draw on the twelve virtues highlighted at the end of each tale and summarised at the end of the book, you will attain a state of power and balance.

Over the years, I have sat in sessions with men and women from all walks of life, of different ages and many nationalities. I have counselled an array of people from housewives, businessmen, celebrities, professors, doctors, to therapists and even renowned spiritual teachers. No matter what a person's identity may reveal, beneath the surface, we are fundamentally all the same.

We all think and feel, and the quality of our thoughts and feelings determines exactly what we experience. Even beyond who we 'think' we are, the most important thing of all is how we genuinely feel about ourselves. This became very apparent to me when I met with one of the most talked about celebrities in Hollywood who despite her obvious beauty and talent, struggles with addiction and fluctuating body weight. What was missing in her world? There was one important feature—a generous amount of self-love.

CHAPTER ONE

A CHANGE OF ATTITUDE BRINGS A CHANGE OF HEART

The way we alter the quality of our life is to know we are worth the effort it takes and care enough about ourselves to make those changes.

As I entered the gates of my client's Hollywood Hills mansion for our first session, I was reminded of the grand villas in Tuscany. Pulling up in the driveway, a friendly, young girl, who introduced herself as the actor's personal assistant, greeted me. She escorted me into the library, which housed an impressive collection of paintings and artworks. On the mantelpiece was also a touching collection of family photographs. Looking at them, it seemed plain to me that the woman I was about to meet had a passion for life and a sensitive nature. Portrayed in the photos as a mother, a lover and a devoted daughter, her charms extended way beyond the parameters of what her vast audience saw.

She has been acclaimed as a living goddess who, at times, has fallen out of favour with the media because of her emotional frailty. Despite her vivacious, worldly demeanour, she is vulnerable to judgment and criticism. This was to be my first meeting with her, which proved to be a very valuable one. Not only for her, as she found solace in my counsel, but it also reminded me of the pitfalls of competition and comparison. Here was a woman who had graced the covers of top fashion magazines and yet she still wasn't convinced of her intrinsic beauty.

As my client entered the room, I was a little taken aback. At first glance, she seemed much smaller in stature than she appeared on screen. Her long hair pinned up loosely with a few stray locks falling about her face. Wearing little makeup, her skin was clear and a little flushed. She wore a pair of tight yoga pants, highlighting the sculpted contours of her thighs. Being someone who also works out in the gym regularly, I know how much effort it takes to develop that level of muscle tone. I complimented her on the wonderful shape of her legs, knowing at times she battled with her weight. She told me she had taken up jogging with her husband. It may seem strange that someone who carries the title of 'spiritual teacher' would raise the topic of body sculpting. But even after all my years of meditating on the essence of life itself, I am still susceptible to exalting the human physique.

I found it somewhat surprising she referred to her jogging partner as 'her husband' rather than using his name. The man is an icon in his own right, an acclaimed actor and 'sex symbol'. Living with a partner who is admired by millions would surely be a test for anyone's confidence. Especially when the critics are constantly scrutinising your looks and performance. Perhaps that was why she wanted to meet with me—to clarify, once and for all, why she was constantly in a state of unrest.

We sat together quietly as I realigned my focus by going into a light meditation. My attention moved beyond the boundaries of the physical world and through my intuitive abilities, I entered the sanctuary of her inner thoughts and feelings. Peering through a window into her soul I began to sense what she was experiencing. In this moment I sat before one of the most attractive, charismatic and highly talented women in America and yet, I could see she was plagued by insecurity.

My first impression of what she was experiencing was a sense of powerlessness. I described an image of her drifting down a narrow river looking very frail, with no oars in the boat. As I continued to interpret the metaphor, the tears began to roll down her cheeks. Her deepest emotions had been suppressed for so long that when she started to cry she felt a sense of relief. She had fought most of her life to maintain the profile of being gentle, demure and loving to such a degree she had compromised her strength of will. Her fear of moving beyond her restricted self-image was diminishing the assertive side of her nature. For fear of being viewed as tough, she watered down her strength and vigour at the very times she needed to take a stand for what she really believed in.

There were times she felt lonely, wanting her partner to engage with her emotionally, but instead of communicating her needs, she would give way to his headstrong nature. She wanted to share her deepest views on life with him but he seemed more concerned with his sensual gratification and bolstering his own career. Her desire to please him led her to play the role of the supportive, yielding companion and in the process she denied her own preferences and betrayed her heart. Both her past relationships and her current marriage exhibited the same behaviour.

Rather than expressing her anger and frustration, she'd suppress it by reaching for comfort food. Consequently, she then felt heavy and unattractive. The heaviness was based on her feelings of powerlessness or being 'stuck' and so she'd drink alcohol to escape or 'feel lighter'. In those moments, the childlike, playful side of her nature would surface and her partner would re-engage.

This cycle continued repeatedly and she remained trapped, betraying herself to satisfy her lover. What she really wanted was to be taken seriously, but her core belief was that men couldn't take her seriously because she was unable to fully hold their attention. She attracted partners who flirted with other women, and while she outwardly dismissed that as part of their personalities, she was deeply hurt. Such flirtations simply reinforced her belief that she wasn't good enough.

We talked about what specific qualities she needed to develop to alter this destructive pattern. The first thing was to communicate her dissatisfaction and request her partner make the effort to support a more intimate relationship. This meant she would need to be assertive and take a stand for her feelings. She would have to risk being seen as aggressive or selfish, which was her greatest fear. Interestingly enough, those are the very qualities her partner sometimes displayed and which had a detrimental effect on the relationship.

I suggested she consider finding the middle ground. Rather than become aggressive or demanding, she could choose to be more assertive and still maintain her gentleness. If she were willing to clearly communicate her preferences rather than explicitly telling people what to do, she would retain her sensitivity and no longer feel a need to manipulate through weakness. For her to be receptive to seeing herself as a powerful woman of substance, she had to be willing to release her preconceived ideas of what that really meant. To her way of thinking, a woman is tender and loving, or independent and outspoken. She needed to realise she could be both.

The universe was telling her it was time to expand the stage she played on and walk with pride wherever she was. As an actor, she had no reservations setting her sights high. Being remarkably creative and a free spirit, she loved to perform. For her, acting was fun. While acting, her focus was on self-expression without seeking approval. She was able to bypass her self-doubt and give way to her passion. In contrast, when it came to affairs of the heart, she sought outside validation for her self-worth. This left her susceptible to attracting men who were difficult to please and competed for status in the relationship.

Her choice in partners simply aligned with her negative beliefs and she saw herself as weak and powerless. She was afraid of having too much impact on men apart from being the seductress. That was acceptable to her; being domineering or forceful wasn't. Her partners were then given free rein to play the dominant role. At times she would subtly manipulate them by playing helpless and they would feel compelled to comply. Although she would eventually get her way, her dignity was stripped bare and her sense of worth suffered.

This woman longed to feel powerful. It was clear she needed to get to the core of the issue rather than search for a coping mechanism. This was the only way she would ever change her behaviour once and for all. Her anxiety had nothing to do with the men in her life; it was all about her limited perception of the value of her love. She felt unappreciated in her romantic relationships simply because she didn't fully appreciate herself. If she did, she would have responded to her partners differently when their arrogance and vanity surfaced. Her compassion and kindness alone were enough to attract adoration. Ironically, if she were to incorporate those two distinct qualities into the relationship with herself, her change of attitude would have transformed her life.

Compassion and kindness are also traits that give a person substance. I suggested she reflect on that statement until the penny dropped. She was known for taking a stand for others less fortunate than herself. Yet she would continually downplay the power of her love when it came to making a difference. She needed to turn down the volume on the cynical part of her mind, which constantly berated her generous efforts. I recommended she change her priorities from magnifying her faults to taking stock of her attributes. Not once, not twice, but continuously throughout the day.

Those internal words of encouragement would help her develop her inner strength, which in turn would boost her confidence and courage. She needed to take on the role as a loving guardian in the relationship she was developing with herself, rather than projecting that responsibility onto her partner. Her childlike qualities needed to be balanced with discipline and discernment. If she were willing to adopt the attitude of being a thoughtful caretaker, she would naturally make more positive life choices.

When it came to being a loving mother for her children, she was extremely conscientious. With the men in the world, she had no problem nurturing their needs and considering their feelings. But when it came to taking care of herself, the guardian went to sleep. The protective, gentle sides of her nature were overruled by overindulgence and self-punishment. The harsh critic that dominated her thoughts provoked negative behaviour and left her feeling fractured.

It is not as if she was incapable of change. There were times when she paid particular attention to her diet and exercise program. Unfortunately, it was during pre-production for a film or when she had a significant public event. During those periods she would hire a personal trainer who would closely monitor her behaviour. Her partner would also train with her at times, which would inspire her to make the effort. But left to her own devices, she lacked motivation. Until she was ready to make those positive changes for herself—not for the director, not for the public, not for her partner, but for herself—she would continue to fluctuate from one extreme to the other.

As our session together progressed, I offered my client the following counsel, 'Any superficial or half-hearted decisions you make in order to seek approval will leave you feeling empty. It is important that your head and your heart are in harmony to bring substance to your choices and actions, otherwise you will feel as though you 'have to' or 'should' rather than have a genuine desire to do something beneficial for yourself. Whatever you do will feel like a chore, a struggle or even like torture, unless you are willing to enjoy the benefits and are open to reaping the rewards. It is impossible for you to wholeheartedly enjoy anything unless you are in touch with your feelings. And unless you are sensitive to your feelings, you will continue to make detrimental choices.

'The key is to consider what you ultimately want to experience and then give yourself permission to have precisely what you want. Not an extra slice of pie, not a second margarita, not a cigarette or another dose of pills, but what you really want, which is to feel better about yourself. If you make the effort to feel good about yourself as often as you can, you will instinctively sense what will genuinely satisfy you and take the steps to bring it about.

'Whenever you feel powerless, you are just like a child rebelling when it's told it can't have another cupcake. You struggle internally for control. And in the same way a child does, if you defy your caretaker, you end up feeling sick after sneaking an extra chocolate bar and regret your actions. You ignore the better judgment, opt for instant gratification, and then suffer the long-term consequences—all under the pretext of pleasure or fun. That 'instant hit' of getting your own way makes you feel powerful and you are temporarily satisfied, which turns out to be a pleasure that is short-lived. Eventually, the feelings of powerlessness return and you simply perpetuate the cycle all over again.

'So how do you break the cycle? Before you make a choice or decision, be very clear on where you are coming from. Which part of you is giving direction? Is it the benevolent caretaker that lives in your heart or the unruly child? Be mindful of how you ultimately want to feel before you take action. Every choice and decision you make is based on how you see yourself and who you believe you are. If you let the self-doubting parts of you drive your thoughts, you will drive yourself into the ground. It takes discipline to be mindful and you are worth the effort. If you remain sensitive to your feelings, you will know when you have gone off track. The bottom line is—unless you are compassionate and generous with yourself and willing to take positive action to support your best interests, your life will never change.'

After the session, I drove through the gates of that majestic property, thinking about how so many people are deceived by outward appearances. What really counts is the quality of the relationship we have with ourselves. No matter how many worldly possessions we have or how many accolades we receive, if we are not at peace with ourselves, we will still feel incomplete.

LOOKING BENEATH THE SURFACE

What can we learn from this 'Hollywood star'? Although many actors seem confident on the surface, when it comes to their emotional lives they are challenged like the rest of us. There is nowhere to hide in intimate relationships, unless you close down and restrict your self-expression. Unfortunately, that is precisely what many of us do when we are afraid of criticism. We play a specific role we believe is safe and are careful not to overstep the boundaries—which is exactly what an actor does.

With my client, it was obvious she needed to be honest with herself and her partner and express her true feelings. Unless she was willing to be more assertive, she would remain powerless and continue to disregard her worth. Whenever she felt overly sensitive or anxious, she needed to be acknowledged. Unless she was willing to pay attention to her genuine desires, she would continue to stuff her feelings down by reaching for substitutes such as food, alcohol or pills. Those feelings would simply resurface because she wasn't getting what she really wanted.

She expected her partner to make her feel better about herself. When she felt connected to her partner she felt secure, and when she didn't she felt incomplete. When she wasn't being loved in a way where she felt acknowledged, she felt empty. She would then look at herself to assess what was missing rather than tell herself that she was already enough. It was the way she related to her husband that was the problem and not that she was deficient.

She needed to love herself first and then take action to change the situation. If she were willing to forget about everybody else just for a moment and consider her feelings first, she would start to realise how important her happiness was. Yet this seems to be the most difficult thing for all of us to do. Staying true to herself, while she remained sensitive to the feelings of her loved ones was her greatest challenge. In fact, it turned out to be her most significant life lesson. Despite her countless admirers, her greatest fear was loneliness. It was essential she give up her attachment to having the 'perfect' identity if she was to achieve self-love. Otherwise her ego would continue to take control and she would be left feeling incomplete.

For my client it came right down to two choices: she could continue to be critical and hard on herself, or practise self-acceptance. At the end of the day, she is the one who determines her own value and is ultimately the caretaker of her life. Her desire to change and grow was prompted by the critical side of her nature and not her sense of worth. No matter how many people came to offer their aid and support, unless she was willing to take responsibility for her own wellbeing, it would have little effect. Self-love was the component necessary to spark her growth and that meant changing the way she saw herself.

Like our Hollywood star, we all need to remember the basic rule—'every decision you make in your life is based on how you see yourself and who you believe you are'.

This screen goddess was ultimately responsible for what she created in her world. If she wasn't willing to own that power she would remain susceptible to being a victim. Far too often she looked at the people in her life and questioned how much they loved her. A more substantial question would have been: 'How much do I love myself?'

Our celebrity needed to take a stand for her feelings. In order to break the recurring pattern, she needed to stay alert and deal with what was in front of her instead of numbing the pain through substance abuse. Unless she was absolutely genuine in her desire to give up the pain permanently, she would continue to carry the burden.

Like all of us, she needed to realise she was worth the effort.

THE CARETAKER
BECOMING YOUR OWN BEST FRIEND

What we can all take from her story is how important it is that we consider our feelings and stop being so hard on ourselves. If we don't consider how important our feelings are, no one will. Asking for help and being open to support is a positive step towards change. Taking the first step independently is an absolute must.

It doesn't matter how small your first step is; if it is a positive action prompted by self-love, it is a step in the right direction.

Good health and vitality are essential if we want to make the most of our lives. If we feel good emotionally, we are more apt to feel better physically and our energy increases. When we are bogged down by negative emotions, we struggle to get through the day. That is why it is imperative we consider the way we treat ourselves and then request that others do the same.

If you find yourself in a position where you don't want to be honest with someone because you prefer to avoid conflict, then you need to get clear that you are surrendering to fear rather than protecting yourself through love. When you accept the position of being the caretaker in your life, then you are no longer susceptible to being a victim to circumstances. Caring for yourself will allow you to intuit your best course of action. Following the gentle voice of your heart will keep you safe and nurtured and help you avoid careless choices. You are then protected by decisions, based on seeing yourself as valuable.

If you feel powerless in any area of our life, you are likely to sabotage yourself. If you have an uncontrollable urge to do anything that you know is detrimental to your physical, emotional or mental wellbeing, then you are at the mercy of your habitual behaviour. At this point you need to let the heroic part of your nature come forward and remind yourself you are worth the effort and there is another way. Take a stand in the name of self-love. If you are willing to summon the courage and be more resourceful, you are going to feel far better about yourself in the long run. You will then make way for more of your power and beauty to come to the surface.

We can go to great lengths to change our appearances but unless we learn to respect our feelings, our emotional experience will remain the same.

KEY QUESTIONS TO ASK YOURSELF

This is a checklist to see how on track you are with being *The Caretaker* in your relationship with yourself.

1. Are you open to making positive changes to alter the quality of your life?
2. Why do you want to change?
3. Who do want to change for—yourself, because you care about the way you feel, or to make a good impression on someone else?
4. Do you attend to your needs and consider your preferences?
5. Do you nurture yourself and allow yourself to enjoy the benefits?
6. How important do you make your feelings in comparison to other people's feelings?
7. Are you willing to take affirmative action to protect your best interests?

Chapter Two

GETTING THE BIGGER PICTURE

*If we constantly compare ourselves to others, we will form unrealistic ideas of who
we are supposed to be in order to be loved, or what it takes to be successful,
then we will continue to believe we are 'not good enough' on some level.*

Working as a stylist and art director in the advertising industry for many years, I spent a lot of time behind the scenes watching people transform their appearance in a matter of minutes. Fresh-faced young girls wearing jeans and t-shirts would enter the makeup and wardrobe departments and emerge as glamorous cover girls.

There were also occasions when models would arrive early in the mornings, hung over and dishevelled, and I would wonder what the hell the casting agents were thinking. The models would throw their overstuffed tote bags on the floor and take a seat in front of a mirror ablaze with lights. Every sign of minor neglect was visible on their faces. After a couple of cups of black coffee and a few drags on a cigarette they would lean back, close their eyes and surrender to the make-up artist and hairdresser to perform their magic. With the twist of a curling iron and wave of a mascara wand, they evolved into high fashion goddesses.

After stripping down to a flesh tone g-string, they wriggled their tiny hips and squeezed their lithe bodies into their outfits. Over the years I helped dress some of the most graceful, well-proportioned bodies imaginable. Sadly, I also saw many girls who were so emaciated I was concerned for their health. I noticed when the crew stopped for lunch these models would bury their nose in a book or talk on their mobile phone, rather than sit and enjoy a proper meal. Others would survey the caterer's table, searching for any morsels free of fat, sugar or carbohydrates. Occasionally I came across extremists who carried out clandestine activities in the ladies room after lunch. Judging by the amount of dessert they'd consumed, I suspected they were getting rid of the evidence...with a quick flush of the toilet.

Not surprisingly, many of these girls felt tired and weak after a typical twelve-hour shoot, yet they'd still push themselves through a gruelling workout at the gym. Couldn't they have waited until the next morning, when they weren't booked on a job? Of course not: they had casting sessions. And besides, the following day they needed to work out again—and again—and again! Had they ever considered the word 'balance'? Then again, with the way their measurements were scrutinised, they had a hell of a lot to live up to. After dressing the models, I would escort them on to the set to gain the director's 'approval'. I lost count of how often the order of the day was long legs, lean thighs and well-rounded breasts. I would cringe when the director would ask, 'Can't we have more cleavage?' My response was always, 'Nothing that a little tape and padding can't fix'.

It is remarkable what tricks the art department can perform. And now with the help of computer editing, you can shave a girl's thighs or embellish her curves with a simple 'drag and click'. Trying to live up to those fantasy figures has prompted ordinary women to pursue more unrealistic dietary restrictions and surgical cuts than ever before. But what have we sacrificed in the process? From my observation, we've devalued our uniqueness. Do we really believe having the 'perfect' face and body will win us the ultimate drawcard in life? Looks can be deceiving, and so can our egos.

After taking a six-month sabbatical to write my second book, I returned to the advertising world with fresh eyes. It took me a while to acclimatise to the fast pace and shift of priorities after living very simply in a sleepy coastal town. Spending long periods on my own in retreat gave me the opportunity to commune with my soul.

My sense of what was important altered. Unlike many women, I was finally free of angst when I faced my wardrobe each morning to ask, 'What am I going to wear?'

My first booking when I arrived back in Sydney was for a well-known hosiery company. It was redesigning its packaging and wanted a new, more sophisticated image. My inspiration would be drawn from the pages of English *Harper's Bazaar*.

I turned up one morning for a casting session at the photographer's studio. I took my place on the reviewing panel. As the girls came in one by one they were asked to hitch up their skirts to reveal the shape of their legs. The specifications for the list of candidates were: extremely lean, and preferably close to 6-foot tall or 185 centimetres. Not one ounce of excess flesh would be tolerated, so the girls were viewed with an exceptionally critical eye. Now, more than any other time, I understood why many young models drop out of the industry because they resented being seen as 'a piece of meat'.

At the end of the day we laid out the Polaroid photographs to make the final selection. Each of the models was compared, examined and assessed. One by one we cast the rejects aside. Out of a list of at least one hundred girls, ten were chosen. Of these, just one would be labelled, 'the optimum choice'. While the other girls would be photographed wearing short, tight dresses, this specific model would be photographed naked, wearing nothing but a sheer pair of hose. All eyes scanned the photos with great discernment. Finally, we chose Sarah. She had just flown in from Europe and was noted as 'a fresh face with a great behind'! Sarah was a striking 6-foot blonde with a compelling smile. With long, graceful limbs, she resembled a porcelain sculpture crafted by the gods.

I wondered how it was physically possible for a woman to be so tall, maintain her curves and have such a tiny waist. I had worked with hundreds of models over the years, but Sarah's body took the prize for its sheer grace and elegance. My inquisitive nature led me to probe a little deeper on the day of the shoot. Was this woman naturally slim or was she vigilant with her fitness regime? Sarah arrived at the studio that morning with her hair pulled back and wearing a loose, white, cotton shirt and a pair of comfortable jeans. The clients on the job were gathered in a corner enjoying freshly brewed coffee, a basket of fruit and a selection of fine pastries. Our photographer was renowned for his appreciation of good food and wine. Working with him usually meant we were treated to gourmet fare—except Sarah. She introduced herself, grabbed an apple and headed for the makeup room.

Over the next couple of days Sarah avoided the caterer's table. I noticed when we broke for lunch she nibbled on a small bowl of salad and sipped a glass of mineral water. The 'mother' in me asked her if she was going to be satisfied with just a small snack when she'd been working since 7 am. She'd had nothing but a diet coke and a piece of fruit. She told me she didn't want to feel bloated. I wondered if standing naked in front of a camera had prompted her concern. Somehow I felt there was more to the story, and so back in the privacy of the makeup room, where many a girl's secrets have been divulged, we started to talk.

I shared a little with Sarah about my work as an author and intuitive counsellor. At first she was taken aback. I reassured her I wouldn't 'read her mind' and offered instead a sympathetic ear. After dealing with an eating disorder in my teens and early twenties, I was one person who could read the signs, and someone she could definitely trust. Sarah began to tell me that although she had graced some of the most prestigious catwalks in the world and featured in the most elite magazines, she was plagued by self-doubt. While she talked, I thumbed through her impressive portfolio. Portrayed in everything from bikinis to haute couture, there was no doubt as to why she had risen to the height of her career.

Although Sarah seemed composed and confident at the casting session, she inwardly became anxious, as she compared herself to each and every girl. Sarah was exceptionally vulnerable due to a recent split with a long-standing boyfriend. While her ex remained in Europe, Sarah had returned to Australia for some respite from her emotional unrest. But her internal conflict remained.

The previous year, her boyfriend had nursed her through an eating disorder so severe that she was admitted to hospital, where she was officially diagnosed with anorexia. Before hospital, she'd shrugged off people's comments about her extreme thinness by saying, 'You can never be too thin or too rich.' Besides, she was a model, and 'You know the camera puts on five pounds.' Sarah could have been fifteen pounds heavier and still escaped the model management Gestapo. Her critical attitude went far beyond her agent's stringent criteria; she had gradually developed a distorted body image. From what I could gather, Sarah was fading away because she saw herself as 'insignificant'. This seemed like a strange point of view for someone who was glaringly visible on newsstands all over the world.

This young woman was beautiful both inside and out. But she continued to compare herself to others and magnify her flaws, hard as they were to find. Inwardly she saw herself as gawky, with large thighs and disproportionate shoulders. She thought she was too 'simple' and not sophisticated enough, despite the fact that most of her clients were the world's top fashion houses. It is amazing what a Chanel gown, a pair of Prada shoes and a tube of lipstick won't do for the way a girl sees herself on the inside! Just as her potential clients would do in casting sessions, Sarah would constantly critique herself, looking for imperfection.

Sarah's insecurity was amplified by her boyfriend's behaviour. A young model himself, he was often away on location and found it difficult to resist the temptation of other beautiful women. He undoubtedly loved Sarah, but claimed he was unable to curb his amorous nature. When he and Sarah were together, he was a caring, supportive companion. When they were apart, his thoughts would stray and so would his hands.

Sarah compared herself unfavourably to the other woman who captured his attention. How were they better than her? Were they smarter, funnier, sexier or more attractive than she was? Rather than believe she was more than enough to satisfy a man and realise her boyfriend was fickle, she made his infidelity mean she was somehow inferior. Sarah was very hard on herself and her self-criticism had deprived her of a valid sense of worth. Her abstinence from food was a symptom of her denial of love. Every time she rejected herself, she deprived herself of nourishment. Sarah was unconsciously punishing herself for not being good enough.

Sarah's story was so compelling I temporarily deserted my post as fashion stylist and perched on a stool to listen to her story. I asked Sarah if she'd resolved her problems. She shared the details of her recovery and said she'd gained twenty pounds since hospital. There were still days she felt stressed and ate like a bird. On good days though, Sarah made the effort to nurture herself. She was far less obsessive about her work and curbed her tendency to 'size herself up' or down. Our conversation was interrupted by the camera assistant, who called Sarah into the studio for the last shot of the day. It was time for her to take centre stage again. This time her figure rather than her heart would be the focal point, and once again Sarah's self-doubt would be masked by her ability to strike a pose.

After the shoot, I went into the advertising agency to meet with the packaging designer who was orchestrating the job. I walked into Karen's office to find her reviewing the mock-up packages from the art department. She sat shaking her head. 'Take a look at what they've done to Sarah's body.' Her hips and legs had been trimmed through computer graphics to such a degree that she resembled a malnourished adolescent. Both Karen and I were stunned. Here was a woman over 6 feet tall, with micro-measurements, and apparently that wasn't enough to impress the consumer. Was the marketplace flooded with women who resembled toothpicks? Although on the day the clients had seemed happy with Sarah's graceful curves, after transferring her image to film, they thought she needed to look much slimmer. I asked Karen how she thought Sarah would react if she went to buy stockings and discovered her distorted body image? Karen said she didn't think Sarah would care—little did she know.

What would other women think when they looked at Sarah's thighs? Would they sigh with envy or roll their eyes in disbelief? Would they compare their bodies to Sarah's carefully contrived, computer-generated image or revere their current shape?

The answer rests on their level of self-worth and what they have determined makes them lovable. Would these women celebrate their uniqueness or aspire to change their shape in order to be admired, in the same way Sarah had done?

LOOKING BENEATH THE SURFACE

If we were to learn something from Sarah's story it would be to stop comparing ourselves to others. We may not be models, but if we use casting sessions as a metaphor, how often do we believe there is an invisible panel reviewing our attributes? Do we have an internal critic constantly sizing us up and evaluating our worth? In at least one aspect of our life, most of us do. That critical voice normally shows up in areas where we have experienced disappointment in the past and are therefore susceptible to insecurity or self-doubt.

Like Sarah, if we look at ourselves under a microscope, we blow things out of proportion. If we pull back and gain the bigger picture, we can see how inconsequential things can be in the grand scheme of things. That is the nature of the illusion of this world; it tempts us to forget that we are so much more than what we see with our physical eyes. We all have so many magnificent qualities to offer, and yet we are obsessed about the shape of our body, our level of status, or the size of our wallets. We continue to highlight our faults and ignore the value of our intrinsic worth.

One of Sarah's major concerns was keeping a check on her internal dialogue and silencing the voice of doubt. When she remained detached and became an objective observer, she would see things in the proper proportion—including the shape of her body and the size of her meals. She noticed that when her self-criticism stopped, so did her negative behaviour—repeatedly telling herself she wasn't good enough would leave her feeling miserable. She would then lose her appetite, not only for food, but also for life.

After her spell in hospital, Sarah realised what was important and in this case it was her health. Her body, which was the means by which she earned a substantial income, was now wasting away. As her boyfriend sat at her bedside, she became very clear on the conditions she had placed on being loved.

For Sarah to bring the strength and life back into her fragile body, she needed to take her power back from everyone she had ever given it to. That included her peers, her clients, her boyfriend, and most of all, her inner critic. Sarah needed to stand as an equal when she faced other women and simultaneously value her uniqueness. If she did this process sincerely, she would regain her power and overcome self-doubt. Sarah would then no longer rely on the opinions of others to validate her worth. She needed to pay particular attention to the tone of her internal dialogue and be mindful of negative comments.

THE OBSERVER
SILENCING THE INNER CRITIC

Most of us, to a certain degree, are challenged by our doubts and fears on a daily basis. Every time we start to feel uneasy or apprehensive, we need to steer our internal dialogue towards acknowledging our gifts and strengths. This is the best way for any of us to increase our confidence. It is also important that we accept, rather than resist, where we are and stay focused on what we ultimately want to achieve. Our opportunities automatically increase when we stop doubting ourselves because we not only see ourselves differently but we think in a more creative way.

Every time we find ourselves judging ourselves for our past experiences, we need to practise forgiveness.

Although Sarah's boyfriend was responsible for his infidelity, she labelled herself a failure for not satisfying his needs. As a part of her healing, Sarah needed to forgive herself for not being 'perfect'. When she did, she finally felt free. Just like Sarah, if we are ever going to stop comparing ourselves to others, we need to be generous enough to consider our full potential. We can then hold an image of who we want to become, rather than focus on who we don't want to be. Most of us have no idea what we are really capable of achieving.

With Sarah, she was so consumed with winning back her boyfriend's affection that she dismissed the option of moving on. Eventually she did, but not until she increased her level of self-esteem. It takes humility to know things can be different. And there is nothing humble about judgment and criticism. Whether it is directed towards us or someone else, it is destructive and hurtful.

It takes discipline to stay awake and challenge our negative thoughts. So what is our incentive? Just as the case was with Sarah, when we carefully monitor our internal dialogue we feel better about ourselves, which will open us up to receiving more from life.

If we remain sensitive to our feelings and pay attention to our internal dialogue, we will eventually recognise we have the power to change our emotional experience.

We all love to surround ourselves with people who offer us praise, encouragement and support. So why is it so difficult for us to do the same for ourselves?

The media frequently endorses a particular image as superior. We have the 'best dressed', 'worst dressed', 'top ten', 'most eligible', 'pick of the bunch' and what's hot and what's not. They often set the standard of what is important and what is acceptable. There is a huge difference between striving for personal excellence and wanting to impress others. In the same way Sarah did, if we compete for recognition, we will only propagate seeds of self-doubt.

When we evaluate ourselves as superior or inferior to someone else we are buying into the negative side of our egos. The truth is, we are all unique which, by definition, makes us incomparable. Many models have similar features and adopt a certain style, yet they are all distinct in some definable way. It is the essence of an individual that ultimately shines through. After spending time with Sarah, it was the depth of her character that left the most indelible impression on me, not the length of her legs!

Every person we meet is going to have a different opinion of who we are and what we deserve. So who is right and what is accurate? If a different panel of 'experts' had cast the hosiery job, Sarah may never have been a contender. The old saying, 'one man's meat is another man's poison' is ultimately true. If we look to someone else to determine our worth, we are setting ourselves up to be crucified. So does this mean we shouldn't listen to other people's feedback? If a person is generous and objective in their appraisal, they are usually worth listening to. If they are motivated by ego, we'd be wise to bypass their comments.

When I was a young teenager I struggled with my weight. To my mother's dismay, I was always trying different diets. Like many European mothers, she encouraged me to eat more. As a rebellious adolescent, I wanted to take charge of my own life and figure. Every time I opened a fashion magazine I wanted to push my plate aside. This frustrated my mother no end, and so whenever we went shopping, she would point out obese woman and say, 'See, you're not fat, look at her.'

Similarly, when my mother put on a few extra pounds, she compared herself to extremely large women, to make herself feel better. However, when I put on the extra weight, I compared myself to stick-thin models and consequently felt depressed. Neither one of us was willing to assess our weight based on how we actually felt about ourselves.

We always have two choices: we can either pull back, which allows us to be an objective observer, or we can listen to the negative chatter of our ego. If we give it permission to take the driver's seat in our life, we are in for a bumpy ride. Sarah learnt that lesson the hard way. She pulled back and stopped her obsession with being the 'chosen one'. Instead, she started to focus on the quality of her own personal experience. The only thing that is real is what we are experiencing right now in the moment, which brings us back to our feelings.

The most significant lesson I learnt in the advertising industry was that 'you can't judge a book by its cover'. And yet we can all be so quick to judge at times, labelling people and pigeonholing them. How often do we assess a person on their appearance and then on closer inspection find we are disappointed or pleasantly surprised? Then we wonder why we didn't follow our intuition in the first place. But if we don't silence the incessant noise in our minds, our deeper perceptive voices can't be heard.

The world of ego can be deceiving and trends can be very fickle. At the end of the day, changing our outward persona doesn't change a thing unless we also alter the way we view ourselves. If we look at someone like Sarah, who changed her clothes, her makeup, the shape of her body and even the countries she lived in, it made very little difference until she was willing to stop and genuinely accept herself.

When we finished our job together, Sarah thanked me because I took the time to find out more about who she really was. After recovering from her eating disorder, she was careful who she confided in. At times Sarah had been judged as superficial and was hurt by people's misconceptions. By contrast, I found her quite soulful and have no doubt she went on to create a rich and rewarding life for herself. Her newfound attitude gave her the freedom she rightly deserved and her increasing confidence assured her a promising future.

If we are always comparing ourselves to others, we will continue to create more separation in a world where far too much prejudice already exists.

KEY QUESTIONS TO ASK YOURSELF

This is a checklist to see how on track you are with being *The Observer* in your life:

1. Do you frequently compare yourself to others?
2. Where does it show up specifically—is it in the area of your appearance or your performance?
3. Do you ever catch yourself trying to impress others to substantiate your self-worth?
4. Do you acknowledge your uniqueness or try to live up to other people's standards?
5. Which do you do more often—encourage or criticise yourself?
6. Do you spend more time acknowledging your strengths or focusing on your faults and weaknesses?
7. Are you willing to take on a challenge to develop your skills and broaden your experience or do you admit defeat and avert the opportunity?

CHAPTER THREE

MASTERING THE ART OF BALANCE

*Our ego will waver in determining our status. Given reign,
it will conclude we are either superior or inferior, but never equal to others.
We are the most important player in the game of creating our life.
Our wins and losses are based on how we evaluate ourselves.*

Alec looked remarkably healthy for a man who drove himself into the ground.
Blessed by good looks, his classical square jaw and impeccable smile attracted the
attention of many admirers.

Most mornings he started at 6 am, ready to handle a 'to do list' that would make
most people dive back under the covers. Although Alec lived in a glorious house
with views that stretched to the ocean, he rarely took time to enjoy the ambience.
His bedroom overlooked a swimming pool bordered by manicured lawns and
crimson bougainvillea. His mind was so consumed by his business affairs that he
often neglected to enjoy the comforts that this lavish environment offered.

After working through his gruelling agenda, Alec would often look at his watch
to discover it was after 11 pm. The lid on his trusty laptop would finally close and
his depleted mobile phone was put to rest.

Although Alec was an extremely intelligent man who graduated from Harvard,
when it came to affairs of the heart, he often appeared quite ignorant. In the business world, he stood like a captain at the helm of his ship. He remained alert,
resourceful and progressed steadily forward. In his personal relationships, he
would fall asleep at the wheel.

It took seven years of persistence and a lot of talent for Alec's wife to completely
win him over. Her feminine charms and her corporate skills were put to the test. An

extraordinary woman in her own right, Stacey was both powerful and magnetic. Her delicate features were accentuated by a mass of chestnut hair that fell softly around her doe-like eyes. Stacey's devotion to ballet as a child had clearly enhanced her poise and grace. Although petite, she was quite voluptuous, and took great care maintaining her appearance. Despite her busy schedule, she exercised religiously and managed the upkeep of her perfectly manicured nails. Like Alec, she was intensely ambitious and prone to overwork. Her artistic nature and marketing degree led her into advertising. She quickly advanced up the ranks to head her own marketing firm. With a team of young executives and talented designers by her side, she proceeded to climb the corporate ladder. Stacey was no urban princess, and she certainly didn't need Alec to rescue her from mediocrity.

The story of their tumultuous courtship is a testament to her patience and intense loyalty. It seems that just like everything else in Alec's world, Stacey was always under scrutiny. He went through the early part of their relationship with one eye fixed on spotting 'Miss Perfect', while the rest of him was completely in love. Consequently, Stacey was driven to also compete, not only with her girl-friends but also with the men in her life. Stacey refused to be left behind, and judging by Alec's cadence, she needed to shift into overdrive. While Stacey was busy keeping up with Alec, he was more concerned with evaluating his competition. What they did, he did, and what they had, he wanted. Just as well Stacey was dynamic and popular, or perhaps Alec would have passed her by.

When Alec woke in the mornings, Stacey was still sleeping. When he finally went to bed, his head hit the pillow with a thump; his brains were normally fried and he was totally exhausted. What happened in between? There were projects to develop, building sites to find, plans to be approved, foundations to lay, bankers to sway, and of course, people to woo. Unfortunately, Stacey was rarely at the top of his list. Such is the life of 'an empire builder'. It can be lonely at the top...unless you stop to take a breath and realise that people surround you.

Alec was a man caught on a treadmill set on high speed. The question was: What was he in training for? When Alec set out to conquer the world his motto was 'be prepared'. Even though he was accomplished in most areas of his life, in his 'not so humble' opinion, he was always falling behind. Being competitive proved to be Alec's biggest emotional setback. He was ruthless in his appraisal of his achievements, always contending for supreme status, with an intense desire to eliminate obstacles. And yet, no matter how far he escalated on the stairway of success, there was always another level to climb.

When Alec finally agreed to sit with me in a session, he had come to his wit's end. He had worked painstakingly on a property investment deal for months, but his competitors won the tender. He was frustrated and angry. After constant cajoling from his wife, he reluctantly conceded to seek my counsel. Stacey was finding it difficult to deal with her husband, who was acting like a spoilt six-year-old. For days he walked around chanting the mantra that life wasn't fair. For a man who lived in a four-million-dollar house, had a beautiful wife and two adorable children, life just wasn't fair.

Alec worked extremely hard to build his current life; the question was, was he willing to enjoy it? He was so busy trying to compete with the Rockefellers that he had lost sight of his countless blessings. There was no doubt in my mind that Alec needed to reshuffle the deck of his priorities.

The day Alec walked into my house, he seemed a little surprised. After hearing about the nature of my work, he half expected me to live in a Bohemian dwelling with incense, embroidered cushions and a selection of crystal balls. He was expecting me to arrive at the door wearing a tie-dyed caftan, Birkenstock sandals and a gemstone talisman around my neck. Probably. It is funny how we try to label people and put them into a box. We love to make up stories of who we think they are. Our ego loves to embellish the information we gather from the outside world. It adds meaning to everything and draws its own unfounded conclusions.

In Alec's world, he defined distinct boundaries. They were originally drawn to maximise his time and spare him the trouble of dealing with fools. Unless you stood out in a crowd or excelled in some way, you would quickly escape his attention. There were very few people who crossed the intimacy line with Alec, and it took a great deal of effort to win his confidence. At times he was construed as being self-important; I saw him more as a man who was rarely willing to trust. Being in control was imperative. In Alec's way of thinking, trust was earned and built on merit, which left him less vulnerable to being let down. Despite his valiant attempts to avoid disappointment, his safe guard offered him little protection.

I invited Alec to take a seat in the living room and offered him a glass of cold water. He seemed a little hot under the collar, and I sensed it wasn't because of the heat. When I closed my eyes to meditate for a moment, I could hear him fidgeting in his seat. It was a challenge for Alec to sit still for more than five minutes, but after I started to speak he was completely engaged for over two hours. He had a list of people he wanted me to 'tune into'. One by one, he began to identify his relationship patterns and how destructive his competitive behavior had been. Alec competed for recognition, for control, for space, for power and even for love.

Like many misguided corporate leaders, he believed that arrogance and dominance equalled power and control, and equated humility with being weak and invisible.

Alec was often left disappointed after dealing with his co-workers. Living up to his standards was no easy feat. In the same way he pushed himself to the max, he was unyielding with the demands he placed on others. If you were a player on Alec's team, you had to play to win.

His fear of failure often held him captive. Alec was imprisoned by the commentary of his ego, which emerged like a tyrant from the depths of his own mind. His internal dialogue mimicked the tone of a strict and critical parent. Good enough was never enough; he always had to be better. Rather than celebrate his achievements, he would dwell on his rival's conquests. As a property developer, rather than take pride in his portfolio, which included artfully restored apartment buildings in Boston and New York, he compared himself with entrepreneurs in the league of Donald Trump.

Alec told me he had met with some of his Harvard buddies for lunch the previous day. They had gathered at an exclusive eatery in Soho to catch-up on one another's lives. Although this was a social event, the conversation had naturally gravitated towards business. As each one of his friends talked about their recent endeavours and accomplishments, Alec's hunger began to diminish. An extra bottle of wine was ordered as the topic of company revenue and annual gross profits were discussed. Alec's comrades instantly became his competitors and he immediately began to doubt the value of his merits. A couple of his friends had recently moved into the internet business and literally made a fortune overnight. They were smart, sophisticated and savvy, just like Alec.

So what was the difference? Was it luck, fate or destiny? More accurately, these men were willing to play big, think big and see themselves as big! They followed a hunch and were willing to take a risk. They trusted their instincts and relied on the support of a highly creative team. Each one of these men was a team player who held a grand vision of what was possible, and was willing to step into those shoes. When you are starting a new company, in a new arena that is unexplored territory, as the internet was at the time, who are you going to compete with or compare yourself to—Mr Yahoo? In fact, Alec's buddies were talking big figures, the kind that added a couple of zeros to the end of their revenue stream. Their earnings were ten times greater than Alec's, and Alec's were twenty times greater than the average person in America!

Rather than sit in this wonderful restaurant and enjoy the food, the atmosphere and the company of his adventurous friends, Alec deprived himself of the pleasure of being in the moment.

I suggested to Alec that he consider his feelings the next time he was tempted to beat himself up. Taking the 'inner tyrant' to lunch would leave him feeling miserable. If one of his Harvard buddies would have blatantly laughed at his earnings, told him he was a loser and called him hopeless, he would have halted him in his tracks. And yet that was precisely the conversation Alec was having with himself. I asked Alec if anyone had called him hopeless when he was a child. He nodded his head and told me it had happened often. He had heard the words, 'you're hopeless' and 'it's hopeless' more times than he cared to remember. No wonder Alec wanted to fight back. He subconsciously fought against being 'useless' by being an overachiever and a workaholic. In the process, his health and intimate relationships deteriorated.

At the end of our session I suggested Alec go home and have a leisurely weekend with his family and enjoy the fruits of his labour, rather than focus on creating more. I presented him with an analogy: 'If you are not willing to enjoy the food on your plate, there's no point ordering more.' I assured him that I wasn't accusing him of being greedy; I was simply stating the fact that unless he was satisfied with himself, he would never fully enjoy his life.

Alec's eyes turned away for a moment and he looked down towards the floor. He was finally getting in touch with his feelings. To allow him to fully digest what had been said, I paused for a moment before I continued. I told Alec to contemplate how much his attitude would change if he practised being grateful. Because I had become accustomed to Alec's way of thinking, I assured him that being grateful wouldn't make him complacent. It would simply take the pressure off his mind and he would feel less compelled to 'perform'. If Alec were willing to let go of his 'control' and simply celebrate life in the moment, he would automatically open up to receiving more.

There were the occasional times when Alec did let go. But like most corporate heads who operate under immense pressure, he was an extremist. Alec turned out to have quite a lot in common with many Japanese businessmen. They are committed to building 'the empire', as they chant their communal motto, 'never lose face'. They work obsessively all week long until their heads are ready to explode. Come Friday, when it is time to relax, they lose sight of the meaning of the word 'moderation'. To release the pressure they have built up during the week, they drink themselves blind and are often found sleeping in the corner of the subway. Alec was the same. He occasionally discovered the delights of tequila, and the emperor's throne was exchanged for a stage and a karaoke microphone. Las Vegas is a long way from Tokyo, but it is one place in the world you can easily get lost in the fantasy. He was known to forget his name and social security number after the first five margaritas. After that, he simply took on a different identity.

I felt tremendous compassion for Alec. Even though most people saw him as arrogant, his harshness was merely a front. Beyond his forceful persona, he was a sensitive man who was driven by insecurity. Never satisfied with himself, he was a man on a mission to prove his worth. The more he struggled to win control, the more contempt he had for himself. He was only in his mid-thirties and he was showing signs of burning out.

If Alec could only learn the art of balance, he may slow down long enough to hear the voice of his heart. The inner tyrant kept him on his toes even at times when he needed to rest. It kept him away from his family and his authentic dreams. Who was he building the empire for anyway? If he were doing it to silence the inner tyrant, he would have a long list of tasks ahead of him. His ego would never be appeased: its slogan was 'Conquer or be conquered.'

That equation leaves very little room for enjoying supportive, harmonious relationships that inspire our lives. Being humble means we approach others with very few preconceived ideas of who they are, and what they are capable of achieving. Alec also needed to do the same with himself. If he continued to let his ego rule his relationships, someone was always going to come up short. So I suggested he refrain from judgment and tell his ego to stand in the rear. After all, Alec wasn't God in totality. Therefore there were times he may not know everything about himself, life and everyone else's potential.

That treadmill he was walking on may have been strengthening his stride, but it was certainly taking its toll on his body and his emotions. Life was attempting to teach Alec how important harmony is. Through little signs and quiet whispers, life would tell him to slow down and stop pushing to compete. Our sessions together were strong evidence of those messages. But at the end of the day, Alec had to realise what was at stake. With his iron will and stubborn nature he would have to make the decision himself; after all, he wasn't a man who liked to be pushed—unless, of course, he was pushing himself.

LOOKING BENEATH THE SURFACE

Although most of us are not as 'intense' as Alec, we can all learn something from his story. How often do we push ourselves unduly to gain control, rather than be receptive to more graceful alternatives? Whenever Alec felt insecure, he would lash out at the world rather than remain open to being supported. This would alienate him from his staff and put a lot of pressure on his wife, who had to deal with his frustration and anger. Alec only felt threatened with his business rivals because he wasn't willing to trust his resources—internal or external. He focused on what was missing in his world rather than what he had. He then concluded there must have been something wrong with him, and took every setback far too personally. Whenever his expectations weren't met, he was left feeling disappointed with himself. Like all of us, Alec needed to realise he still had things to learn, rather than judge himself so harshly.

It is so easy for us to judge ourselves when we are dealing with disappointment or failure. And just like Alec, whenever we criticise others or are hard on ourselves, we end up being defensive. We do this to shield ourselves from further hurt and it usually doesn't work. We attempt to hide the things about ourselves we don't like and so we either opt for 'false bravado', or retract and withdraw like a wounded dog. At the end of the day, we still have to look at ourselves in the mirror and there is nowhere to hide. That is why self-acceptance is so important; no matter where we are in the world, we still have to live with ourselves.

Because of Alec's competitive nature, he would push for what he wanted until the very end. People would often get hurt in the process. This is exactly what happens when we operate from ego and compete for power in a relationship. We may not use our fists to attack and defend, but a sharp tongue can be just as painful.

Whenever Alec felt threatened, he would struggle for control to feel less vulnerable. He had no tolerance for people who were supposedly weak or hopeless. When they did show up in his world, they were simply mirroring parts of himself he wasn't willing to be with. And so, of course, Alec would voice his disapproval and abruptly shout, 'next'. Then when he came across someone he thought was better than him, like his buddies in New York, the flip side of the recording would play and he felt inferior. His esteem would rise and fall, like a barometer, depending on whom he was with. All of us are susceptible to this sort of tedious behaviour, unless we have the confidence of Adonis. Alec believed he had to compete to reinstate his shaky footing.

How was Alec going to defeat the inner tyrant and reinstate his balance? Logical advice for our boy from Harvard would be to search for deeper understanding and use more compassion—both for himself and others. Alec would then naturally become more humble and feel less threatened.

After judgment, punishment normally follows, and Alec was in the habit of punishing himself often, through his own internal criticism. He needed to pay attention to his fluctuating mood swings. When Alec was pleased with his performance and achievements, he felt up. When the tyrant came out, he was down.

I remember Stacey calling me one Friday afternoon after picking Alec up from the airport, when he arrived home from New York. Driving back to the house, her husband, who was having a 'mini meltdown', started to resemble the toddlers in the back seat. Like them, Alec was in need of a little attention, support and inspiration. It takes time to change old patterns, and Alec was again frustrated with his progress. I had visions of him carrying his emotional burden all through the weekend and Stacey having to shoulder the brunt.

Alec may have been deluded into believing he was working hard to create wealth and security for his family, but all they wanted was to spend more time with him. He was often too busy to exercise, eat sensibly or even have sex. All in the name of wanting to feel better about his life, so he could ultimately feel better about himself.

Love is born from humility and instantly dissolves arrogance. When Alec practised self-acceptance, he enjoyed much more satisfying relationships. This became very apparent to me when I watched Alec with his kids. He silenced the inner tyrant and stood with a tender heart. The innocent, childlike parts of his nature came to the forefront, and creativity and play naturally replaced competition. Would Alec ever be brave enough to remain that vulnerable playing the corporate game in America? I know one thing for certain; if he were, he would have received a lot of support and definitely had much more fun!

THE PEACEMAKER
BRIDGING THE GAP BETWEEN OUR HEAD AND OUR HEART

Sometimes we can make the world so real, and take things so seriously, we lose sight of what's really important. Misleading ambitions can easily cloud our authentic dreams; and the pressure from our heads suppresses our hearts. This was precisely what was going on in Alec's life. His head ruled his heart to the degree that his chest literally felt constricted. Rather than pull back, to recharge his energy and contemplate, he would push on. That is a great way to have a heart attack. And with many headstrong individuals, it takes a crisis that intense to make them slow down.

If our identity becomes more important than our real self, we will always feel a sense of being incomplete. This is where Alec's, 'do more to have more to be more' belief came from. His wife would often tell him that if he weren't careful, he would drive himself into his grave. Well Alec didn't go quite that far, but he certainly had a very close call that inspired a dramatic shift in his priorities.

It was September and Alec was visiting Boston to meet with potential investors and oversee one of his building projects. Although he usually travelled with a personal assistant, on this trip he was alone. That particular morning, on his way to his first appointment, he picked up a copy of the *New York Times* and stopped at one his favourite cafés, which was renowned for its great pancakes. This was to be one of the rare occasions where Alec would stop for a moment and treat himself rather than charge into his day.

As he glanced over his newspaper, he became disturbed by the themes of the headlines and was alarmingly conscious of how much violence there was in America. Alec started to think about the sensitivity levels of his kids and realised how vulnerable they were in a world that was primarily ruled by domination and control. He sat in the middle of this large, industrious city, unnervingly aware of just how far he was from the people he loved. It was only 5 am in California, far too early to call his family and talk to them for reassurance. Blasting horns and wailing sirens invaded Alec's moment of contemplation. For the first time he felt a strange sense of loneliness in a city he normally loved.

He switched on his pocket computer and checked his schedule. Alec then made one of the most important decisions of his life. Rather than stay in Boston another night, he decided to cut his trip short and take an afternoon flight to Los Angeles. He was originally booked to leave early the next morning but his urge to be with his family prompted him to call the airlines and change his original booking. That evening Alec spent a peaceful evening with Stacey and the children, with a new deep sense of appreciation in his heart. His trip to Boston had been a long one, and he realised just how often he was away.

The next morning Alec slept a little later than usual; he was probably still tired from his flight the previous day. Rather than automatically slip into his regular routine, he switched on the television in his bedroom, to catch the morning news. After only seconds of taking in the graphic images on the screen, he turned up the volume on the remote control. His mouth dropped open as shivers started to run through his body. He called out to Stacey as he watched the second United Airlines plane slam directly into the Twin Towers building. Alec was so overwhelmed, he wondered if he was still asleep and having a nightmare. He sat on the edge the bed with Stacey by his side, and clutched her knee. Flight 175 from Boston to LA had been hijacked by terrorists and turned towards New York. Alec's stomach churned as he realised he was originally booked on that specific flight before he serendipitously changed his plans. If Alec had stuck to his original schedule, he would have been on the plane that dived nose first into the core of the building.

Was this a strange twist of fate or divine providence? No matter which way you look at it, Alec was being given a direct message to rethink his priorities. September 11 was undoubtedly one of the worst disasters for the western world in modern history. Does it take a tyrant like Osama bin Laden to help us recognise what is important? A wave of compassion and brotherhood swept over the world after this terrible tragedy. The question was, after this life-altering experience, would Alec stay awake or fall back to sleep? Would the voice of his ego lure him back into a trance? Or would he have the courage to break the spell permanently, and finally follow his heart. It was time for Alec to jump off the treadmill, stretch his thinking and alter the course of his life.

Material wealth and physical attributes don't necessarily lead to happiness. The quality of the relationship we have with ourselves does. Success is not just based on how many times we win, or how much we accrue; it is based on how much joy we experience and how secure we feel in the process. Our internal dialogue will indicate just how much care and respect we are willing to uphold in the relationship we have with ourselves. Generosity and humility are by far our greatest strengths when it comes to fostering security and trust.

We can see how Alec's headstrong nature was overriding his feelings and causing him to put far too much pressure on himself. We are accompanied by our thoughts every second of every waking day. If those thoughts lean towards criticism and uncertainty, we will place ourselves through unnecessary stress and anxiety. To remedy the situation, we need to make the effort to be sensitive to our own feelings and handle ourselves gently, in the same way that we would any other precious commodity. After Alec's 'wake-up call' on the morning of September 11, that is precisely what he did. The quality of his relationships and his general well-being were thrust to the top of his priority list.

As in any healthy relationship, we need to offer ourselves acknowledgment and encouragement. After the time that Alec and I spent together, that message was finally driven home. The more he was willing to acknowledge himself and others for their efforts, the more satisfying his experience was. And just like Alec, if we do fall short of our goals or make mistakes at times, we need to be patient and remind ourselves we are in the process of growing and learning with every step we take.

As was the case with Alec, one of the reasons we disregard our true worth is because we have been disappointed, which has left us disheartened. There were times that he felt he had let himself down because he wasn't able to create or achieve everything he set out to do. At some point in our life, we have all felt powerless to change our circumstances. And yet our intuition is always there to guide us. If Alec had stubbornly adhered to his schedule and not been touched by the voice of his heart, he would have lost his life on September 11.

There were times Alec feared being taken advantage of or being overpowered. He learnt that fighting back or trying to gain control only creates more struggle. When Alec felt powerless, he would fight to validate his position or blame other people. He would become domineering and controlling or end up feeling hard done by. No matter which position he took, he was operating from a place of fear. Just as Alec did, if we blame others or ourselves for our circumstances, we will become a victim to our own ego. It is hard to believe that someone as powerful as Alec, who played out the tyrant, could also take on the role of being a victim. That is specifically how the ego works. If we choose to compete, we will either win or lose. And in Alec's case, when he lost, he felt powerless. If Alec were willing to be humble enough to forgive himself for his past mistake, he would silence the 'internal critical parent' who told him he was hopeless. He would let go of his arrogance, which was only a defence, and move steadily forward. It was also imperative that Alec acknowledge the impact of his love, both in his relationship with himself and his family.

Although he still sets his sights high, he no longer lets the competitive side of his nature defeat his spirits. He sets himself a healthy challenge by defining his personal goals and developing his skills. If we refrain from comparing ourselves to others and simply remember our goals, we can all move smoothly towards success without depleting our energy. It was important to Alec that he learn to enjoy what life had to offer in the moment, rather than obsessing about his future. By reflecting on his past, he could see how much emphasis he had placed on performance and not on the quality of his experience.

Since that fateful day in Boston, Alec has operated from a completely different place. He cashed in most of his holdings on the East Coast to spend more time with his family in California. Strangely enough, because he was willing to release the fixed ideas he held around his identity, his creative projects have taken on a new depth. In following one of his own personal dreams, he has ventured into a new business arena that allows him far more freedom and flexibility, with larger streams of income. Alec started to notice that the more he was willing to just enjoy the creative process, the more successful he was. He gave himself permission to take on projects that inspired him, rather than solely increase his wealth. He is now far less attached to developing his status and is much more interested in enjoying the game.

It is a misconception to believe we have to work really hard, and compete to achieve results. We will have much more energy if we make a steady effort and stay open to being supported as we go. In the same way Alec eventually did, we can take the pressure off our mind and stay open to receiving from life in unexpected ways. We are then free to create from our heart and allow our love for what we do to inspire us. Our creativity gives us the opportunity to dip into our internal resources and enjoy the fruits of our actions. We can give and receive and discover more of ourselves in the process.

There is always an alternative route to get to the same destination; we simply have to expand our vision, stay receptive and be willing to give up control.

KEY QUESTIONS TO ASK YOURSELF

This is a checklist to see how on track you are with being *The Peacemaker* in your life:

1. Do you find there are times you push for control?
2. Are you more conscious of the level of your performance or enjoying the creative process?
3. Are you open to support, or do you insist on doing everything?
4. Do you see yourself as a person who has made mistakes and failed on certain occasions or labelled yourself as a failure?
5. Are you driven to be productive to validate your worth?
6. Do you remain sensitive to your feelings and take time to consider the consequences of your actions?
7. Do you run on automatic pilot or stop to consider your most favourable options?

CHAPTER FOUR

BEYOND THE MIRROR

*Our identity needs to be flexible and adaptable for us
to be completely self-expressed and enjoy a full life. It is wise not
to lean too heavily on our laurels in one area and admit defeat in another.*

As the gay mecca of Los Angeles, West Hollywood is a city of extremes. It is not uncommon here to encounter men who want to be women and women who want to be like men. However, this was far from the case with Cindy, who was all woman, from head to toe. Tall, lean, leggy and very blonde, she was a magnet for men with an eye for grace and glamour. Men, both gay and straight, worshipped this sex goddess on heels. My dear friend Scott Taylor was not spared from Cindy's allure; he offered her a heart, inspired friendship, and a strong shoulder to lean on when the going got tough.

My first encounter with Cindy took place when Scott arranged a rendezvous at his home, which was always a wonderful place for a gathering. Like his house, this tall Australian man stood apart from the crowd. He was talented, witty and handsome, and if you didn't know he was gay, you'd call him 'a man's man'. A gentle soul at heart, he was always helping 'lame ducks'. Over a hot cup of tea or a vodka martini, Scott offered friends and strangers alike, comfort, counsel and a few good jokes. After spending ten minutes listening to opera on his plush, velvet couch, even the most diehard worrywarts would forget their woes. Scott had a particular soft spot for struggling artists too, which is how he first met Troy, who then introduced him to Cindy. The three of them became close friends and significant in each other's lives.

Troy was a photographer, painter and writer. His good looks and extraordinary talent had won both Cindy and Scott's affection. Tanned, blonde and extremely sophisticated, he was a rare commodity because of his childlike nature. Troy and Scott were both playful and refined; the difference being Troy was prone to self-sabotage.

Troy and Cindy would play most of the day, which distracted Troy from being productive. Scott, on the other hand, was creative, inventive and industrious. He would start his day at 6 am, and at 10 am would pass you by in a whirlwind of activity, saying, 'Half the day's gone and nothing's been done.' By this early stage of his day, he would have accomplished what most people would do in eight hours. He approached life like a man on a mission; whether he was designing the interior of a house or ordering Chinese takeout. His trusty golden retriever Leona was often by his side. She would let out an agreeable bark when he cursed the traffic, or put her head on his knee and sigh when it was time for their walk in the hills. When they stopped for turkey sandwiches, she always got the bulk of the filling.

Scott was a pushover for beautiful females with gentle manners. That is why both Leona and Cindy ran high on his list of priorities. Scott was like a shepherd in their lives, protecting them from prowling wolves. Keeping men at arm's length was one of Cindy's greatest challenges. Although she had been married for almost fifteen years, she had no shortage of suitors. Her husband Kurt supported her lavish lifestyle, and because he was often away on business, she operated on 'standby' to support his needs and accommodate his erratic schedule. As an ex-flight attendant, this was something Cindy was used to.

When he was away, Cindy had a lot of time on her hands. Her list of daily priorities read like a selection of options at an exclusive day spa resort. In the morning, she would brief the housekeeper and gardener and then welcome her personal trainer to her private gym and pool overlooking the canyon. Above all, Cindy was committed to maintaining her physical beauty and her glamorous image. How many women do you know who work out on the treadmill with a glass of chardonnay in their hand? After a gruelling day at the races in Del Mar, there was no better way to ease her tension.

Cindy's morning workout was usually followed by a short trip down to Beverly Hills for some retail therapy. Cindy was the perfect clotheshorse. She always looked immaculate, no matter what the occasion. She favoured beautifully tailored, feminine suits with very short skirts. Her shoes were always delicate and extremely expensive. In Cindy's world, the higher the heel, the more the appeal. She had impeccable manners and deportment and was usually accompanied by a gorgeous man, either gay or straight, to accent her charm.

Troy was one such faithful escort. He would frequently accompany her to lunch at an exclusive Beverly Hills restaurant for Bollinger and a round of Caesar salads. They'd often invite an assortment of multi-talented people such as scriptwriters, fashion designers, producers and actors. Cindy's eyes would widen as she listened in awe to their stories. Troy was less enthusiastic, and occasionally felt intimidated by their success. He had no shortage of talent, but his efforts were inconsistent. Whenever he was strapped for cash, he would whip up a painting overnight and sell it to one of his clients the next day to pay his expenses for the month. So when his lunch companions would go on about their laborious efforts, he would simply check out of the conversation.

Cindy, by contrast, was fascinated by her creative friends and at times was confronted by her apparent lack of inventiveness. She mentioned it once during a moment of quiet reflection over lunch with Scott. Most of her friends would dismiss her concern and remind her that she had a wealthy husband. However Scott took her inquiry seriously. He was one man who celebrated his uniqueness and couldn't imagine a world without creativity. He suggested Cindy have a session with me to unravel the mystery around her 'soul's purpose' and her life's lessons.

The appointment was set for Friday morning and we decided to meet at Scott's house. Looking delightfully feminine, Cindy arrived wearing pink and beige.

Leona was there to greet her at the door and started spinning in circles. Scott instructed Leona to sit and behave, and left the two of us to enter 'the zone'. Cindy sat in one of the large club chairs in the living room. As she made herself comfortable, I started to set up my portable tape recorder. She gracefully crossed her legs and brushed her soft, blonde hair away from her face to reveal a large diamond earring. She seemed a little nervous about recording her session. After we started I realised why.

It seemed that Cindy's discontent had started to affect her marriage. Although she loved her husband Kurt dearly, after almost fifteen years of the same routine, things were becoming tedious. Although her life may have looked exciting, she craved stimulation. Her marriage had become 'comfortable' and the passion had started to wane. When she started looking beyond her marriage to seek stimulation, she justified her behaviour by telling herself her husband was doing the same.

Kurt started staying away from home a little longer than usual and Cindy was tired of following him around. She craved a life outside the marriage, yet when her husband was away, she felt quite alone. Neither the men nor the money seemed to satisfy her longings. What would it take for her to feel whole? While she and her husband had decided not to have children, Cindy still needed to give birth to her own creative self-expression.

As we continued our session, she was inspired when I talked about her latent talents and undeveloped skills. This gave her insight into why she felt so frustrated. I suggested if she continued to deny the value of her own essence and the power of her creativity, her life would present her with a series of messages until she finally took the plunge. She asked if that meant she should leave her husband. I told her it had little to do with Kurt. What needed to be addressed was the relationship she was having with herself. Finding another man, no matter how attentive or interesting, would not resolve her unrest. Cindy needed to stop living in someone else's shadow, otherwise she would always feel deficient. She needed to set aside time to explore her creative, inventive nature, rather than taking her artistic friends to lunch.

I suggested Cindy take a good look at the 'icons' in her world and the lessons they were teaching her. Our dear friend Scott was a wonderful example of someone who wasn't afraid to put his signature to his creation and take it out boldly into the world. He viewed his work as a contribution from his heart, and others embraced it in the same way. If Troy had been willing to do the same, he could have created a similar life to Picasso. Both Troy and Scott had equal amounts of talent. The difference was, Scott was willing to create for the sake of exploring his creativity and Troy was more concerned about making a good impression. Troy's father was a powerful man who ran a successful company. Standing in his shadow, Troy assessed what he did by comparison, as being inconsequential. He was more inspired to find a partner who was 'an empire builder' like Cindy's husband, than take on the responsibility himself.

Through my observation, Troy was standing in Cindy's shadow and wanted to be like her. Cindy was standing in both Scott and Troy's shadows and wanted to be creatively gifted, like them. Scott was the only one being himself. It can get very dark if we stand behind another person and expect them to compensate for our weaknesses. If we continue to dim the light on our inner resourcefulness, we will feel incomplete.

Shadow play can be interesting to watch. We are often drawn to people we admire who exhibit the attributes we wish we had. Then we come across someone who demonstrates the qualities we are threatened by and we're repelled. There is nothing missing inside any of us; we are all whole and complete. We just need to accept ourselves fully and then choose who we want to be.

Cindy told me she didn't know what she really wanted to do. This was a sure indication that she was out of touch with her true feelings and clouded by self-doubt. It would have been an affront to her soul if I told her what career path she 'should' take. After all, who knows us better than ourselves? I suggested she look at what she loves to do and then explore those ideas. Cindy loved to cook and entertain and did it with great pleasure. Would she be wise enough to see that this was possibly an avenue for tremendous self-expression and potentially lucrative?

That was to be her greatest challenge. Cindy was quick to denounce the potency of her skills. A little more imagination and a lot more ambition was in order. Where would the likes of Martha Stewart and Nigella Lawson be if they had denied their creativity? They were willing to do what they naturally loved to do and share it with the world. Instead, Cindy was hiding behind her husband, a brigade of fabulous gay men, and the persona of being a trophy wife. Cindy was an intelligent, beautiful and charismatic woman with all the makings of a celebrity. But like many idealistic women, she wanted to be rescued. In looking to men to support her stride, she had sacrificed parts of herself. What if her prince charming decided to nudge her off the back of his horse? To me, one thing was clear: unless Cindy was willing to start taking her latent talents seriously, she would continue to mask her pain with champagne, shopping and sex.

Twelve months later, after a downturn in his career, Cindy's husband Kurt decided to leave California and accept a job offer on the East Coast. Cindy and Kurt made a mutual decision to split. Kurt moved on to a more intimate relationship with a woman he had been seeing during his travels. Cindy was left with the house in the Hollywood Hills and a small settlement. It was time for her to start a new chapter, and now there were no distractions.

She stood at the crossroads in life. What assets and skills would Cindy rely on, as she set off into the world to create a new life? Would she put on her stilettos, coiffure her hair and stride down the runway of life in search of adoration and attention?

Or would she walk down an unfamiliar path, exploring her ingenuity and creativity leading to growth and productivity? Would Cindy draw her inspiration from the pages of her gourmet recipe books or her little black book? If she were really clever she would both develop her skills and align with people who supported her talents.

There were many days Cindy pondered her options over lunch with Troy and Scott. Scott had visions of Cindy hosting her own cooking program and becoming a celebrity chef. She had all the right ingredients: charisma, culinary skills and contacts. He also suggested she bottle her fabulous pasta sauce and market the line through Bristol Farms. He came up with one suggestion after another until his creative well ran dry. Cindy then turned to Troy and asked for his opinion. He looked at her vacantly through his rose-coloured glasses as he sipped his glass of Bollinger. From his perspective, there was only one option: 'Find yourself another rich husband.'

During the next two years, Cindy spent all her time and resources trying to find 'Mr Wonderful'. There were blind dates, parties, exclusive matchmaking services and even internet hookups. Her candidates appeared one by one, and read like the 'who's who' of Hollywood. There were even a few imports, like the coffee plantation owner from South America. Cindy was whisked away to islands, flown around in private jets, escorted to mountain hideaways and paraded alongside champion racehorses—but still found no suitable life partner. Cindy's gay friends would hold up scorecards when she talked about her latest suitor's traits and material assets. Looking for one person to satisfy your every need can be very tiresome, and the search was draining both Cindy's spirits and her bank account.

Cindy's test came when she met Brian, a gentle man with a fascinating mind and a whimsical sense of humour. His character was rich and deep, unlike his pockets. This scriptwriter and poet with a generous heart and a soulful nature intrigued Cindy. Brian had managed to carve himself a comfortable niche in the Hollywood film industry. A man of high values, he was selective about his work rather than driven by ambition. His vast collection of rare books and fine ceramics were evidence of his love of the arts and he enjoyed a fruitful life.

Cindy felt a strong connection with Brian, reminiscent of the early days with her husband. They laughed and cooked great meals together and spent many nights sitting in front of the fire talking about philosophy. Cindy had finally met a man who touched her heart. There was just one problem. Brian's income didn't meet Cindy's checklist for a 'suitable' husband. As far as Brian was concerned, when he met Cindy, he felt as though he had died and gone to heaven. Unfortunately, that trip was curtailed by a short detour to hell. When Cindy finally told Brian it was time to spread her wings and move on, he bid his 'angel' farewell and nursed his broken heart.

One night on her way home from a cocktail party, Cindy drove down the freeway towards the Hollywood Hills, with a little too much champagne under her belt. She was frustrated and bored by the advances of a few insensitive men at the party. To further amplify her anguish, a group of young guys driving a blue Mustang, cruised alongside her car trying to get her attention. To them, she looked like a girl who was out to have some fun. After playing cat and mouse over four lanes on the freeway, Cindy had come to her wits' end. She reached over and pulled out a small handgun from her bag and pointed it directly at her annoying pursuers. Completely overwhelmed, the young would-be playboys stepped on the accelerator and sped off into the distance.

Cindy shed a few tears and turned off the freeway. She was tired, in more ways than one, and was starting to lose her composure. If she were willing to take that fighting spirit and channel it into her creative endeavours, she would make progress. If she wanted men to see her in a new light, she had to see herself differently first and then take an alternative course of action.

LOOKING BENEATH THE SURFACE

Cindy needed to move beyond the character traits she knew and trusted and build new ones. We all ultimately choose who we are and what we will experience. There is no human strength that is missing within any of us. If we feel we are lacking in some way, we have disregarded our potential. It is up to all of us to choose how resourceful we become, and whether we are willing to allow our talents to bring us rewards. As Cindy's story reveals, our world acts as a mirror, reflecting back what we believe about ourselves.

Troy played Cindy's devil's advocate. He idealised her glamorous image and was quick to downplay her creative and productive potential. He did the same thing with himself, despite being extremely gifted. Scott showed up as an avatar. He encouraged her in every way, and when all else failed, he played the rescuer. Scott often came to Cindy's aid after her husband left. He held the vision of her finally attaining success.

Cindy could have learnt something very valuable from Scott by observing his resourcefulness and developing some of those same qualities. If Cindy had more faith in her internal resources, her external resources would never have dwindled. If our behaviour is counterproductive in any area, we can always reach back into our 'creative well' and try a different approach. If we are not willing to grow, parts of us will die of undernourishment. This was definitely the case with Cindy; she started feeling like a flower without water. And having an extra glass of champagne wasn't going to quench that thirst.

When we discover we have the ability to do something new, then we acknowledge a little more of our personal power. That's why it's important for us to continue searching deeper within ourselves to uncover more of our attributes. It was obvious that Cindy needed to accept responsibility for her own happiness. What we all need to remember is that whether we wish to build more satisfying relationships or further our careers, the answer always lies within us.

Cindy continued to look at others and say, 'They are creative and resourceful and I am not.' Her ego had fooled her into believing she didn't have enough substance. Every time she denounced her power, she recited her mantra, 'If I don't find my prince, I will end up being a pauper.' If we recite a line long enough, it becomes a prophecy. Cindy was scared. And when we operate from fear, we compromise our integrity. We also start to lose our confidence, which in Cindy's case only made her rely more heavily on what had worked for her in the past.

Now in her early forties and still very beautiful, she insisted on playing up her feminine charms. If we overuse one part of our identity we can become too rigid, and eventually our life will start to break down. In the same way a bodybuilder trains, if some muscles are heavily worked and others are ignored, they develop weak points. A good bodybuilder will train each and every muscle to gain strength and balance and augment all their features.

When people saw Cindy from a limited perspective, they would only ever compliment her on her looks. She started to resent that they weren't seeing anything more. If we choose to 'advertise' one part of ourselves in order to get what we want, we will end up feeling insecure. It isn't surprising that she started to feel far too vulnerable when she was left to rely on her own devices.

The young guys in the metallic blue Mustang appeared in Cindy's life as messengers. They were playing out her shadow. As they hounded and harassed her on the freeway that night, she saw them as being immature and reckless. They showed no concern for the ramifications of their actions and were only concerned with having fun. As she looked in the rear vision mirror she asked herself what they were thinking. The question is, what was Cindy thinking before they showed up? Her thoughts drifted towards having more security and substance in her life; she was tired of playing the field, going to parties, taking drugs and drinking too much. She started wondering why, although she was in her early forties, this was still happening.

If I had told Cindy she had a lot in common with those boys she probably would have pulled a gun on me! And that is how subtle, yet powerful, shadow play can be. You can't eradicate your shadow, you can only own it; then it simply becomes a part of you. Rather than retaliate, Cindy needed to simply turn off the freeway and take a new course. That is also precisely what she needed to do with her life— change direction.

Swinging the pendulum from one extreme to the other never works. Playing 'tough' rather than demure didn't make Cindy feel any better. She needed to find the middle point. If she were able to develop her 'light' or radiance, she would dispel her shadow. The qualities Cindy needed to take on were wisdom, responsibility, vigilance and foresight—the same qualities the boys in the blue Mustang needed to consider. Cindy had been projecting those qualities on her partners instead of owning them herself. That little outburst in her car was prompted by sheer frustration. If you keep a lid on any part of your nature for long enough, it may break out in an extreme way. Cindy was fortunate that her counterparts didn't retaliate. Otherwise she could have been destroyed by the hostility that was suppressed in her own shadow.

THE EXPLORER
CLAIMING THE HIDDEN PARTS OF OURSELVES

If we are willing to accept all the parts of ourselves, we acknowledge our full potential and true heritage, which is an empowering place to be. Otherwise, in the same way Cindy did, we will continue to live in fear of being incomplete, and will overcompensate in certain areas. For Cindy to be at peace, she needed to depend on herself and have confidence in her resources. If she were willing to see the qualities she admired in others in herself, and then take action, she would awaken her power.

Are we willing to embrace all the beautiful qualities we have within us and recognise the depth of our creative powers? I suggested to Cindy that she pinpoint the limited opinions she had formed about her potential over the years and change her point of view. We will never move forward unless we are willing to challenge our limited beliefs. In the same way Cindy did, we all have the opportunity, and the power, to create any identity or personality we choose.

Cindy was tired of other people seeing her as the stereotypical 'fun-loving blonde'. And yet she was unwilling to move beyond the pigeonhole she'd created for herself. Our liberation lies in our power to choose. The labels we give ourselves based on our past experiences will warrant our expectations in the future. Cindy saw herself as helpless and therefore was always looking for someone else to hold her hand.

Whenever we enter a relationship with the intention of bolstering our own limitations, we deny our full potential. Cindy had an underlying belief that she needed a partner to become whole and complete. She was gentle and receptive, which drew her to men who were dynamic and assertive. They were also practical thinkers who were disciplined, whereas, she was more nurturing and sensitive. Cindy looked for a partner to 'complete', rather than 'complement' her. When I suggested she bring up the strengths she was looking for in a partner in herself, her response was, 'I have never been good at those things.' It is easy for any of us to make excuses when we know we need to change our behaviour or face a challenge. If we are not willing to stretch our self-image, we will close the door on opportunities and deny our true potential.

It was important for Cindy to consider her motivation and intention when forming a relationship. Wanting someone else to pay her mortgage would do nothing to help her self-esteem. If she were willing to take on the challenge herself, she would discover her own talents, which was what her soul was calling her to do. If she had explored her creativity in the financial security of her marriage, she would not have given in to panic once the pressure started to mount. Cindy ended up losing her house in the hills and was forced to move to a more modest neighbourhood. It was time for this princess to get on her horse!

Just like Cindy, when we feel insecure and are overwhelmed by fear, many of us make sacrifices and compromise our integrity. It is much more powerful to stay focused on what we ultimately want to experience and know we have what it takes to uphold the vision. We can then invite others to join us, and mutually navigate the course as we travel. Like many of us, Cindy just wanted to weave a beautiful dream with someone else. But that aspiration would only be a fantasy unless she believed she was capable of sustaining her creation. This would only happen when she knew the strength of her character. By playing the role of being helpless, Cindy was unconsciously manipulating others through her weakness. This is how co-dependent relationships are born.

The first rule to embracing our power is to stop denying its existence. Then we need to take our power back from everyone we have ever given it to. In Cindy's case, this was every man on the planet.

Why would someone like Cindy, who had absolutely everything going for her, sell herself short? Because she had too much energy invested in the outcome. When she was married, she attracted men like bees to a honey pot. Now she was single, the men still appeared, but things didn't quite gel. When we create from fear, rather than from a desire to experience more, we block the creative flow. Our feelings are like 'glue'; they bring substance to our experiences. Anything built on fear will quickly fall apart. That is why Cindy's fleeting relationships didn't last. Cindy was making romantic relationships far too real instead of seeing them as a playful self-expression.

So where is Cindy now? She started to reminisce about her time with Brian. She missed his poignant stories and his handy work in the kitchen. Cindy remembered how peaceful she felt sitting on the back porch of Brian's house, looking at the stars and listening to his music collection. A glass of red wine in hand, he would remark on how childlike she looked in the candlelight. His sensitivity and strength had left an indelible impression on Cindy's heart. She attempted to reconnect with Brian but it was too late; he wasn't willing to take a second chance. There was no turning back for him; it was time to move on.

Troy formed a relationship with a partner who was completely committed and supportive. Their compatibility list was cross-linked in every way imaginable— except for one. Derrick was an attorney who ran a successful law firm and Troy, of course, was far more laid-back. Because he was a professional person, who was normally very productive, Derrick found it difficult to watch Troy's talent being dampened by alcohol and drugs. The boys played together beautifully, but building a life as a couple was challenging. Derrick became influenced heavily by Troy's lifestyle and developed a fondness for cocaine. Derrick's 'dabbling' in drugs escalated to a habit: he would begin his day with a line of cocaine before he left for the office. Derrick struggled with his willpower and was torn between his love for Troy and maintaining order in his world.

It got to the point where Derrick's financial security was threatened by his addiction. He knew that unless he gathered his strength, he would eventually go under. Although he didn't want to lose Troy, Derrick finally mustered the courage to give him an ultimatum. They would either have to give up the drugs or separate. Love can be a powerful catalyst for change and they decided to go into rehab. Troy not only gave up cocaine, he enrolled in a journalism course in college. Troy started to channel his energy into his creative skills and his relationship with Derrick flourished. As partners, they were a strong support for one another and their love inspired them to overcome their weaknesses.

Troy wasn't the only one who became more productive. Cindy started catering for private dinner parties, a wonderful outlet for her culinary skills. One of her closest friends asked her to oversee a formal celebration and offered to pay her handsomely. Cindy was inspired by the prospect of preparing a fabulous feast for twenty and designed an enticing menu. She arrived at the house with a small entourage to carry her pots and pans and whipped up a storm in the kitchen. Cindy's European delicacies were an instant hit, and so were the exotic cocktails. The word spread quickly about her cooking talents and Cindy was offered a number of jobs 'spicing up' soirées for the Hollywood set. She began to create an independent life and slowly developed her confidence.

Cindy was also offered a position overseeing an exclusive day spa resort in Florida. The qualifications for the job were like second nature to Cindy. She was an ambassadress of style who knew exactly what it takes for a person to feel pampered and indulged. Can you think of a better way for Cindy to spend her day and generate a great income? Well at least it would be a step in the right direction. You never know who you might meet when you are busy doing the things you love.

If Cindy were willing to write a new chapter in her life, she would undoubtedly broaden the depth of her experience and discover more of herself. Life may not always be a fairytale, but there is definitely a hero and heroine inside all of us. We essentially have the power to create miracles in our lives if we are willing to step out of the shadows and stand in our greatest light.

Our lives can unfold as a dream, a nightmare, or a state of mediocrity, depending on who we believe we are and who we choose to be inside our creation.

KEY QUESTIONS TO ASK YOURSELF

This is a checklist to see how on track you are with being *The Explorer* in your life:

1. Are you well rounded—or do you overuse your strengths to compensate for your weaknesses?
2. Are you willing to rely on your internal resources and take risks?
3. Do you compensate for your own weakness by depending on others?
4. Do you expect your partner to exhibit certain qualities you haven't developed personally?
5. Are you in the process of discovering more of your potential?
6. Are you willing to try a new approach and stretch your character?
7. If you ever feel inadequate, do you develop a new strength or hide your weaknesses?

CHAPTER FIVE

SHEDDING THE ARMOUR

If we build a defence structure around us it not only keeps out the things we don't want to experience, it also separates us from experiencing love.

When I sat down to lunch in a sunny Sydney café with my good friend Mark, I immediately sensed that something was bothering him.

'What's wrong?' I asked. 'You seem agitated.'

'It's my boss. She's stressed and she's taking it out on her staff,' he said. 'If you don't snap to attention when Monica appears, she thinks you're being impertinent.'

Although Mark was annoyed by Monica's gruff manners, he was also sympathetic to her heavy workload. He knew that underneath her strong facade was a sensitive woman, suffocating under the pressure of both her status as a business owner and her sheer physical bulk. Monica's once voluptuous figure had become far heftier since her rise to the top of the corporate ladder.

I had worked quite closely with women with weight issues, and suggested to Mark that perhaps Monica could benefit from a session. He agreed wholeheartedly and set about trying to coax his boss to see me.

Monica had already met me in my role of art director. Perhaps this would allay her concerns that I might be a new age 'fruitcake'. Monica was an academic, who had little time to waste on speculation. It did seem ironic that a woman with a will of steel had so little discipline when it came to food. And now Monica's doctors were also scrutinising her obesity as a possible cause of her infertility. Monica's disappointment and frustration at not falling pregnant were escalating, and her staff was absorbing the brunt of it. Her concern about her infertility and her sagging energy levels finally convinced her to have a session with me. Mark was relieved; he felt this was an opportunity to take the pressure off both of them.

I agreed to meet with her at her office, when most of her staff had left for the day. Mark decided to stay behind and tie up a few loose ends. I told him he could dismiss the notion of pressing his ear up against the wall. My sessions were confidential!

I walked into Monica's office and she closed the door behind me. She took the 'power seat' behind her desk, and I was offered the visitor's chair. For a moment I felt we needed to switch positions. This was one occasion where it would be wise for Monica to give up her control. If she was going to gain anything from the session, she had to be totally receptive and let the information filter through her head and land in her heart. My eyes surveyed the fabulous collection of photography and design books lining the shelves of her cabinets. The artist and the sage in me were tempted to explore the contents of their pages and consume my concentration. Monica's office was ablaze with colour. An abstract painting laced with splashes of red hung boldly on a pale, ice blue wall. By contrast, Monica was wearing basic black. Her pale, delicate skin was framed by long waves of shiny, dark hair. Her striking, blue eyes were, without a doubt, her most prominent feature.

As I started to sense Monica's energy, I was hit by a wave of resistance. Her defence structure was so strong I was slightly intimidated. In fifteen years of sitting in sessions, I have only come across four other people who were as heavily guarded. Three of them were men, and the other was a high school headmistress who had just come out of a torturous thirty-year marriage. For a moment, I wondered if I would be able to cut through Monica's force field. It was going to take a hammer and chisel to break it down. I adjusted my focus, took a breath, and reminded myself that I was working with her soul. I placed my ego to one side, and was ready to take the plunge. Monica reached for a pen and notebook. I requested that she refrain from taking notes. As an option, she could listen to the recording of her session at a later date. She looked at me as if to say, 'Don't tell me what to do.' I suggested she stay present, and just relax. Monica placed her notebook and pen neatly in the drawer and leant back with her arms folded. There was no point tiptoeing around with Monica; I had to get right to the core of the matter, to impact her heart.

Monica had both power and presence. She commanded respect by promoting her intellectual prowess and her strategic skills. Her father had always taught her that her brain was her greatest asset, and that if she wanted to get ahead, she had to stand out in a crowd. Her mother knew all about 'being visible'. She was strikingly beautiful and was the perfect socialite wife. Monica's father enjoyed the attention she gave him. Her life revolved around waiting on him, and fulfilling his every request. Monica was put off by her father's arrogance. There were times when he was condescending towards his wife and complained that she was vague. It isn't surprising that Monica's mother found solace in the bottom of a martini glass. Monica's father was a perfectionist, and often self-righteous. He was proud of his daughter and yet, at the same time, highly critical. Rather than acknowledge Monica's achievements, he would highlight her mistakes and emphasise the areas where she needed to lift her game.

Monica's father expected her to have his brains, her mother's beauty, and a touch of her own mystique, a tall order for a girl who also had her own aspirations. When Monica was a small child, she had an expansive imagination. She loved to dream, to enter an internal playground of pure possibility where she would become different characters and express herself freely. Her mind would take her on delightful journeys to explore her full potential. Monica's inner world was a safe haven, where 'the romantic dreamer' came to life. As an innocent, impressionable child, Monica was vulnerable to her father's rigid temperament. The soft, feminine side of her nature began to retreat.

Her outward persona took on a strong, vigilant edge, which allowed her to stand sturdily in her father's presence. Monica started to believe that unless she was on the ball she would fall behind or be dominated. After all, if she were vague and docile, like her mother, she would end up being stepped on, or bridled and saddled like a show pony. Would anyone notice if Monica put the sweet and sensitive side of her nature to sleep? Monica's mother was concerned about her daughter's tendency to shut down. She didn't appreciate her aloof manner and told Monica she was being selfish. Monica started to feel as though the world was against her. Somehow, she needed to find her freedom.

As Monica got older, she forged ahead to build her own life, and protected 'the romantic dreamer' at all costs. Her assertiveness and practical ingenuity became her greatest strengths in protecting herself from further hurt. She drove herself long and hard, not unlike her father. She was fiercely independent and reluctant to ask for help. Being controlled, or told what to do, was one of Monica's greatest aversions. How many times did Monica's father disapprove of the way her mother prepared his meals or ran his errands? He insisted on having the final say. And how many times did she watch her mother reach out for her father's emotional support and end up feeling dumped? Monica believed she couldn't rely on anyone to act as a tower of strength in her world. So she simply decided to take on the role herself. 'The romantic dreamer' was locked in a tower, just like the character of Rapunzel in the fairytale. Monica started to feel shut off from other people.

Armed with a degree in marketing, commerce and fine arts, Monica entered the advertising industry. As she forged ahead, she noticed her body starting to change shape. The more intense Monica's determination became, the more weight she put on. Whenever she felt challenged, she would override her fear and push down her emotions. Rather than maintain her feminine grace, Monica's manoeuvres resembled the tactics of a football player. Fighting for equality, and eventually superiority, she refused to be vulnerable. Yet underneath her tough exterior was a frightened little girl who was afraid of being hurt.

Monica got to a point where she just needed to breathe. Her weeks were crammed with appointments, meetings and job tasks. Far too often, on a

Saturday night she would sit at home in front of her computer writing proposals for the following week. All she had to keep her company was her cat and a tub of chocolate-chip ice cream. It isn't as though Monica wasn't attractive; she was curvaceously striking and a wonderful conversationalist. Her emotions were so overwhelmed by the intensity of her thoughts that she simply lost her spark. This escalated to the degree that she eventually became numb and her heart froze over. All work and no play made Monica a dull girl. She felt fatigued and uncomfortably fat. She was carrying the weight of the world on her shoulders, with no one to lighten her load.

Deciding it was time for a long-overdue sabbatical, Monica set out from America to Australia. Perhaps a sea change would expel Monica's inner demons. But despite leaving her job, her family and her country, her parent's emotional legacy remained wedged in her heart. The spirit of her parents followed her like a silent mentor. Monica made a vow never to be as weak as her mother and unknowingly continued to seek her father's approval. Although she managed to put an ocean between them, she was still caught in the cycle of comparison and competition. Australia was like a new frontier for Monica, and it inspired her pioneering spirit. Her arrival in Sydney presented a promise of hope—and it was there she met her future husband.

John was a quiet, mild-mannered young man who spent most of his time glued to his computer, navigating his way through cyberspace. His fascination for technology was rivalled only by his passion for reading. He often devoured the entire contents of a good book in an evening. John had a wonderful imagination, which enriched his sensitive nature. A man of few words, he remained receptive to what life had to offer, and was humble enough to accept its blessings. John had a distinct twinkle in his eye and a boyish charm. His playful spirit and affectionate nature warmed Monica's heart; so much so, that she vowed to accompany him as his faithful companion in life.

The beginning of their relationship allowed Monica to rekindle the secret dreams she had buried in her childhood. The sensual, spontaneous side of her started to blossom, and 'the romantic dreamer' began to see the light. As Monica gave voice to her heart, the excess weight began to slowly melt away.

Monica felt a sense of peace when she was with John. Unlike the men in her past, he took the time to listen and didn't try to compete with her. Although he was extremely intelligent, he was fairly unassuming, and allowed Monica to take centre stage. She had finally found a sympathetic soul, with whom she could share her aspirations. Although John was extremely resourceful, he wasn't overly ambitious. He preferred to take his time with things and had a remarkable eye for detail. When they first met, John tempered Monica's stride as they explored each other's worlds. John was on his home turf and felt confident supporting Monica while she adjusted to the Australian way of life. As he introduced her to the colloquialisms, quirks and customs, she enjoyed being guided for a change. Once Monica's feet were firmly planted right next to John's, it was time for her to pick up the pace.

After planning their future together, Monica picked up the blueprints, surveyed the terrain and hit the pavement running. She was not in the habit of waiting for anyone to 'get her a life', so she set about creating a life for both of them. How did John feel about this? He was happy to continue following his own path and include her in the process. He built foundations slowly; Monica built them fast. He liked to contemplate which were the best bricks to use, and she was more concerned about having enough bricks to build a second storey. John loved Monica, and fortunately for both of them, he was born with a liberal amount of patience and tolerance. Was John too slow for Monica? In her mind, most people were. As playful lovers they were gracefully on course; as architects designing a life, they were way out of step. Rather than tread on John's toes, Monica decided to streak ahead. As a sensitive, supportive partner, John remained steadfast; as a 'monopoly player', he was not up for the game.

By the time Monica and I came together in session, she had built many levels to her material world. Unfortunately, in the process, 'the romantic dreamer' had retreated behind her fortress of excess weight. She regained the weight she'd lost when she met John and had even piled on more.

She was protecting the feminine side of her nature, while her masculine side worked overtime. Where was John? Watching from the sidelines, waiting for her to give up the fight with life. Consequently, she began to suppress her feelings again. Although Monica's life was growing externally, her inner world seemed empty. Her sexual experiences with John became less frequent and intimacy became blocked by her fear. She was self-conscious about her size and no longer felt desirable. To attempt to fill the void, Monica turned to food.

When I broached the subject of her sex life, Monica began to swivel in her chair. Her eyes looked at the corners of the ceiling and she became detached. For a woman who normally looked people straight in the eye, she was struggling to keep her composure. This was obviously one topic she wanted to avoid. I sensed that this was an important matter, which is exactly why I persisted. In my sessions, there is nowhere to hide, and it was futile to try to skirt the issue. I would simple change my approach, and go in through the back door. She was not going to surrender easily, and I had to tug on her heartstrings a little until she opened up. I talked about her underlying fear, which was masked by a layer of anger and guilt. As I communicated exactly how she was feeling, she shed a few tears. I handed her a tissue and when the conversation was finished, she breathed a sigh of relief.

Both John and Monica had talked about having a child. The problem was, Monica was finding it difficult to conceive and was frustrated. As with everything else in her life, she tackled the problem 'head on' and was determined to accelerate the process. But where was Monica's heart when it came to this delicate matter, and what were her deeper intentions?

There is often a split between what we consciously think we want and what we desire on a deeper level. In her rational mind, Monica decided she wanted to have a child. But subconsciously, she didn't trust John to support her completely, and was terrified of depending on him. Would he be a 'tower of strength' in her world and catch her if she fell? Being pregnant and surrendering to her feminine side would leave Monica feeling vulnerable—one of her greatest fears. Monica had also drawn parallels between motherhood and her own mother's unhappy life. She equated playing 'the nurturer' with submission.

This woman was also unwilling to give up her desire to prove to men that she was just as strong as them. I sensed Monica's hurt and her belief on a deeper level; she wasn't soft and gentle enough to be a mother. Her defensiveness was keeping powerful men at bay. Unfortunately, it also kept the love out. Monica's potential unborn child was on the other side of that blockade, trying to find an entrance. Staying unreceptive meant she would never allow herself to have a baby. This was one time she couldn't force her will or control the situation. The child needed to grow on fertile ground; it was time for her to embrace her femininity.

I talked in depth with Monica about her childhood preference of wanting to be a boy. Although there were many things about being a girl she enjoyed, she felt boys had more freedom. It was time for Monica to reassess her beliefs around being a female. She needed to create her own paradigm, rather than rely on her mother's example. Because she swung the pendulum to one side in order to avoid her mother's weaknesses, she denounced her mother's positive traits in the process. For Monica to feel fulfilled, she needed to retrieve the sensual, nurturing muse—characteristics that were prominent in her mother. And yet Monica had judged these as being useless. What would Monica's first step be? She needed to honour her feelings and allow 'the romantic dreamer' to inspire her path. Her early childhood dreams held the key to how beautiful life could be. In recapturing her innocence, she would become receptive enough to embrace the idea of motherhood and give birth to a new part of herself in the process.

Whenever we give birth to a new part of ourselves or more of our potential, our opportunities multiply. As fearful as she was, Monica needed to trust that she had everything it took to be a good mother. Out of fear, Monica had become locked in her head. Which is why she insisted on controlling everything and everyone. If she were willing to allow the feminine side of her nature to complement her masculine energy, her intuition would guide her gracefully into motherhood.

After our session, Monica was clear that she needed to surrender her control and replace it with a strong desire to become a mother. 'Gentleness' and 'receptivity' were the key words for her to remember. I assured Monica that she wouldn't become weak and dependent. In actual fact, she would potentially become more powerful. Her energy levels would increase and she would create far more harmonious relationships. Her life would be based on the principle of 'giving and receiving', rather than always feeling depleted.

Monica needed to allow people in her life to support her, and at the same time, give generously to them. She needed to put her husband and marriage at the top of her list. It wasn't enough for Monica to declare her marriage as a priority; her thoughts, actions and feelings needed to line up with that statement.

It was time for Monica to make a few significant changes: most of all, her attitude. During our session, Monica cried on several occasions. For me, this was a sign that she was willing to be more vulnerable and allow her feelings to surface. Monica gathered up the crumpled, tear-stained tissues she accumulated on her desk. Her eyes were slightly red but her face looked open and fresh. Monica's demeanour had been transformed from a composed, corporate executive to a soft and gentle woman. Her armour had dropped, and the beauty of her essence began to shine through. I suggested she go home, run herself a bath, put on her favourite piece of music and pamper herself. If she wanted to become 'the nurturer', it was wise to start nurturing herself. I told her to imagine the water in the bath washing away the residue from her past, and clearing away her defences.

I gave Monica a hug and told her she was incredibly beautiful. That is the gift that awaits me at the end of all of my sessions. Not so much the hug, but the opportunity to see how extremely precious each individual is. Over fifteen years, not one person has left my company without presenting me with that priceless gift. Some people have more baggage than others. But beyond their physical persona, no matter how hard their armour may be, exists the magnificent presence of their soul. Monica squeezed my hand and thanked me. Our session added a new depth to the meaning of freedom for her and she intended shedding her baggage, both emotionally and physically. After all, there was a lot at stake. She had finally realised the importance of liberating 'the romantic dreamer'.

Dreams born from the heart never die; they simply lie sleeping.

Mark called me several weeks after the session, to give me an update on Monica's progress. For the first time, Monica was making an effort to directly acknowledge him for his efforts. She encouraged Mark to use his initiative and follow through with his ideas independently. Monica was finally willing to trust others. Her manners had definitely softened and she was even a little more tactile. Mark was stunned when Monica allowed him to oversee the creative team and pitch for a new account single-handedly. When they won the deal and locked in the contract, she even gave him a hug. For someone normally as reserved as Monica, it was one step short of a miracle.

Monica's husband, John, also listened to the tape from the session and now saw his wife in a completely different light. John had always been compassionate, but now he had a deeper understanding of why Monica behaved the way she did. It took a lot of courage for Monica to share her session with John and her openness paid off. It gave John room to support her emotionally and their relationship took on a new dimension. Mark also noticed that Monica started to leave the office earlier and attempted to clear most of her workload by the weekends. Her priorities finally shifted and she wanted to spend more time with John. Contrary to her old beliefs, Monica's company didn't collapse; it continued to prosper. But now, the responsibility for that was shared.

LOOKING BENEATH THE SURFACE

After Monica's session, I realised how often we sacrifice parts of ourselves under the guise of getting what we want. Our beliefs will dictate precisely what we create. Monica didn't feel it was safe to be 'too feminine', so she beefed up her masculine qualities for strength. She wasn't willing to trust her feelings and relied heavily on the workings of her mind. Consequently, she flattened out her feelings, including passion and sensuality.

Our feelings are all set on one dial. If we refuse to feel specific emotions, we deny ourselves the pleasure of experiencing the others. If we turn down the dial on our anger and hurt, we automatically diminish all our feelings. We can turn the volume on our feelings up or down depending on whether or not we are willing to silence our fears. Since adolescence, Monica had denied her feelings to avoid the pain of her father's harsh criticism. She had felt under pressure from him to perform. When her fears surfaced, she would push herself harder to gain control, and reach for food as a source of comfort. When Monica overindulged, she was left feeling numb.

It was imperative that Monica gave herself permission to feel again. She needed to learn how to finetune her feelings, rather than control them. Our feelings are there to guide and nourish us. Changing our attitude and taking positive action always creates new opportunities, which leads to more satisfying experiences. If we block our feelings or distrust them like Monica did, no matter what we create, we simply won't enjoy the benefits. Life lacks lustre when we look at the world through shaded eyes. We can't feel a gentle breeze on our face if we are wearing a balaclava to protect us from the wind.

If Monica was willing to be more flexible in her life, instead of being so wilful, she could have saved herself a lot of pain. That old expression, 'she cut off her nose to spite her face', rings true here. Monica detached from her feelings and in the process felt like only 'half a woman'. Even if Monica were a man, she still would have felt empty, because she created a void within herself. It is essential that we learn to dive deeply into our feelings while keeping a clear head. That way we won't deny ourselves the pleasure of feeling passion, joy, exuberance and love. If we avoid pain, we also close down to pleasure.

Her husband had also suffered in the process. Having a lover who doesn't want to 'play' can be very painful unless, of course, you deny your feelings while you go through the actions. Fortunately, John offered his support and suggested Monica modify her behaviour. He was concerned about her size because it affected her health, dampened her spontaneity and pushed him away from her. He never criticised Monica about her weight; he was simply worried about losing the woman he loved.

His wife's obsession with work was based on a desire to build an identity that was 'impregnable'. Monica's inability to conceive a child was a symptom of her resistance. Her excessive weight was disturbing her hormonal balance, which was a reflection of her denied femininity. Although she thought she was treating herself when she ate rich foods, she would end up feeling both physically and emotionally heavy. When she surrendered to her cravings, she felt powerless and then pushed back at the world with her assertive, masculine energy to regain control. The cycle simply went on and on.

Of course all she really wanted was to feel secure and loved. But that couldn't happen unless Monica realised she was lovable, not for her performance or appearance, but simply for her essence. All of us need to remember that our essence is always perfect. That was unfamiliar territory for Monica, because she was plagued by unresolved childhood insecurities. Even though John was there to offer her love and emotional support, his contribution would remain impotent until Monica was willing to love and support herself.

For Monica to break 'the spell' her father had cast on her as a child, she needed to open up to being loved. This modern-day Rapunzel would escape the confines of her self-imposed prison only when she saw there was no ogre holding her captive other than herself. Just like Monica, we all need to face our 'inner demons' and learn how to accept, rather than fear our emotions. We have the power to determine our own experience. The way we choose to respond to what happens in our world governs how we feel. For Monica to resolve her internal unrest, she had to pay attention to how much love she was, or wasn't, willing to receive.

Chances are we all have an inner tyrant who keeps us imprisoned behind a barrage of shields. We can either form an identity as a vehicle for our self-expression, or use it as a false sense of security as Monica did in developing her academic and corporate profiles. She leant on her identity so strongly that it overshadowed the rest of her character. To be fulfilled, we need to open up to life's bounty in the same way children do. This doesn't mean we should be naïve or childish. It's possible to be open while also being wise and discerning.

Shedding our armour in a world we believe is unsafe, can accentuate our fears. Monica was terrified to be seen as 'the insignificant female' based on her limited beliefs. The only way all of us will overcome our fears is to remember that love is our greatest protection. Monica equated love with weakness, because she assessed her mother's love as powerless. Both Monica and her mother wanted to prove they were worthy of love; they simply went about it in different ways. If they were willing to break the cycle and love themselves first, they would have made better choices and been happier as a result. Monica's father was seen as 'god' in the household. So Monica and her mother went to great lengths to avoid his wrath.

To love unconditionally, we need to accept ourselves fully. For Monica, that concept was extremely confronting. She believed that if she accepted herself, she would remain flawed, and would never change. And yet, the opposite is true. We all need to look at the human qualities we are not willing to own or accept, and embrace each and every one of them. If Monica accepted her mother's legacy of beauty, sensitivity and a caring nature and combined it with her father's sharp mind and strong will, she would have found a point of balance. Instead, she saw one position as being more powerful than the other, and believed she had to choose one of them. We often do this with our parents' traits; we categorise and choose, rather than blend and balance.

Monica was deceived by fear, which blinded her to the truth. There are times where vulnerability is a great strength. Yet like many of us, Monica was terrified of being vulnerable. If we want to receive love, tenderness and support from someone we are close to, it is essential that we open our hearts. During the process, we are obliged to give up control, which is why Monica became so resistant. Many people are terrified of surrendering to love; they believe love is untrustworthy because of their past experiences. There is a huge difference between surrendering to another person and yielding to love. Love is a state of awareness that connects us with our essence. That is why our choices and decisions need to be inspired by love, so our heads and our hearts work harmoniously. Love then automatically becomes our protection, because we make wise choices.

The only way to receive love is through humility, which allows us to be in harmony with the world. If Monica had been willing to be more humble, she would have naturally let down her defences and opened up to being touched. Instead, she shut down, because she was afraid of being criticised. Like Monica, we all have to take the responsibility first. We are the ones who ultimately cast the decree of what is valuable in our world. Nobody else does. John could have told Monica she was beautiful until he turned blue in the face, but would Monica listen? Not unless she was willing to surrender to being loved.

The Dreamer
Uncovering our Power and Beauty

My session with Monica proved to be a wake-up call. After having her fears and aspirations exposed, there was nowhere for her to hide. She saw how much she had tortured herself over the years and how she had kept people at bay. Monica knew that if she genuinely wanted to have a child, she had to start taking motherhood seriously. Whenever we deny our feelings, we simply retract from the source of life itself, which is essentially love. We distract our attention in the hope that our negative emotions will dissipate, in the same way Monica did. Burying our head in the sand or fighting back simply doesn't work. It only brings up more negative emotion.

Monica was attempting to mask her problems, rather than dealing with them. Whatever we push down will resurface, to be dealt with, until we are at peace. Even though Monica was a wife, a corporate executive and an intelligent adult, she was still operating on a deeper level as a child.

We continue to recreate our childhood hurts until we realise the key to our liberation lies in self-acceptance.

Monica's self-consciousness resulted in self-punishment. She denied herself love, sex and intimacy, and overindulged in food. If our emotions remain unexpressed, they will simply stagnate and become lodged in our physical bodies. Monica's weight was caused by stuck emotional debris. It was time for Monica to let go of her core belief that she was insignificant. Her voracious appetite for food and work was only a camouflage for her hunger for power. Monica didn't genuinely believe she could have what her heart truly desired.

Many of us complain that people don't care about our feelings, and yet we are often insensitive towards our own. While Monica resented people's cutting remarks about her weight and her rigidity, she inwardly ran the same conversations. If we are unwilling to acknowledge how we feel about ourselves, then we cannot expect anyone else to do the same. If we get in touch with our feelings, that doesn't mean we have to be overwhelmed by them. They are always there for a good reason, which is normally to show us that our thoughts or actions are causing us grief. If we alter our thoughts and expand our imagination, then our feelings will respond. That is why Monica needed to incorporate 'the romantic dreamer' into her life; it was a simple way for her to lighten her load.

We have the capacity to feel everything and anything we choose. When Monica awakened the 'romantic dreamer', she could explore the entire realm of possibility. Our imagination is a powerful tool that cannot be denied. If we discount the dreamer's potency, we will lead uninspired and monotonous lives. Monica knew that scenario far too well; her life was all about work and feeling completely exhausted. We are the masters of our emotions. Other people have an impact on us, but at the end of the day we are still responsible for the way we feel. It is therefore imperative that we are at peace with ourselves, which brings us back to self-acceptance. We can always choose to be more, and so can the people in our lives. The only way we will know who we ultimately want to be is by using our imagination. If we solely rely on our thoughts, we will end up using our past as a reference and come up with the same conclusions.

Imagination is more important than knowledge. Knowledge is limited. Imagination encircles the world. Albert Einstein

Our rational minds are finite and our imagination is infinite. Which resource do we want to rely on to determine our full potential? Our thoughts will eventually align us with limitation, while our imagination promotes creativity and invention. If Monica was to break free of her rigid patterns, she needed to discover a new way of seeing herself. Monica's father was always telling her to stop daydreaming. As an academic, perhaps he would have been wise to consider Einstein's philosophy. Although it was a challenge for Monica, she needed to start trusting her internal senses, rather than exclusively relying on her intellect. To quote Albert Einstein once more:

We should take care not to make the intellect our god; it has, of course, powerful muscles, but no personality.

If we continue to detach on an emotional level, we start to draw away from others. Closing down will leave us feeling lonely, no matter who we're with. Monica felt very isolated, even though she had a husband, numerous friends and a large staff. We can interact with others and yet because of our fears, there is a part of us that wants to stay separate. We can easily find ourselves going through the motions in a relationship and no longer 'feeling' related. This is a sure sign that we have put up our defences, detached from our feelings, and are operating from our 'heads'. And just like Monica, beyond our fear, we long to be completely acknowledged and loved.

After our session, Monica reawakened 'the romantic dreamer' by becoming more playfully self-expressed in her marriage and work. Sure enough, her weight started to shift, and so did her libido. Monica finally embraced more of her sensuality. Her hemlines went up and she let her hair down. 'Rapunzel' was free to let her long hair blow in the wind.

Monica's transformation didn't happen overnight. It took thoughtful attention and consistent effort. The more of herself she expressed, the more weight she shed. It was like lifting a series of veils to uncover more of her power and beauty. The ultimate reward for Monica was yet to come—the birth of her first child. Monica finally broke the spell and created a new paradigm around motherhood. Not only for herself as a woman, but also for her baby daughter. She managed to create a healthy balance between the masculine and feminine sides of her nature, and as a result, her relationship with John blossomed. When we turn away from being loved, parts of us die. Monica was no longer willing to make that sacrifice.

Our choices will either empower or imprison us. We have the privilege of either honouring our feelings or falling asleep and letting our ego take control. We all deserve to be happy. Denying ourselves the love we know, in our heart, we honestly deserve, is simply a form of self-punishment. Love feeds us emotionally, mentally, physically and also spiritually. We starve ourselves very slowly if we don't allow ourselves to be nourished by its presence. That is why, like Monica, we often reach for substitutes to fill the gap. Ultimately nothing compares to love. We cannot blame anyone else for our discomfort, because we know we have the right to choose. It took Monica some time to come to that conclusion, but when she did, her life took on new depth. We need to accept our strengths and our weaknesses and declare that we are lovable.

Once we remove the covers from the sleeping parts of ourselves we expose the power and beauty of our essence.

KEY QUESTIONS TO ASK YOURSELF

This is a checklist to see how on track you are with being *The Dreamer* in your life:

1. Do you take time to daydream and get in touch with your aspirations?
2. Do you explore your imagination or rely heavily on logic?
3. Are you spontaneous and playful?
4. Are you cynical about romance or does it inspire you?
5. Are you open and receptive or distrustful of others?
6. Are you happy to share openly or do you defend your privacy?
7. Do you value your feelings above all else or find yourself avoiding certain emotions?

CHAPTER SIX

HAVING A REALITY CHECK

If we persistently build a persona to hide what we believe are our flaws,
we will continue to search for outside approval to substantiate our worth.

When Lauren arrived at my house for a session, I was surprised when I opened the front door to greet her. I had no idea we had already met. Some years earlier, I was fortunate enough to hear her give a public talk in San Diego on the value of commitment...little did she know her choice of topic would turn out to be an ironic one. That night of the talk would become a memorable one for me. I was deeply moved by the conviction behind her words and her ability to take a stand for what she believed in. Lauren was a powerhouse on legs. She was strong and courageous as well as delightfully feminine and down to earth. As she addressed her audience, she paced back and forth, gesturing with her hands. I was mesmerised by the size of her diamond ring and wondered if it was real. After talking with Lauren at the end of the evening, I was assured that there was nothing fake about this woman. Lauren's charisma left an indelible imprint in my mind.

Although my first meeting with Lauren was a memorable one, our second encounter would take on a far greater depth. We spent two and a half hours together in session, delving deeply into the nature of her relationships and the harsh consequences of infidelity. Lauren was a beautiful and extremely soulful woman. Her wisdom and clarity stretched far beyond the limits of most people I have encountered. Lauren was a long way down the path in the areas of self-awareness and personal development. She was studying for a BA in Psychology. She'd just turned forty, although she didn't look it. She had flawless olive skin and a petite body. She attributed her fresh and youthful appearance to yoga, grooming and a good diet.

She may have lived in southern California, but Lauren was one girl who didn't subscribe to the virtues of breast augmentation and a bottle of peroxide.

I asked Lauren if there was anything in particular she wanted to gain from her session. She looked at me solemnly and said, 'Relief from a broken heart.'

With a box of tissues on standby, I started to go into the core of Lauren's issues. She sat there for an hour and a half without saying a word. Like an innocent child, she listened as I talked about her life's lessons and revealed her greatest challenges. Lauren had spent the better part of her life strengthening her assets and sharpening her skills. She worked with her dark side, her light side, the outside and the inside. Lauren had done everything she knew to become a better person. But as she went through the process, she was driven by one enduring question, 'What's the matter with me?' Lauren may have had her weaknesses like all of us, but there was nothing 'wrong' with her. To me, she was an inspiration. Lauren was intelligent, attractive, witty and energetic, with a vibrant spirit and a generous heart. So why would Lauren feel compelled to find 'her failing'? Because no matter how hard she tried or what she did, her one 'true love' would not commit.

Lauren had finally enticed Greg to walk down the aisle, but he was still a wanderer. Greg wasn't satisfied with one flavour; he wanted to savour an assortment of 'eye candy', and looking just wasn't enough. Although he went to great lengths to conceal his clandestine activities, he was occasionally caught out. He would swear to Lauren that he would give up his philandering, and use that old line, 'She didn't mean anything to me.' And in the case of his call girl connections, I suppose he was being honest. Greg would promise to bridle his 'untamed spirit' and be loyal to Lauren, and then his ego would get the better of him and his commitment would start to waver.

Before their marriage, Lauren went backwards and forwards, and turned herself inside out, trying to make the relationship work. Lauren experimented with everything from tantric massage to metaphysics, and it still didn't make any difference.

While Greg loved many of Lauren's qualities and they were extremely compatible, he just couldn't quite commit. He was keen to leave his options open, in case something better came along. He was ruthlessly ambitious, and his appetite for wealth and power was enormous.

After five years of going in and out of a relationship with Lauren, he finally proposed. Lauren told him he either had to be a man of his word and fully embrace their relationship or walk his path alone. Lauren stood her ground and told Greg he had to choose—her or the field. Greg didn't want to lose Lauren. The level of tenderness, intimacy and friendship they shared was far beyond anything he had known. Her love was unyielding and her commitment unwavering. Lauren was a constant source of love and inspiration for Greg, which was something he couldn't deny. What more could a man want? Nothing. But it was the 'adolescent' in Greg and not the 'man' that needed convincing. Greg was forty-one years old; it was time for him to grow up and settle down.

Even though Greg wasn't certain if Lauren was 'right' for him, he knew, above all else, that she was good for him. So he finally took the plunge. He dived head first into their marriage after promising to remain faithful. Lauren, in turn, vowed to throw Greg a lifebuoy when he was out of his depth. With her wisdom and knowledge she was well prepared to navigate the course of their marriage and be a supportive partner. Would Greg be able to keep up the momentum or would he get sidetracked again? In a culture where ego is rife, he would need to stay very focused and make sure the 'adolescent' part of him didn't lead him astray, otherwise he would sabotage his relationship. Lauren would need to give up her inner query of what was 'wrong' with her, or Greg would start to think that perhaps Lauren wasn't 'right' for him.

During our session, I became very aware that in most areas of her life Lauren was confident and secure. Her self-esteem was very healthy; it was her self-worth that needed strengthening. I told Lauren her self-esteem was something she had built based on her accomplishments and her level of self-expression. Her self-worth, on the other hand, was inherent, and therefore didn't need validating. Lauren had fallen into the trap of seeking Greg's admiration, rather than acknowledging her own worth. On a deeper level, Lauren believed that her love alone wasn't enough to inspire her lover. She thought she had to be 'wonder woman' to make an impression. Lauren was challenged by her greatest life's lesson, which was to know wholeheartedly that she was more than enough to completely satisfy the man she loved. Lauren's soul was coaxing her to recognise the potency of her love above all else.

The turning point in her relationship was when Lauren decided she wanted a child. Although this was their original plan, when faced with the reality Greg became awkward and nervous. They had been married for almost two years and it was time for Greg to grow into the role of fatherhood. After all, he was in his early forties, fit and extremely wealthy. After the recent sale of his company, Greg walked away with almost sixty million dollars. With all of that time and money on his hands, how was he going to spend his day? Enjoying life with his family, after working like a Trojan for twenty years, or revving his Porsche up to high gear to travelling in the fast lane? This was the exact moment Greg would be confronted by his rebellious adolescent. Part of Greg's initiation into manhood would entail becoming a father. Was Greg's heart inspired? Absolutely. Could Greg get his head around the concept? Not unless he changed his self-image.

Greg agreed to the baby with a few stipulations. Lauren had to promise to regain her figure after pregnancy and to not 'let herself go'. Greg was fine about being a dad as long as he didn't have to look like one or have a wife who resembled 'a mother'. When Lauren was upset by Greg's insensitive comment, he told her he was simply acknowledging how fabulous her body was. If this little outplay wasn't a refection of Lauren's negative beliefs, nothing was. Lauren decided to go ahead with the pregnancy, knowing in her heart that she would be willing to raise the child independently if Greg buckled under the strain.

During her pregnancy, Lauren's femininity blossomed. She rested, walked on the beach, had lunch with her girlfriends and did everything she could to stay fit and healthy. Her study of psychology also helped her understand the patterns in her marriage. Lauren gave Greg lots of freedom and simultaneously nurtured their marriage. It was a happy time for her because she was finally living out her dream. Lauren and Greg lived in a large modern house built on the side of a cliff, with breathtaking views of the ocean. She would often sit by the pool and contemplate how beautiful her life would be as a mother, in the arms of a man she deeply loved.

The day Emily was born, it was as though an angel had shed its wings and descended to earth. She was absolutely divine. Greg and Lauren were blessed with an exquisite gift. It seemed also that Emily was sent to liberate Lauren from the limits of a testing relationship. As she tendered and protected Emily over the first few months, she was inspired by the precious nature of her soul. Here was a baby girl who, in all her innocence and glory, commanded love and attention simply because of the purity of her heart. Lauren started to acknowledge the power of her love and Emily responded with sheer delight. Greg was slightly more awkward around the baby. He seemed preoccupied, and Lauren sensed that there was something wrong. And this time she knew it wasn't her. Was Greg experiencing 'growing pains' associated with fatherhood? Or was he simply restless again?

Greg's long afternoon drives along the winding roads of the Coast Highway started to extend into the early hours of the evening. He'd arrive home just as Lauren was putting the baby to bed. Was Greg held up by an extra round of golf perhaps, or a drink with a business associate? Greg was also spending an awful lot of time at the sports club. Was his personal trainer taking him through a vigorous new routine, or was he admiring the scenery? Rather than accepting his new role as a father, Greg was more concerned about keeping up appearances. Now he was semi-retired, he was perplexed by how he should spend his time. Greg was torn between playing 'happy families' and modelling himself on Ken, who was always chasing Barbie. It seems that Greg's 'adolescent' had taken the driver's seat and was about to drive him right out of his marriage.

Greg left his wife when Emily was just six months old, which is precisely why Lauren was sitting in front of me now. Although she had finally come to a point where she no longer wanted to be with Greg, she wanted to put all the painful memories behind her and move on. She knew it was important to stay calm when she dealt with her ex-husband, for her daughter's sake. All Lauren wanted was to protect her daughter and heal her tender heart. It had been one year since the marriage had dissolved and the divorce had finally come through. Lauren had bought a lovely home for herself and Emily in a quiet, leafy neighbourhood. Meanwhile, Greg had no problem adapting to his new life. He was happily wooing his new love interest in his lavish waterfront apartment.

Mandy was the epitome of the blonde bombshell. When the lean, leggy aerobics instructor walked into Greg's gym she elevated his heart rate in more ways than one. With her mesmerising features and sensual voice, she could lull most men into a trance. Like a hopeless schoolboy, Greg fell under her spell. Although he knew he could get his fingers burnt, he felt a strong urge to satisfy his craving.

Unfortunately, a few of Lauren's 'friends' felt compelled to fill her in on the details of Greg and Mandy's romance. Apparently Greg had started his amorous escapade when Lauren was pregnant—which explained why Greg and Mandy moved in together so soon after the split. The news was like a knife in Lauren's heart. She now knew why Greg had insisted she refrain from flying with him on his business trips during the final months of her pregnancy. She'd thought Greg was being cautious, but now knew he had another motivation.

It wasn't surprising that by the time Lauren landed on my doorstep, she had a few wounds to heal. How do you mend a broken heart? By knowing the value of your love, despite other people's opinions and behaviour. Lauren had given her trust to a man who was more concerned with collecting trophies than enjoying his bounty. Just because Greg wasn't willing to treasure her love didn't mean she was flawed. Greg wasn't looking for substance; he was looking for a partner who would attract his rivals' attention.

Where did Lauren fit into his pattern? She was a blessing in Greg's world, and so was Emily. But was Greg willing to open up to receiving all of their love? Did he honestly believe he deserved to receive that much attention? Based on his rebellious behaviour, obviously not. Groucho Marx once said, 'I would never want to join a club that accepted me as a member.' Sometimes things said in jest can be very pertinent. In this case, Greg abided with Groucho's philosophy, which concealed his self-contempt. Greg's behaviour also fed Lauren's own insecurities, which left her doubting the power of her love.

After becoming a mother, Lauren was clear that she no longer wanted to fight. Her first commitments were her peace of mind and her daughter's welfare. And what about Lauren's heart? I worked with her over the course of a few days, helping her to rekindle her dreams. Her heart needed nourishment and a dose of inspiration. For Lauren to open up to being loved, she had to forgive herself first. For eight years she'd walked down a path strewn with betrayal. By choosing a partner who was unwilling to offer her emotional support, she was betraying herself. Her valiant spirit was dedicated to saving her relationship with Greg at all costs. But how was her heart coping in the process? Without a partner who was willing to match her efforts, she was left feeling abandoned.

At the end of the day Lauren couldn't blame Greg for her misfortune. With her knowledge of metaphysics, she knew she had abandoned her own heart by making Greg's opinions more important than her own feelings. That was the lesson Lauren was to gain from her marriage, and it would eventually stand her in good stead for her next relationship. I suggested Lauren treat her herself with the same degree of love, tenderness and vigilance she gave Emily. Then she would start to acknowledge the power and value of her love.

After our first session together, Lauren started sleeping better, and she regained her appetite for the first time in eight months. After working closely with me in a small group over the course of the following weekend, she was completely recovered. When she left the retreat, she looked like a fresh-faced teenager who was ready to take on the world. Lauren was glowing. Over the two-day period, she fostered a deep, intimate relationship with her soul, which enlivened her spirit.

With her new vision in place and her dreams safely resting in her heart, she approached the next chapter of her life with a skip in her step. The next time Greg called in to visit Emily, he was taken aback by the changes in Lauren. She was far less stressed than usual and spoke to him with a newfound serenity and certainty in her voice. Greg was curious to know what had changed. He suspected Lauren had a new lover. And in a way, he was right; Lauren had started loving herself. She gave him my contact details and suggested he call me. He told her he would consider it. She had learnt not to push him. Lauren was now more concerned with her own aspirations than with wanting to 'fix' Greg.

It took two weeks for Greg to call me. He was intrigued, and slightly nervous. After 'tuning in' to Greg during Lauren's session, I felt as though I already knew him. However, I was surprised when I met him in person. His physical appearance was contrary to his forceful, dynamic nature. He was tall, lean and willowy, with ruddy skin and sandy hair. Driving around in his Porsche convertible left him vulnerable to the harsh effects of the sun. He was casually dressed in a white cotton shirt, a pair of blue jeans and carried a brown buckskin jacket. As he stepped into the living room, he surveyed every detail of the interior, like a person taking inventory. I offered him a seat as I opened the French doors that led onto the terrace. I could see he was extremely curious and wanted to get a better read on who I was.

I told him to relax and give me a moment to meditate. I sat quietly and listened to the gentle trickle of water from the Japanese fountain on the deck. When I finally opened my eyes, Greg was sitting peacefully with his eyes closed, stilling his thoughts. What a wonderful place to begin. But I sensed that under his cool facade, Greg was experiencing inner turmoil. He was frustrated and agitated, like a fish swimming upstream. When would Greg ever find peace? He had more money, more toys and more people catering to his needs, than most men see in several life-times. So what was his problem? Nothing quenched his endless hunger for power and pleasure and he was running out of places to search for a 'fix'. Greg's anguish was wearing him out, and he was carrying a very heavy heart. Neither Mandy nor Lauren could lighten this man's burden. Greg's deep dissatisfaction with himself would never be reconciled through outside stimulus. To heal his unrest and ease his discontent, Greg needed to alter his internal self-image.

I could see very clearly after sitting with Greg that his fervent ambition was derived from a deep desire to compensate for his weaknesses. He had built an unrealistic vision of who he needed to be in order to be accepted. This idealised self-image was born out of an adolescent fantasy, rather than an authentic dream. Greg's father was ruthlessly critical when he was growing up and expected him to excel in every endeavour. A very powerful and wealthy man in his own right, Greg's dad was harsh, rigid and controlling. His mother was very different. Greg was her favourite child and she showered him with love and attention. However, his mother's affection wasn't enough to soften her husband's harshness. Although she tried to protect Greg, her love seemed feeble.

Greg attempted to use the strength of his will to overcome his emotions. He vowed that one day he would find his freedom, and be far more powerful than his father. Greg studied hard and used every ounce of his energy to compete for intel-lectual status. He relied heavily on the capacity of his mind to guarantee him a bountiful future. All the while he felt emotionally and physically vulnerable, and mostly kept to himself. When Greg began college, he was faced with even more pressure to perform. Not only academically, but also socially. While his peers were developing their 'masculine prowess' and dating ' the cream' of the campus, Greg was usually hitting the books. He compared himself unfavourably to the out-going, good-looking guys who were popular with women. Greg's desire to prove his worth became more and more intense. His vow to become more powerful than his father extended to all men.

Greg aspired to become invincible. His aim was to be popular, powerful, and physically alluring. And the older he got, the higher his expectations became. He wanted to be a cross between Bill Gates and James Bond. Greg was building his dreams on a shaky foundation. Underneath his confident facade, he saw himself as an unimpressive geek. Greg's fractured internal self-image was based on his dis-torted childhood beliefs. He secretly saw himself as boring, inconsequential and lacking substance. His biggest fear was being exposed as a fake. Greg's father had undoubtedly made a very strong impression on his son in more ways than one.

Greg was an intellectual giant, an extraordinary businessman, a wonderful friend, a playful lover and a loving son. He was creative, inventive, humorous, and deeply philosophical. And yet none of those things was enough to stop him from seeing himself as undesirable. As I sat in front of Greg, I felt like crying. I could not only see his distorted self-image, I could hear his cry for love and feel his emotional pain. I spoke to Greg about his relationship with Mandy and told him I sensed that although they had only been living together for a few months, he already had one foot out the door. I shook my head and told him I sensed that she was concerned about his lack of commitment.

The woman who Greg thought was Miss Right turned out to be less than perfect. When Greg met Mandy he thought he'd finally met his match. He said he had dreamt about being with a woman like her his entire life, and now it was finally happening. To Greg's dismay, he still wasn't satisfied. All of those years in college when he sat back and watched the popular guys walk off with the beauti-ful blondes, he was left in the dark, dreaming about being 'the chosen one'. Now his turn had finally come, and after the first round, he didn't want to play. Greg's fantasy was about to turn into a nightmare. I could feel Mandy's emotional storm about to erupt. Greg already sensed her anger and asked me what he should do. Mandy needed to be acknowledged in a deep and soulful way. If he were willing to support her emotionally, her unrest would subside. Otherwise, he would recreate the same pattern he had played out with Lauren.

Above all else, Greg needed to strengthen his internal self-image by choosing to be a different person. He wouldn't be able to touch Mandy unless he was willing to give from his heart. In order to change his behaviour, he had to start seeing himself as a different person from the inside out. He needed to go deeper and create more intimacy in his relationships, rather than hiding behind a mask. If he were only willing to communicate on a superficial level, his heart would never be satisfied and neither would his partner. I suggested that Greg work on fostering sex and intimacy together rather than viewing them as unrelated. He would have to risk being vulnerable, but this was the only way he would overcome his fears. If he were willing to let his partner get really close to him and refrain from running out the door, he would eventually open up to being loved. It was time for him to let people in and allow them see who he genuinely was.

If Greg wasn't willing to be honest with himself, how could he be honest with others? Similarly, if he wasn't willing to love and cherish himself, he had little chance of letting a woman love him deeply. He was too busy telling himself there was something 'wrong' with them, while on a deeper level he believed there was something gravely wrong with himself. Neither Lauren nor Mandy had any idea how to make Greg happy, because Greg had no idea.

It was time for Greg to wake up. He was running around, searching for an appendage to make him feel better. I told him that every time he had a new lover, it was like putting a bandaid on a large wound which needed serious attention. The part of Greg that needed healing was the part of him that he wasn't willing to expose. All the lovers in the world wouldn't help Greg unless he was completely receptive to being loved.

Greg needed to rethink his priorities and start aiming for substance rather than frivolity. He was skirting the real issue, which was his addiction to overcompensating for his childhood hurts. He needed to strengthen the fractured parts of himself and stop projecting his insecurity onto others. Mandy was doing precisely the same thing with Greg. She had no issue about the way she looked, but she was extremely sensitive when it came to her intellectual capacity. She was forever telling Greg that he didn't think she was smart enough. Greg's arrogance was starting to push Mandy's buttons because she believed he wasn't taking her seriously. Was Mandy inwardly concerned about being labelled a 'dumb blonde'? The three things that build security in a relationship—generosity, acknowledgment and gratitude—Greg rarely practised. And although he was generous financially, he withheld parts of himself.

Unless Greg lifted his game with Mandy, he would continue his search for 'Miss Right'. At the end of our session, I suggested that Greg do a little soul searching. If he gave up his fantasies he could build a life based on what he felt in his heart rather than his ego, which promised the world and delivered nothing.

There is great truth in the saying, 'Love is blind.' Unless we let ourselves be impressed by the beauty of a person's essence, we will never know the potential of their love. Greg also needed to see himself with generosity and acceptance.

At the end of the session Greg said he would reflect on what we'd discussed and asked if I was willing to give him further coaching. As I was leaving for Australia ten days later, it wouldn't be possible. I suggested he listen to his tape and use it to stay focused. He looked quite sad as he left. I was very aware of the innocent, childlike part of his nature coming through to the surface. Although Greg knew he and Mandy needed to talk, he was reluctant to let her in. His commitment to his own personal growth would ultimately have to come first.

LOOKING BENEATH THE SURFACE

Although Greg is a man who lives in a world of extremes, there is definitely something we can all learn from his behaviour. To cover up his fractured self-image, Greg went to great lengths to conceal his insecurity. He was driven to build an impressive facade in order to be accepted and combat his deeper fear of loneliness. Lauren, who was far less aggressive, aspired to be a resourceful 'super-woman' to prove she was worthy of Greg's love and devotion. Our aspirations may not be as exalted as Greg's, or as philanthropic as Lauren's, but we all have our fantasies.

There is a distinct difference between a genuine dream and a fantasy. Lauren's dream was to be a therapist to help people grow. Becoming the 'perfect wife' was simply a fantasy. Greg had a dream to take over a company, use his skills and expertise, and grow the profits to considerable heights. His aspirations were based on positive ambition. Greg's desire to become one of the wealthiest guys in southern California, so he would stand out in the crowd and be Mr Popular, was an adolescent fantasy.

Our idealised self-image is driven by ego and usually based on seeking approval. It has nothing to do with developing our substance and character. If we insist on upholding an impressive persona, we often deny our deepest feelings and discard our genuine dreams and loves. Just like Greg, we work to keep our mask in place for fear of being exposed. It was difficult for Greg to create intimacy in his relationships because he was hiding behind a mask.

For Greg to ultimately feel satisfied in his relationships, he would have to risk being vulnerable and open himself up. How else was he going to receive his partner's love? When he complained that Lauren was not enough to satisfy him, he should have asked himself how much he was willing to receive. Having your heart impressed by love is a memorable experience. Conversely, the bedazzlement of someone's appearance is relatively fleeting. At some point, we have to dive deeper to feel truly satisfied.

Like Greg, many of us attempt to impress, rather than allow our true essence to shine through. Greg was like a child in a sandbox enticing others to come and play with his fantastic toys. He may have been in his forties, but a part of him was still playing out the lonely, awkward child. Greg had a great deal of substance, and yet he still didn't fully believe it. If he lost everything tomorrow, would Mandy still want to be with him? That was one question Greg asked himself over and over. Perhaps he needed to ask Mandy the same thing.

I spent a lot of time in the wealthy parts of southern California doing sessions. Quite a few young women chose their partners as if they were shopping at Neiman Marcus. They had their checklists ready, and their engagement rings already picked out at Tiffany's, even before 'Mr Wonderful' had showed up. If he wasn't driving a prestigious car he never got a second date.

If we base our 'powers of attraction' on a persona, rather than on the qualities of the heart, we will end up feeling estranged in the same way Greg did. Although his intention was to experience more love, his identity, not his feelings, became his priority. When I sat with Greg in his session, I felt his undercurrent of sadness. Because he was denying his 'real self', he wasn't being nourished. The 'boring, inconsequential, unimpressive geek' will stay locked in the cupboard forever. And yet this tiny part of him was running most of his life. He was exerting far too much energy trying to hide this part of him. He needed to fully accept and integrate this aspect of his nature if he were to be healed.

His wounded child was crying out for love and self-acceptance and there wasn't a woman on the planet who could take that pain away. Greg had to take responsibility for loving himself. Then he could open up to really enjoying an intimate relationship. Mandy also suffered from a fractured self-image around her level of intelligence. If Mandy was able to heal this part of her, she may have built her own business empire. Where would Greg be then? Would Mandy have passed him by? Would she put up with Greg's noncommittal attitude and his arrogance? She also needed to 'get' the value of her worth; otherwise she'd continue to feel unappreciated.

There are few of us who have reached a level of self-love that allows us to consistently uphold our preferences without compromise. Most of us feel incomplete in some way. Whenever we search for someone, or something, to validate our worth, we are attempting to fill a void.

Lauren mended her broken heart and fortified her self-worth by re-establishing her vision based on authentic dreams rather than her ego. Her love for her daughter Emily was the catalyst. After her divorce, Lauren was eventually able to look at her past and say, 'I have failed, but that doesn't mean I am a failure. I have learnt through my experiences and know I am a stronger, more loving person.'

In the same way Lauren did, it is incredibly important that we all hold a strong image of the person we ultimately want to become, based on our genuine dreams and aspirations. Lauren saw herself as an attractive, intelligent, dynamic woman, who had a great capacity to love. This put her in a strong position to create a wonderful future. Lauren had to be willing to let go of the past in order to stop projecting her failure into the future. If Lauren had placed more emphasis on her performance and appearance after splitting with Greg, rather than on the depth of her character, she would have continued wanting to prove her worth. She could have done what many women in California do after a divorce—go shopping!—not just for a new look, but for a new husband. Lauren was committed to fully healing her heart and giving up the struggle. As a result, she is at peace and feels much better about being herself.

Greg was still battling with his ego. After finding his 'dream girl' and living with her for several months, he still wasn't happy. He was put off by her demands for more attention and more commitment. Mandy would come home from work every now and again and sulk in the kitchen while cooking dinner. She'd rattle the pots and pans and slam the cupboard doors. Greg would attempt to soothe her by taking her out somewhere fabulous for dinner. But Mandy didn't want to be entertained, she wanted to be acknowledged. Why didn't she just express her feelings to Greg? Because like most people, she had poor communication skills and was afraid of telling Greg she wasn't happy. She'd then 'withhold' in the bedroom, which is when Greg would get really annoyed. Greg wasn't a man who liked to argue. Mandy, however, was full of passion. Greg just needed to learn how to keep up or get a clue! Like all of us, Mandy just wanted to be loved.

THE HEALER
OPENING UP TO BEING LOVED

Even though Greg was a powerful man with millions of dollars in assets, he still had difficulty accepting his inherent worth. No matter who we are in the world or what we achieve, unless we learn to value our essence above all, we will be plagued by our ego. It will demand that we live up to a list of unrealistic standards. If we don't measure up, we go unloved. Greg knew that experience well, based on his childhood relationship with his father and his adolescent dealings with his class-mates. He was intimidated when he felt he didn't fit in or belong. His identity didn't match up to what he considered 'valuable', and he felt like an outcast.

Rather than feel left out, Greg wanted to find a way to 'fit in' and 'stand out', all at the same time. The only way we can do that is to know the value of our essence and honour our uniqueness simultaneously. In my sessions, I've met many people who have struggled for years with this dilemma. They compromise themselves because they want to be accepted. Like Greg, if we follow the treacherous path of our ego, we'll be estranged from love.

Greg placed so many conditions on being loved that to him, love became nothing more than a concept. Why? Because he wasn't feeling love, he was merely thinking about it. He was trying to calculate who was worthy of his affection. And if the person didn't promote his stature, he was rarely interested. When it came to his intimate relationships, he was afraid to love deeply for fear of making a mistake. To gain a sense of being in control, Greg turned down the volume on his love. What if Greg gave his love wholeheartedly and was rejected? To overcome his fear of disappointment, he harnessed his love like a bridled horse and measured its merits with his rational mind. Most of us saunter through life waiting for love to arrive, rather than claiming love in the moment as our divine birthright.

Life is a gift, and so is love.

Our 'real self' is both profound and inspirational. If we always seek others' approval we give away our power. Which is what Lauren did with Greg for many years by making him 'god' in her world. She waited for him to decide whether she was worthy of being loved. Greg did the same with every tall, blonde 'goddess' on the planet. He desperately wanted their approval.

Who do we make 'god' in our world? Every single human being is worthy of love. It is up to us whether we are willing to receive that love. Once Lauren gave up her self-criticism and practised self-acceptance, she could let go of Greg and heal. Lauren now celebrates her uniqueness and doesn't compare herself all the time to other women—even the tall, blonde, leggy variety. She no longer needs Greg to 'define' her, and is blossoming on her own.

The last time I spoke to Lauren, she was about to graduate with her BA in Psychology and was excited about the future. She wanted to work specifically with women to heal their hearts and enliven their spirits. Her life experiences have prepared her well and she wants to share her wisdom with others. Lauren is also happily dating again, but this time, with a new level of discernment. If a man wearing hunting boots turns up on her doorstep, she simply tells him to move along. She is very clear that she wants a man who has the strength to commit for the long term. Although she hasn't met her ideal partner yet, she's at peace being on her own with her daughter for the time being. That is a far cry from the 'old Lauren', who would have been asking, 'What is wrong with me?' Every morning when she opens her daily journal, she reads the memo on the front page: 'Remember the value of your love.'

Lauren has finally learnt to listen to her heart and is now more receptive to being loved. I told her to be wary of the 'voice of doubt' and suggested she pull the plug on her ego whenever negative thoughts kicked in.

The more we listen to the ego, the further we move from our 'real self', which is a source of love and power. If we continue to give our ego permission to define who we are, we will always sell ourselves short.

Our ego looks for our Achilles heel and grinds away until we are defeated. It doesn't help to argue or reason with it, or even try to annihilate it. We simply need to nip it in the bud and shut it off.

When we move away from our 'real self', we can find ourselves struggling or vying for power. Greg lost sight of his real self and got caught up in the illusion of life. Rather than judging him, or condemning him for being selfish, we need to recognise that Greg simply fell asleep. He was looking for a woman's touch to awaken him, but was unwilling to acknowledge the power of their love, or his.

Just like Greg, at times we may feel empty, and we may attempt to fill that void with alcohol, food, sex, drugs, work or even too much partying. On a deep level, he felt powerless in intimate relationships. All of our unfulfilled dreams will point towards a distorted self-image. Underneath the rogue was a scared little boy who was looking for love. There were times when Lauren and Mandy saw that side of Greg, which is why they fell for his boyish charms.

Unlike Lauren, Mandy was still trying to win Greg's approval. She was demanding an official commitment, but the mere mention of marriage made Greg very nervous. All of a sudden he developed selective hearing and tuned out, hoping she'd drop the subject. But Mandy wanted to be fully loved and wasn't willing to give up.

It would have been very wise for Mandy to ask herself one important question. If you have to push a man to acknowledge the value of your love, is he worth spending your life with? If a man is so fearful of commitment, he is not committed to experiencing more love.

Just a few months after moving in with Mandy, Greg already had one foot out the door. Six months later, he was revving up the Porsche with his hunting boots on. When will it ever end? Perhaps when he finds a Swedish model or an exotic Brazilian dancer? At this point, I would suggest to Greg that he enter a monastery rather than keep playing the field. Well, for a short time anyway. Just long enough to reconnect with his soul and make a commitment to loving and accepting himself, otherwise he will end up searching for love in all the wrong places, until he finally comes home to himself.

Any form of addictive or obsessive behaviour simply doesn't work in the long run. It will never satisfy our desire to be loved.

KEY QUESTIONS TO ASK YOURSELF

This is a checklist to see how on track you are with being *The Healer* in your life:

1. Do you have authentic dreams which serve as a platform for you to express your talents and which help you grow in love?
2. Do you indulge in adolescent fantasies based on substantiating your worth?
3. Do you work hard on maintaining your image rather than developing your character?
4. Are you awkward or hurt at times and pretend to be OK?
5. Do you attempt to change things externally, and create more in your world, to overcome feeling empty or fearful?
6. Do you reach for a 'quick fix' or look deeper to see what ails you?
7. Do you take time to reflect on the value of your love and the beauty of your soul?

CHAPTER SEVEN
HOOKED ON LOVE

Unless we wholeheartedly acknowledge the power and value of our love, we will continue to search for someone or something on the outside to fill the void.

Living in La Jolla, California gave me the opportunity to meet an eclectic group of people. La Jolla is known for its lavish estates and wealthy inhabitants. When I first arrived in La Jolla, I lived in the pool house of a huge property with a tropical garden, high above the ocean. The house was designed by Frank Lloyd Wright's son, and was beautifully refurbished by an LA designer for my dear friend, Brad. The architecture was sleek, white and ultramodern, with floor to ceiling glass windows and an open plan living area overlooking a serene, edgeless swimming pool.

This magical hideaway became an idyllic setting for me to hold my sessions. It was here I first met Lucy. She was going through a challenging period in her marriage and was searching for clarity and direction. On the day we met, I watched Lucy through the glass doors, as she strolled around the garden looking for the entrance to the pool house.

Brad noticed the 'lost maiden' meandering through his garden and came out from the main house to offer his assistance. A handsome bachelor with a keen eye for attractive women, Brad was more than happy to chat with Lucy as he ushered her to my front door. This mini-skirted sex goddess was only 5-foot 3 inches but what she lacked in height she made up for in attitude. She had striking Eurasian features and wore a flimsy floral dress and high heels, and smelled of jasmine.

Lucy told me she was nervous and excited to meet me. Apparently she had a strong interest in spirituality and a passion for exploring alternative methods of healing. She twisted her wedding and engagement rings around her finger as we talked. As I closed my eyes and began to meditate, I became very conscious of Lucy's underlying sadness. Images came to me of a nightingale in a gilded cage, sitting motionless on its perch, longing for freedom. I shook my head and began to talk to Lucy about her feelings of imprisonment. Her frustration about feeling 'trapped' had surfaced as intense eczema on her legs.

Lucy's strict Chinese father had always cautioned her against laziness and promoted productivity. He ruled with an iron fist and wanted to be proud of Lucy and her brothers. He insisted they make the most of their opportunities in America and take their studies seriously. Being raised in a poor family, Lucy's father worked extremely hard to provide his children with a college education. He detested indolence and ignorance. Lucy was the 'little butterfly' in the family, but he still wanted her to take a strong place in society where she would command respect. He expected his daughter to be intelligent, obedient and a good mother and wife.

Both Lucy's parents worked conscientiously to upgrade their humble lifestyle. Lucy was something of a rebel and resented her parent's puritanical attitudes. She wanted to feel safe and protected in the world, but also longed for freedom. She felt imprisoned by her father's expectations and her mother's unsophisticated manners. Although Lucy desperately craved attention, she resented being controlled or told what to do. Integrating her Chinese heritage with her American heritage was a challenge, and at times Lucy felt like a misfit. She wanted to prove that she was just as good as, if not better than, her peers, and was terrified of being dismissed as an outcast.

So what talents would Lucy use to weave her web of intrigue when she went out to find her place in the world? She chose to accentuate her sensuality and play out the role of being the 'temptress'. Although Lucy was not 'classically' beautiful, she used her sex appeal to command attention. When it came to attracting lovers, she was unrivalled. Her success with men was based on her level of self-esteem and not on the law of statistics. She learnt to 'wiggle those hips' and totter on her high heels, and played the 'helpless female'. Underneath that girly facade, she was one shrewd cookie. In no time at all, Lucy noticed that her behaviour brought an avalanche of attention, which is exactly what she craved.

Although Lucy was quite bright, she forfeited her intelligence at times and didn't believe in the power of her mind. Aside from dating a string of men in college, she felt slightly inadequate. She partied hard, and was more interested in filling her 'dance card' and exploring the music scene than in furthering her studies. Although she was usually drawn to handsome, athletic men, she entered into a serious relationship with a studious young man called Dan. When Lucy first met Dan, she thought he was a little 'nerdish'. She finally surrendered to his persistent requests to date her and became impressed by his brilliant mind, tenacity and ambition. Dan tried every trick in the book to win her over and eventually succeeded. He promised to adore her, make her feel like a princess and take good care of her. And in exchange, Dan won a partner who boosted his confidence, popularity and social skills.

To the chagrin of her parents, when Lucy graduated from college she took a job as a waitress. She went through a long period trying to determine what she really wanted to do and finally settled on studying massage. Dan was happy to support Lucy in whatever she wanted to do, and after a year of living together, they were married. Dan's father had taught him the ropes of being a good businessman. Majoring in economics, he went out into the world to start his own mini empire. With a little backing from his parents and a hell of a lot of chutzpah, Dan began to build a strong platform for success. The more his empire grew, the more hours he was forced to work.

In the meantime, Lucy grew frustrated and bored. She wanted Dan to 'come out to play', but he was more concerned about driving his business forward. The more money he earned, the more money she spent. Although Dan loved Lucy deeply, he found it difficult to keep up with her demands financially, physically and emotionally. She complained about his lack of initiative both socially and in the bedroom. Despite working a sixty-hour week, Lucy accused Dan of being lazy, boring and uninspiring. She craved adventure, wanted to explore new horizons and longed for excitement. Dan didn't want to lose Lucy, so he gave her the freedom to socialise with her friends and picked up the tab for most of her expenses. To alleviate her restlessness and boredom, Lucy would often travel independently and spend extended periods away from home. All the while, Dan continued to work like a Trojan, and was exhausted by the weekends. Over a seven-year period they slowly drifted apart.

By the time I met Lucy, she had one foot in her marriage and one foot out the door. She had recently decided to study holistic healing practices in Los Angeles four days a week. To avoid a long commute, Dan agreed to set Lucy up in an apartment in Venice Beach. Although Lucy was in her early thirties, she had the demeanour of a twenty-two-year-old. As I 'tuned into' Dan in her session, he felt like someone in his late thirties, yet he and Lucy were almost the same age. Dan was not inspired to party as much as Lucy, and she was not inclined to settle as much as her husband. So as their priorities shifted, Lucy was not getting the attention or acknowledgment she desired from her partner, and her 'intentions' started to stray. Lucy wanted to take on the world. Although she had her independence in Los Angeles, she was like a butterfly caught in a net—she needed complete freedom.

I talked to Lucy about how she had recreated the situation with her parents in her marriage with Dan. She wanted to feel secure and protected, but underneath, she resented being 'trapped'. Lucy felt powerless in her marriage. She wasn't being acknowledged in a way that satisfied her, but at the same time she was afraid to leave the marriage and face the world on her own. I talked to Lucy about why she married Dan in the first place; she had compromised, and wanted Dan to be responsible for her welfare. Lucy wasn't ready to settle down and play 'happy families'. The more he gave her, the more she wanted. The more he tried to pull her closer, the more she pulled away. Dan's cadence was more like a caterpillar than a butterfly; she chose a partner who would 'ground' her, but then she felt tied down. Lucy not only wanted Dan's support, she wanted him to inspire her, entertain her, and make her feel better about herself. That was ultimately Lucy's downfall.

She was angry with Dan for seeing her as a fragile 'sex object', and accused him of thinking she was dumb. That seemed a little strange for a girl who had built a persona based on those particular qualities. The things she was initially attracted to in Dan, she started resenting. His stability and ambition were driving her nuts, as were his sensitivity and gentleness. She was always criticising Dan for not being good enough. Lucy rarely wanted to have sex with him, and when she did, it was all about her pleasure. Dan became so despondent with their sex life that he stopped trying. That was the last straw for Lucy, who had an addiction for being desired and pursued.

The more Lucy criticised Dan, the more he tired to fulfil her demands. On one occasion, she suggested she would be more inspired to have sex with him if he developed a 'six pack' and gained more muscle tone. Dan went out the next day and enrolled in the gym. The more he gave, the more disdain Lucy felt for him. And the more anxiety Dan experienced, the more he shut down emotionally. He was going through all the 'right' actions, but underneath, his heart was broken. Although Lucy was attached to Dan, she thought he was weak and dull. She wanted a 'real man' who made her feel like a 'real woman'. Lucy concealed an emptiness that was almost impossible to fill.

During Lucy's session I sensed that she was straying in her marriage. She told me she had been spending time with a 'friend' of hers called Tom. He was a tall, tanned playboy from Del Mar. Unlike Dan, he was outgoing, adventurous and sporty. He and Lucy partied often and would laugh and dance until the early hours of the morning. There were even times when Dan would escort her to one of Tom's parties. After midnight, Dan would be tired and bored and Lucy would want to stay, so Dan would leave her in Tom's 'trusty hands'. He would escort her home; or if they were too drunk, he would promise to put her to sleep on his couch. Hmm, interesting story. Dan turned a blind eye to Lucy's extracurricular activities. She promised to be faithful and that was good enough for him.

How could Dan be certain that Lucy wouldn't betray him? Several years before, Lucy was out of town studying at a holistic workshop. After the course she and a few girlfriends went to a party. Lucy had far too much to drink and ended up spending the night with a young man who captured her desire. One of her friends was shocked, and threatened to tell Dan.

Lucy was terrified that if Dan heard about her weekend romp from someone else, he'd throw her out. So she decided to tell him herself, at a moment when she knew he wouldn't go crazy. She told him one evening at dinner with a group of his business associates. Dan's face turned white. He excused himself from the table and asked Lucy to join him.

As they walked out into the cool night air, past the valet parking attendant, Dan attempted to restrain his anger. His first question was, 'Why are you telling me this, and of all the times to choose, why now?' She burst into tears like a vulnerable child, and told him about her friend's threat. Lucy told Dan that she had learnt her lesson and didn't want to be scolded. Through the mask of innocence, she proclaimed her love, and expressed her fear of losing him. Dan mournfully shook his head, then reached out and took Lucy in his arms.

It almost destroyed him to see her breakdown and look so unhappy. Was he completely gullible or just astonishingly forgiving? If the truth were known, Dan was just hopelessly afraid of losing Lucy. He asked her to promise she would never do it again; if she would not promise, the marriage was over. Dan requested that she sign a contract stating that if she ever left him she would leave with nothing. Lucy signed the document and was grateful for a second chance. Sticking to the agreement was easier said than done; by this stage Lucy had developed an appetite for seducing good-looking men. The little butterfly was trapped.

A few years later, Lucy started to really feel the pressure. Dan was a secure marriage partner who owned the deed on their house and ran a thriving business. If she left, Lucy got nothing; if she stayed, she had to curb her desires. I suggested to Lucy that she was more than capable of supporting herself. She wasn't a child any longer and her soul was encouraging her to claim her power to create a full and rewarding life. Lucy also needed to learn how to speak her truth, without criticising or blaming her partner. It was time for her to be responsible, regardless of whether she chose to stay in her marriage or go out on her own. Sitting on the fence and complaining would only leave her feeling miserable. Lucy couldn't expect Dan to fulfill her needs if she wasn't willing to consider his. It was time for her to be truthful with her husband, and talk to him about what she honestly felt. Not about him, but about their relationship, in regard to her genuine desires and aspirations. Then Dan would at least know where he stood.

After we discussed her marriage, I talked to Lucy about her desire to be a holistic healer. She wanted be a strong independent woman who had the ability to alter people's lives. I suggested she practise using compassion and thoughtfulness, and being the nurturer in her partnership with Dan, which would in turn develop her self-esteem. If she wanted to be seen as a gentle woman with substance, Lucy needed to allow her self-image to mature and expand beyond the parameters of being an elusive, captivating, butterfly. Flitting from one thing to another, and one man to the next, was dissipating her energy. She was still suffering from a fractured sense of belonging, which was destroying her marriage and compressing her heart. She didn't want to be with Dan, she wanted to be with someone 'better'. And yet, she was imprisoned in the relationship because of her lack of self-worth.

Lucy was always looking for someone to rescue her from her own her self-doubt, even if it was a temporary companion to provide the next thrill. Lucy had completely disregarded the impact of her actions, and had no faith in the validity of her love. Tom wasn't Lucy's only hobby; flirting with the opposite sex became one of her favourite pastimes. Being a masseuse brought her into intimate contact with an array of attractive men. If Lucy weren't willing to take her marriage seriously, and build solidarity in her relationship with Dan, their partnership was destined to end. On one level she was pushing him away with her lack of acknowledgment and her criticism, and at the same time she was terrified to let him go. It was time to jump off the fence, or she would end up getting splinters in her delicate behind! Lucy needed to choose her path and stick to her convictions; otherwise she would continue to feel helpless.

Lucy told me she would attempt to heal her relationship with Dan and see if she could make the marriage work. I reminded Lucy to have patience with herself and Dan, and to curb her impulsive behaviour. She looked at me like an innocent child and nodded in agreement. I sensed that this little butterfly was more powerful than even she suspected. When a butterfly flaps its wings it can trigger a storm somewhere else in the world.

After Lucy left, Brad came to my door and asked me about the delectable 'honey' who had wandered up his garden path. I rolled my eyes and told him Lucy was married. 'That's funny,' he said, 'she didn't give me the impression she was a married woman.'

I wondered how many men had fallen into Lucy's lair. The impact she had on men was astounding; if she were able to channel all that energy into her career and marriage, she could be a Chinese–American empress!

A few days after Lucy's visit, her husband Dan called to book a session. When Dan walked up the pathway, my first impression was that he had far too much on his mind. His shoulders were slightly hunched and his hands were tucked into the pockets of his charcoal suede jacket. With his jet-black hair and pale, luminous skin, he cut a striking figure against the muted sky. I greeted him at the door and offered him a seat. Dan seemed like an extremely gentle man who was carrying a very heavy heart. His boyish smile brought occasional relief to his otherwise startled gaze. His eyes were large and mournful. After probing deeper into Dan's emotional state, I noticed that he had taken on the brunt of life like tiny little shocks, which had jolted his psyche. Those disturbances had built up to the degree that he was completely disassociated from his feelings.

The images that came to me around Dan were of a man climbing to the top of a mountain carrying a heavy load. As strange as it was, I then saw him sitting on the side of the escarpment rolling a cigarette. I found out later that Dan was partial to marijuana. Every evening after work he rolled himself a joint and his problems seemed to disappear in a puff of smoke. For a man who ran a large company, Dan managed to 'keep it together', and even excelled at his game. But how were his relationships? In most cases they were non-existent. Dan was in physical contact with people at all hours of the day, but was completely estranged from them emotionally.

Dan's main lesson in life was to learn how to create affiliation, co-operation and unity. Although he was president of his company, he had very few 'people skills'. His staff members were always complaining about his lack of communication. Dan attempted to build rapport but ended up being a 'people pleaser' rather than a negotiator. Dan would stuff his own feelings down, say very little and end up being railroaded. He needed to develop the assertive side of his nature. Even though he was academically brilliant, and had extraordinary technical and inventive skills, he liked to work in the dark. Dan preferred to retreat to the 'bat cave' than to step out into the limelight.

That was Lucy's job. She was the party girl, the performer, the attention seeker, and he loved to bask in her glory. Lucy was playing out Dan's 'light shadow'. He had projected onto his partner parts of himself that he wasn't willing to own. The little butterfly inspired the bat to come out of his cave and have fun. The only problem was that Lucy wanted to play with other butterflies too. On one level it was understandable that Dan was so transfixed on Lucy. He was blinded by her magnetism to the degree that he lost sight of his own. When Dan had Lucy on the end of his arm he felt secure and confident. When Lucy had Dan at her side, she felt safe and protected. But that contract was wearing thin.

Dan was tired of Lucy's criticism. He felt completely unacknowledged in the relationship but was willing to put up with her behaviour because he had a companion who built his status. Dan took great pride walking into a room knowing that most of the men around him wanted to sleep with his wife. The downside of the equation was that most of them actually did.

Dan saw himself on a deeper level as gawky, unattractive, boring and unpopular. In reality, he was a tall, intelligent, attractive guy, with a generous nature. Most people would have thought his self-esteem was higher, but take him out of the business world and he was searching for crutches.

With a workaholic father who rarely took time to share the spotlight, he got off to a rough start. His academic mother was frustrated with her husband's self-absorption, and stuffed her anger down each day with an endless supply of joints, chocolate and cigarettes. When Dan was a child and sat in the kitchen with his mum in the afternoons, he wasn't waiting for a batch of cookies to bake. He was playing 'mother's little helper' as he siphoned out the seeds from her latest bag of grass. There was very little nurturing in Dan's childhood. He used to make his own sandwiches before school, because his dad was out the door early and his mother slept late.

When Dan was twelve, his mother packed her bags and moved out. Dan was left with his grieving father, who had a complete emotional meltdown. Young Dan was left to pick up the pieces. To make matters worse, his father went into another relationship almost immediately. When his new bride moved into the family house, Dan locked himself in his room, night after night, and refused to come out. Television became his escape; it blocked out the noise of his stepmother's loud cackling, and his father's compulsive moaning. Dan dreamed of someday being rescued from this mayhem by his adventurous mother. He missed eating ice cream with her late at night on the porch, and their endless games of Scrabble. She may not have been the classic nurturer, but she was usually fun, and life with her was rarely dull.

'The nurturer' was a foreign concept in Dan's world and its absence took its toll. It is interesting that Lucy rarely cooked dinner for Dan or even made the bed. Although she was a masseuse, she was also reluctant to give him a massage because it was too much like work. There was a lonely young boy trapped inside Dan who needed a large dose of love. Dan equated love with rejection. Ouch! No wonder Dan married a woman who treated him like an errand boy. It was never about him; it was always about her, and Dan was simply a backstop.

As I covered Dan's issues in his session, I talked to him about the importance of discernment and taking a stand for his feelings. If he persisted in acting like a door-mat, people would continue to walk over him. His power was muffled under a timid voice that needed to be vented. Dan was not expressing his concerns or his preferences; he simply avoided conflict at all costs. Dan wanted to be a lover, not a fighter. To assuage his hurt he turned a blind eye and lit another joint. At times he would wake up in the middle of the night with anxiety attacks. Rather than stir his sleeping wife, he would head for the kitchen, munch on a couple of chocolate chip cookies and wash them down with a swig of milk, just as he did when he was a kid. Dan was craving love, support and tenderness.

I told Dan he needed to start treating himself with love and respect, and that until he did so, no one else would. I suggested he take back his power from Lucy, and learn to say 'no'. Then he needed to express his preferences; this was difficult, because Dan didn't know what they were. He was so caught up in pleasing everyone else that he'd lost sight of his own personal dreams. Hello Dan, why are you building your empire? Oh, to keep the princess happy.

Dan's fear of abandonment and loneliness had left him trapped in a prison of self-sacrifice and martyrdom. His ego told him Lucy was his ideal partner because she kept his self-contempt in place.

I suggested Dan take a few days off, head for the wilderness alone, and do a little soul searching. He gasped and his eyes opened even wider. I was serious, and I had no qualms in telling him. He had no idea Lucy was thinking of leaving; he was too busy trying to win her approval. Dan needed to go away and come back to La Jolla with 'the nurturer' as an escort and not the 'critical parent'. No more cracking the whip of self-punishment, Dan needed to leave his bondage ropes in the past.

The next time I saw Dan, he and Lucy were together. They booked in for a couple's session to gain a deeper understanding of the dynamics in their relationship. As they sat in front of me on the couch, Dan placed his hand affectionately on Lucy's knee. She was agitated. I felt she expected me to tell Dan to pull his socks up and give him a lecture. As far as I was concerned, Dan had already been scolded enough in his life; he was more in need of a little compassion. I 'tuned in' to them individually to gauge what they were experiencing. I then turned my attention towards where they stood as a couple. There was a wall of separation between them: although Lucy was physically still in the marriage, emotionally and mentally she had completely checked out. The small rift in their relationship had turned into a chasm. Their union had no solid foundation, and as a couple, they had no mutual vision.

Something had transpired since my last meeting with Dan that had driven a wedge between them. It was going to take a miracle to keep Lucy and Dan together, and one of them needed to be responsible enough to create it. I sensed that this chapter of their lives was about to come to a close. So what had prompted the demise of their relationship? The saboteur in Lucy was primarily running the show. To ful-fill her sexual fantasies, she enticed Dan to 'walk on the wild side' and partake in a little couple swapping. Dan had obviously gone deaf in his personal session when I suggested he practise discernment and consider his preferences. He disregarded his better judgment and was led right up the garden path with Lucy holding his hand. Lucy took Dan's consent as permission for her to entertain new playmates. Dan had no idea about Lucy's solo escapades, although he was quite clear that she was drifting away and had little interest in spending time with him.

Placing their attention outside the relationship was a great way to feed their egos. Rather than nurturing their partnership, they were flirting with disaster. Dan's insecurities mounted and Lucy's desire for freedom increased. That is a great recipe for divorce. I looked across the room and noticed the dark circles under Dan's eyes; he was working himself into the ground, and the nurturing side of his nature was in a coma. His addictions to dope, cyberspace and sugar were keeping him comfortably numb. Lucy was indulging heavily in her sex addiction. Her pleasure cup was spilling over and yet she was still feeling frustrated. She had an insatiable appetite for passion, which was masking her desire for love. Underneath their compulsive behaviour, they both felt empty, powerless and lost. Although I was facing two intelligent adults, I felt as though I had two wayward children sitting in front of me.

Dan finally acknowledged that his marriage was in dire straits one weekend when he and Lucy flew to Las Vegas for their wedding anniversary. To celebrate their union Dan suggested they have identical tattoos on their ankles. He wanted the world to know they were bonded eternally. Lucy flatly refused. Instead, she had a small delicate, butterfly tattooed onto the side of her hip. If that wasn't a sign for Dan, nothing was. Rather than sit down with Lucy and ask her about her intentions, he went straight into a tobacconist and bought a pack of cigarettes. He lit up, took one long drag, and started a brand new addiction.

And now, a week after their anniversary in Los Angeles, they were sitting on my couch. What did they really expect me to tell them? They were both unwilling to take heed of their previous sessions, so all I could do was give voice to their doubts. It never ceases to amaze me how many couples can sleep in the same bed year after year and yet find it such a challenge speaking the truth. They not only disengage emotionally; they also withhold their conversations and refuse to listen to one another.

Denial and ignorance may defer confrontation, but those unexpressed thoughts end up festering, and eventually breed hostility. In my sessions, I give voice to those unspoken words and bring them to the surface. I painted a clear picture for Dan and Lucy, and they knew exactly what they were dealing with. It was time for them to choose. They had the option of reinstating their vows and backing those words with integrity or untangling the web of deception and opting for their freedom. I suggested that the only way they could move forward was to create and uphold a mutual vision which would inspire them to recommit. Without detours or diversion, they needed to focus on instigating greater intimacy—not just sex, but intimacy. They were both hungry for love, so I suggested they open their hearts and give to one another generously. Their love could potentially heal the scars in their relationship, enliven their spirits and nourish their ailing hearts.

A month later, Lucy came home one evening, packed her bags and told Dan she was leaving. There was little explanation; she simply told him she needed her freedom. Dan asked Lucy if she was leaving him for another man and she said she was going to stay with a girlfriend. Even at the last moment she found it difficult to be honest with Dan; Lucy fell straight into the arms of Tom, who had been waiting on the sidelines. Dan was completely shattered. He cried for three days until he was so exhausted that he fell into a deep state of calm. Dan had finally transcended his state of being numb, to release an avalanche of despair. His family and friends rallied to give him strength and support.

How much would it take for Dan to realise that he deserved more in his life and that Lucy wasn't good for him? Although Lucy had signed a financial agreement with Dan and was legally entitled to nothing, he still gave her a settlement. Dan covered her expenses for the next twelve months, so she could continue her studies and feel secure. To the dismay of his family and friends, Dan wanted Lucy back. He was still in a state of delusion and refused to accept the fact that she had betrayed him. Dan was reliving the childhood abandonment he experienced when his mother left.

Life was presenting him with a few hard facts and his soul was encouraging him to move on. When Dan found out Lucy was living with Tom it shook him up a little, but he still prayed that Lucy would change her mind and come back to him. Then the full picture of Lucy's betrayals was revealed. One evening Dan received a call from Cherry, the wife of one of his close friends. She tearfully told Dan she'd found a letter in her husband's briefcase—it was a love letter he'd written to Lucy almost a year ago.

Dan slumped in his chair. It was bad enough that Justin was his friend and Cherry and Lucy were close, but Cherry had also just had a baby and had now thrown her husband out.

Dan put his hand over his eyes and wondered how Lucy could stoop so low. Cherry asked him if he would like her to read out the letter. Dan told her he thought he had already heard enough. Cherry then asked Dan to promise her he would have nothing to do with Lucy or let her back into his life. He half-heartedly agreed and said he was sorry she had gone through so much pain. Cherry cautioned Dan once more and warned him that Lucy was evil.

Dan couldn't sleep that night; he had Cherry's words running through his mind. He didn't believe his little butterfly was evil. He saw her as lost, simply misguided. He turned and sobbed in his pillow, longing to hold her close and protect her from harm. When Dan finally fell asleep, he had a nightmare about Lucy destroying his house. She took an axe to the furniture, ripped things off the wall and smashed his favourite possessions. All the while, he called out to her to stop and give him a break. Lucy ignored him and seemed to be in a trance state. Dan was undoubtedly having a dream about the destructive part of himself. His soul was still trying to get a message through to him to snap out of his childish nostalgia. If Dan weren't willing to protect and nurture himself, his heart would never heal, and his self-worth would never be restored.

The next day Dan called Cherry and asked her to fax him the letter. He was willing to know the truth. Dan was at work when the fax came through. He closed the door of his office and sat quietly to read the contents of the letter. As each word permeated his brain, his heart pounded in his heavy chest. Justin had declared his undying love for Lucy and told her she was his inspiration and gave him a reason to face each day. The letter went on to expose the delights of their lovemaking and the intensity of their passion. It was the next part of the letter that pushed Dan over the edge.

Justin expressed his frustration and anguish at having to wait in line to receive her attention. He then proceeded to list all Lucy's lovers, in order of priority. Dan was number one on his list, because they were married. Second on the list was Tom; Justin followed a close third. As Dan read the long list of names he came across the name of his best friend, Craig. Dan was absolutely appalled. Shock waves ran through his body like the current running through an icy stream. According to Justin, Lucy's affair with Craig had gone on for many years. He closed his eyes and prayed he was having another bad dream. There was no way now for Dan to escape the truth; it was time for his reality check. Dan thought of Cherry and wondered how crushed she must have been after reading Justin's words. At least she had the good sense and the self-worth to ask him for a divorce.

Dan then rang Craig to tell him their friendship was over. Next on the list was Lucy. He told her about the letter, and about Justin and Cherry's separation. Lucy burst into tears, and for the first time was speechless. There was no denial, no counter blame and no justification; all that was left was a sincere apology and a wave of remorse. If this wasn't a lesson for Lucy to clean up her integrity, nothing was. Dan told Lucy that if she didn't leave California, he would send a copy of the letter to her father. Blackmail, perhaps, or just a reassuring safeguard? Dan wanted to wash his hands of Lucy once and for all. He finally took a stand for his feelings. Although his actions were quite extreme, both he and Lucy had dragged things out for so long that it took a severe crisis to pull them apart.

LOOKING BENEATH THE SURFACE

Both Dan and Lucy chose to take the hard road rather than learning by their mistakes. Looking at their behaviour, although it was extreme, allows us to observe the ramifications of addiction and destructive behavior. Most of us have felt disappointed in our relationships at times and have found ourselves going through an emotional tug-of-war. A part of us wants to be closer to the other person, but because of our fears, we also pull away. Our internal conflict normally outweighs the external conflict, until something gives way. Dan ignored all the signs because of his fear of losing Lucy. He was completely unsatisfied in his relationship but didn't want to be alone. Didn't Dan realise there was no joy or freedom in making that sort of sacrifice? Apparently not. He masked his pain with his addictions. Neither Dan nor Lucy would find resolution until they both assessed their full potential and located where they had given their power away.

Lucy gave her power to Dan by expecting him to be the source of security and protection in her world. Dan expected Lucy to boost his attraction powers and his ability to experience spontaneity and adventure. If they had been willing to own those qualities within themselves, they would have been more discerning and honest with each other. We all have the right to choose our own behaviour. If a person's actions are causing us grief, it is our responsibility to seek resolution. Sitting on the fence and complaining simply leaves us in pain.

Deep down, Lucy and Dan both believed they were unworthy of being fully acknowledged for their love. It was easy for Dan to take a stand for Lucy, because he deeply cared about her, but why couldn't he take a stand for himself? Because Dan didn't believe he was important enough. Dan needed to acknowledge himself, and so did Lucy. Then they both would have been confident when they stood independently, without a partner to tell them they were lovable.

There are times when we are unable to effectively communicate our feelings. Lucy seemed impervious to Dan's hurt, which is why she continued to criticise him. Dan, on the other hand, was resistant to Lucy's cry for emotional support. At times Lucy asked herself if Dan was deaf, dumb and blind, and wondered if he even cared about her. The only reason Dan cut off from her emotionally was because he was plagued with self-doubt. He didn't honestly believe he was enough to satisfy Lucy, and he attempted to hide his insecurity. His self-doubt was mirrored back to him when Lucy started pursuing other men. Dan was going through the motions in the relationship but he avoided developing intimacy because he was afraid of being hurt. If we continue to create partnerships with our mind rather than our heart, we will end up frustrated and disappointed. Dan and Lucy's relationship became a chore, instead of a joyful expression of love.

Whenever we close down to love we become defensive. Dan was shut down because he feared being attacked. Lucy turned her back on Dan because she felt unappreciated. Lucy attempted to control Dan in the relationship by subtly attacking him. She wanted to have power over him so she was less susceptible to being hurt. There was no equality or sharing in the relationship because of their lack of intimacy and communication. Because they weren't growing together, they started to grow apart. If our mind is in conflict, our heart is distressed. If we get caught up in a relationship where we are at odds with the other person and are unwilling to resolve the situation, we will continue to struggle for power. Dan and Lucy were both addicted to staying with one another because independently they felt powerless. Their marriage was built on a lie, because their union was a disguise for their underlying feelings of helplessness or hopelessness.

Whenever we feel powerless in a relationship, we compromise our integrity. We often go into denial in the same way Dan did and tell ourselves things are OK. Or we withhold information from our partner, which is what Lucy chose to do. The only reason Dan and Lucy stayed together was they didn't honestly believe they could have what they wanted. They also made the mistake of thinking there was something missing within them, rather than seeing that there was something missing in the relationship. The dynamic that two people create in a relationship is always based on how they see themselves. Therefore it helps to ask why we would allow ourselves to be in a relationship that upholds our negative self-image. Dan yielded to Lucy's constant criticism and Lucy was willing to put up with Dan's unwillingness to express his emotions.

I suggested that Dan and Lucy ask themselves honestly how much love they were willing to give and receive. The quality of a relationship is based on those two important values.

It is essential that we are devoted and committed in the relationship we have with ourselves. Neither Lucy nor Dan nurtured themselves or their relationship. The scales tipped more towards addiction and self-punishment than balance and harmony. Unless they stopped devaluing their feelings and communicated authentically, they would be trapped in a prison of pain. It takes humility to release the preconceived ideas we have about ourselves and recreate ourselves anew. We need to take the time to review and release our limited beliefs, while we discover our true capabilities. Unless we are absolutely genuine in our desire to give up the pain, we will still carry the burden. For Dan, letting go of Lucy was almost impossible, because he was addicted to self-punishment. He completely disregarded his true potential.

The desire we have to punish ourselves can be incredibly subtle. If we look at the choices we make on a daily basis, we will gauge precisely how much we care about ourselves. Our choices need to empower us to grow, rather than deplete our energy. If we continue to take negative options, we simply deny ourselves the right to succeed and enjoy a full life. Like Lucy and Dan, we start to give our power away, which often leads to addictive behaviour. We stuff our feelings down and compromise our choices because we don't believe we can have what we truly desire.

Although Dan was extremely successful, he was frustrated with his chosen career path. And even though he worked long hours, he did so under duress. When we deny ourselves comfort and pleasure and push ourselves relentlessly, we override our feelings and are driven by our mind. Dan operated from that space for the better part of his day, until he reached for a joint to temper his stride. He opted for the quick fix and the easy way out. Was Lucy willing to nurture her relationship with Dan, rather than seek adoration from other men? She needed men to admire her, to reinforce the identity she had learnt to depend on. If Lucy were willing to expand her internal self-image, she would develop enough strength to gain her independence and create a full and rewarding life. If we are not living a life that nourishes and inspires us, we have fallen prey to the antics of our ego.

When we begin to recognise the precious nature of our soul, we will become our own loving caretakers. Although Lucy had a deep interest in spirituality, she was far more attached to her ego than celebrating her essence. The mother in her heart came into play beautifully in her capacity as a healer, but when it came to her relationship with herself, the nurturer was deemed powerless. That spilled over into her marriage with Dan, because she wasn't interested in 'building a nest', becoming a mother, or nourishing their partnership. Lucy would have felt far more secure if she had created a space for love to enter into her experience. Instead, she was obsessed with being seen as 'the temptress'.

When she was with women who had families or substantial careers, she felt inferior. To reinstate her power, she used her sexuality to gain attention from their partners. The ego can sabotage our progress, or even destroy our lives. It is therefore essential that we align our choices with love and expansion and not with instant gratification. Not one of her lovers, including Dan, was allowed get close to Lucy, so she was left feeling dissatisfied.

Nothing can ever harm us if we are willing to stay receptive to the wisdom of our intuition.

It takes discipline to disengage from the chatter of our mind and focus on the quiet voice of our heart. Our intuition can lead us to shelter and guide us to love when we feel estranged. If we set our intention to stay humble and receptive, and then pay attention to where our thoughts are going, we will develop the skill of remaining peaceful and centred. The more we practise, the greater the benefits. Lucy was partial to yoga and meditation, but when she went out into the world to create an identity, she lost sight of who she really was. She constantly searched for outside validation to support her self-worth, rather than knowing who she was before she left home.

Dan expected Lucy to rescue him from his emptiness and Lucy looked to Dan to protect her from being powerless. Their eight-year marriage came to an end when they had extracted as much as they could from one another; both were left feeling unappreciated. The antidote to heal their marriage was love and careful attention. But sadly, neither of them believed in the power of their love.

THE NURTURER
HAVING OUR BEST INTERESTS AT HEART

The only way any of us can overcome our negative addictions is to replace them with positive substitutes. Dan started smoking on the day of his last wedding anniversary. He'd suggested to Lucy they get identical tattoos, which was his way of 'branding' her to deter his competition. When Lucy declined, he was angry and disappointed, but rather than communicate his feelings he masked his emotions by puffing on a cigarette.

He created a buffer and was withdrawing from life. His only refuge from his stress and anxiety was his ritual of smoking dope. It altered his perception of reality and gave him an escape route from himself. It is fairly clear that Dan was frustrated with his identity but was stubbornly holding on to his old ways and refused to make positive changes. Why? Because deep down, Dan didn't believe he was worth the effort. Very few people in his life had acknowledged his dreams and nurtured his feelings. So why should he? Unless Dan was willing to be responsible for his health and happiness, he would continue to look for a 'stand-in' to compensate for his losses.

If we surrender to our ego, it will keep us feeling trapped and powerless. That often leads to self-pity, which locks our old patterns in place and leaves us feeling weak and defenceless. Dan loved to blame Lucy for his lack of support, but he was unwilling to take on that role himself. They were the two main qualities Dan needed to administer in the relationship he had with himself. It was the same for Lucy who had an identical complaint. They both blatantly refused to be loved.

If we intend to give up a habit, our existing course of action must be intercepted by an alternative response. If we get in touch with our feelings and ask ourselves what we really want, rather than go on automatic pilot, we can make better choices and move towards our aspirations. No matter how small that step is, eventually it will take us in a positive direction. With Dan's cigarette smoking, I encouraged him to look very clearly at the intentions behind his actions. He realised that every time he lit a cigarette, it was because he wanted to hide. He finally quit and started communicating. Rather than please everyone else, he started to do things for himself.

In the process, Dan let go of his obsession with being rejected by Lucy, the 'sex goddess', once and for all. Interestingly enough, when he stopped smoking, he also regulated his business hours and, for the first time in years, started to explore his creativity. He developed an interest in digital photography and started playing the guitar again. He began to see the results of having his best interests at heart.

Most people don't usually sit down and ask themselves why they enter into habitual behaviour. Rather than react, we need to learn how to respond to life in a different way. That is why it is imperative that we think clearly before we act and get in touch with our feelings. If we don't challenge our compulsive thoughts, we will simply continue to override our feelings and struggle to gain control.

When we fully wake up to how much it hurts when we engage in our negative behaviour, we will stop the habit indefinitely. Dan had his fingers burnt more than once trying to hold onto Lucy. It took an overwhelming wave of pain in the form of that love letter to Lucy from his friend to finally collapse his fantasy.

Lucy wasn't an evil person; she was simply immature and lost. She was blinded by her insecurity and was reaching out for love in a very haphazard way. For Lucy to denounce her destructive behaviour, she needed to accept the aspects of her nature she had deemed as inferior and practise self-acceptance.

All of our addictions stem from one primary weakness, which is our obsession with the past. If we continue to dwell on our past experiences, in the way Dan and Lucy did, we will reactivate our fears. Dan's fear of betrayal and rejection stemmed from his childhood and his mother's leaving. Lucy focused on trying to gain attention to make up for her distorted belief that she was a 'misfit'. She also rebelled due to her fear of being controlled, which was a reaction to her father's possessiveness.

Both Dan and Lucy were emotionally trapped in the past and continued to reach for the 'quick fix'. They reacted from impulse rather than collecting their thoughts and remaining clear and centred.

If a relationship perpetuates our negative patterns and we forgo our preferences, we end up feeling powerless. The problem always stems from the way we see ourselves, which determines every single choice and decision we ever make. How often do we do things we know are detrimental to our wellbeing and believe we just can't help ourselves? We watch ourselves repeat the old behaviour and feel miserable. We have to learn to interrupt the cycle by asking ourselves, 'Does this choice empower me and help me to move forward? Are my actions in line with what I really want in my heart?'

If we are in the same position as Dan and Lucy and feel frustrated because we think we are unable to create what we want, we need to see ourselves experiencing precisely what we want in the future. If we allow our imagination to impress our feelings, we will start to view our potential differently. Then we can make choices to support our aspirations. We just have to watch our internal dialogue and stop using our past as a reference to gauge what is possible.

Unless we are willing to give up our old conversations and limited beliefs, we cannot embrace what we ultimately wish to experience. It takes a leap of faith to enter the void, and this is precisely where the source of new creation lies. When Lucy finally mustered the courage to leave Dan, she was left to her own devices and was forced to be more resourceful.

Lucy only stayed with Tom for a short period. After Dan issued her with an ultimatum to leave California, she boarded a plane to China. Lucy wanted to learn more about her heritage and further her studies as a holistic practitioner.

Interestingly enough, once she left Dan, the rebel in her subsided and she started to curb her appetite for seducing men. Lucy focused on developing her strength of character and overcoming her fears. She became intrigued by Buddhism and started practising mindfulness and nonattachment. The adventurous side of her nature was balanced with a sincere desire to ground her spirituality and feel a stronger sense of belonging.

She turned her back on temptation, took off her stilettos, put on a pair of sensible flat shoes and walked into a brand new future. The Asian–American princess began to mature. She realised how much impact her choices had had on herself and others. She was horrified when she discovered that her 'harmless affairs' had caused Cherry and Justin to split and Dan to denounce some of his closest friends. What we sow, we reap.

After being wounded in battle, Dan was determined to jump straight back into the saddle. Although he was cautioned to take his time and heal his scars, he was eager to find a new fair maiden to inspire his journey. We can all take heed from Dan's story—if we do not change our internal self-image and increase our level of self-worth before we enter a new relationship, we will recreate the same experiences. Dan still wasn't committed to deepening the relationship he had with himself, so he was again searching for someone to rescue him from his pain and loneliness. Rather than being discerning, he was still looking for a 'sex goddess' to fulfill his adolescent fantasies.

His confidence with woman was still shaky. His fears of being seen as gawky, insipid and unattractive still haunted him. If we enter any project, including a relationship, with self-doubt, our insecurities will be mirrored back to us.

Rather than acknowledging the value of his emotional contribution, he put the assets he trusted the most out on the end of his fishing hook as bait. He promoted himself as a man of affluence with an impressive sports car and a large house. Dan was a gentleman who treated his potential partners like princesses and was a kind and thoughtful listener. But Dan became more of a page than a prince.

He was looking for someone charismatic and physically striking. He attracted a few women who met his criteria, and one of two things would happen. After getting to know Dan, his companion would complain in the same way Lucy did and give him the flick, because she had her eye on another contender. In this case, Dan would step aside, and another 'lucky' guy would walk off with the prize. There were other women Dan liked, but as soon as they became emotionally involved and treated him with love and respect he would lose interest.

On a deeper level, Dan was still on a mission to prove he was good enough to be loved, and women who told him he was were quickly placed on the reject pile.

In Dan's world, love had nothing to do with sharing. He equated partnership with sacrifice. What did Dan gain from having a partner who was aloof and emotionally unavailable? He got to stay separate and emotionally distant. The only way he could break the pattern, once and for all, was to open his heart and be generous in his choices. Perhaps Dan needed to take women out of the loop for a while and turn his attention towards taking pride in himself.

The last time I spoke to Dan, he was still doing the circuit. He spent far too much time looking for a woman to validate his existence. He wasn't clear on his personal dreams, or the type of life he wanted to create. He was looking for more than inspiration; he was searching for someone to help him build his identity. It may take another few rounds of Russian roulette before Dan learns to stop shooting himself in the foot. Just like Dan, we all need to be clear on our fundamental beliefs and areas of sensitivity or we will continue to give our power away. It is imperative that we remove the restrictive labels we have attached to ourselves which confine our spirit and close us down to love. Those limited assessments strip us of our pride and self-esteem.

When we find ourselves wanting to impress somebody with our appearance or performance, we are compromising our standards. Dan was given all the clues— and even a guidebook on how to change his life—but unfortunately, unless he realises how valuable he was, he will continue to search for love externally and look for someone to hold his hand. Although Dan has all the trappings of a successful man, he is like a lost and lonely child, trying to hitch a ride home.

We are all worth the effort it takes to change our lives for the better.

KEY QUESTIONS TO ASK YOURSELF

This is a checklist to see how on track you are with being *The Nurturer* in your life:

1. Do you run on automatic pilot or question your choices and actions?
2. Do you reach for external relief to numb your feelings and suppress your emotions?
3. How willing are you to give up what you know isn't good for you?
4. Do you focus on what you genuinely desire in life or reach for substitutes?
5. Do you nourish your spirit, nurture your emotions and tend to your needs?
6. Are you willing to confront your addictions or do you make excuses?
7. How healthy are your significant relationships: do they nourish and inspire you or deplete your energy?

CHAPTER EIGHT
THE ROAD TO FREEDOM

We have to be willing to make peace with our past in order to create a new life.
To believe in our dreams, we first have to believe in ourselves.

Several years ago, I was given the opportunity to house-sit for my friend Hayden, who owned a beautiful home in San Diego. The synchronicity was perfect. Hayden was going to Europe for a month and I needed a quiet place to withdraw and concentrate on my writing. However, even the most solidly laid plans can be curtailed by an occasional twist of fate.

I arrived at Hayden's house with my luggage and was ushered downstairs to the master bedroom. This came as a surprise, as I had assumed I would be staying in the guest room. Hayden suggested I would be far more comfortable downstairs with my own private ensuite and direct access to the courtyard garden. As he put my suitcases down he looked at me sheepishly. Hayden was reluctant to tell me that there had been a change of plans and I would have to share the house with one of his friends. He knew how particular I was about my privacy; my bleak expression must have been a dead giveaway.

Hayden went to great lengths to assure me I would be delighted with his friend, who was eager to meet me. His friend, Robert Morgan, was from his hometown in Michigan, and had moved to California to 'reinvent' himself. Robert apparently wanted to start a new life after doing a great deal of soul searching.

Was there anything else Hayden needed to tell me before the new lodger arrived? Perhaps one little thing: Robert had just been released from prison. He had been convicted for drunk driving but had apparently mended his ways. In fact he was at an AA (Alcoholics Anonymous) meeting now and was expected back soon. What had I let myself in for? Hayden suggested I trust him and refrain from jumping to conclusions until I had met Robert.

Over the coming few weeks, I would fill in the blank spaces and put together the complex jigsaw puzzle of Robert's life. I was curious to know how a gay, self-indulgent hairdresser had survived the perils of prison.

As it turned out, Robert Morgan was one of the most extraordinary individuals I have ever come across. He was an extremely tall and robust-looking man in his mid forties. His dark hair and clothing accentuated his pale skin. Looking distinctly sophisticated, Robert took a few long strides across the room, tipped his head and shook my hand. Within minutes, we were chatting about his pilgrimage to California and I was instantly charmed by his wit.

There was never a dull moment around the mysterious Mr Morgan. He won my heart by delivering a charming impersonation of Carol Channing singing 'Razzzzzberries' in his deep, raspy voice. For any man, straight or gay, to take on that song, stone cold sober, was a true sign of courage and passion, in my books. We spent many nights relaxing on the big cream sofas, eating Chinese takeout and sharing the details of our life experiences. The stories unfolded like episodes of *Days of Our Lives* blended with *The X Files* and a touch of *La Cage aux Folles*.

Prior to his stint as a convicted felon, Mr Morgan had managed his own chic hair salon in an elite suburb of Detroit. His skill at colouring hair was only matched by his ability to colour a story. When one of his clients was having a seriously bad hair day, he would instruct them to come in directly through the emergency door. A magician of many talents, he could give you a fashion forecast, dating tips and make your dark roots disappear all in one sitting. In exchange, his clients would tip him generously, invite him to bar mitzvahs and teach him Yiddish. Although he wasn't Jewish, he was fascinated by the culture.

Robert loved the 'high life', and before he swore his pledge at Alcoholics Anonymous, his motto had been, 'the higher the better'. He was known to shout drinks all round at many an exclusive restaurant. He and his clique of friends would party until the wee hours and stumble into the salon after a few hours' sleep, wearing dark sunglasses and an extra layer of eye gel. Robert liked to lift his spirits in more ways than one. When Mr Morgan wasn't dining, he was shopping. If he felt a little low, he would head off to Gucci or Prada and sashay out with a large dent in his credit card. Always dapper in black, white, navy or gray, Mr Morgan was nicknamed 'the style master'. But, as always, there was another side to his nature.

Robert was lonely and craved affection. He and the neighbourhood teenaged boys would often sit on his balcony overlooking the lake, drinking and smoking joints. He would provide the alcohol and dope in exchange for their youthful company. But at the end of the day, or at least the next morning, Robert was usually alone. Although he was an attractive, kind-hearted man, with a wicked sense of humour, he inwardly saw himself as unappealing. In Mr Morgan's world, unless you were striking enough to adorn the cover of GQ magazine, you didn't stand a chance in the relationship stakes. Robert's perfectionist attitude was born out of a desire to be accepted, and at best admired. He had deep sense of 'not belonging'.

Being gay can be challenging for some; for others, being gay and not 'drop dead gorgeous' can be downright confronting. In his youth Robert was sporty, lean and playful. He became a hairdresser because he didn't take his career too seriously and was more interested in being an adventurer. Robert was always driving a speedboat full throttle, or riding behind on a pair of water skis. He downplayed the intellectual side of his nature and expressed his creative side. Working with glamorous women who admired him gave him shelter from the austerity of the business world, or so he thought.

There was nothing overtly 'girly' about Mr Morgan, but internally, he felt inferior as a 'man'. Robert detested violence, aggression and crudeness. He was a gentleman. Women occasionally propositioned him and he would roll his eyes, tell them he was flattered and confess he played on a different team. That was Robert's challenge: he felt very 'different'.

His drinking and his lavish lifestyle were all a cover for this simple Michigan boy with a creative flair that would have inspired Coco Chanel. But underneath his polish lay a trail of unfulfilled dreams and shattered expectations. Robert was plagued by the guilt of letting his parents down. They wanted him to be a fine upstanding citizen and wear lumber-jackets and work in the motor trade and go to church on Sundays. But Robert aspired to be more like Betty Ford than Henry Ford. He also couldn't bear the thought of staying in school longer than necessary. Robert felt like a misfit. When his classmates were checking out girls' legs, he was looking at the colour of their shoes and the cut of their clothes. Robert always had a crush on some athletic 'hunk'. But he had to admire from afar, or watch them from the bench. Downtown Detroit was not exactly 'gay friendly', especially in the early seventies.

Robert's passion was design and architecture but he knew he could make great money as a 'society hairdresser'. He made a beeline straight for the glamorous set and became popular because of his colourful character. He put his design skills on hold, although his keen passion for good architecture never waned. Every month, he waited impatiently for *Metropolitan Home* magazine to hit the stores and drooled over the contents in the back room of the salon with his friend Amy. Between the 'oohs' and 'ahs', they would puff on their cigarettes and dream of living inside those pages.

Although Robert was extremely confident as a stylist, he felt out of his depth when it came to staking his claim as an interior designer. Although he had enrolled in design school, he found study challenging and had been diagnosed with Attention Deficit Disorder (ADD). However, I suspected Mr Morgan's ADD came from 'checking out' due to his lack of academic achievement. His issues around commitment and consistency stopped him from fully 'checking in'. He just didn't quite believe he had the substance to pull it off, and he hated being assessed and compared to others. Although he made a song and dance about his ability to turn a bland interior into a visual delight, he didn't have the qualifications on paper to back up his claim. Was Mr Morgan looking for someone else's permission or approval? Although he already had the talent, the skill and the imagination, there was one ingredient missing—confidence.

Robert was a 'closet designer'. He needed to value his talent and his contribution far more than he feared being seen as deficient. In the areas of romantic relationships and career, Robert compromised his worth. There was no doubt he was a star; he just couldn't see his own light. His authentic dreams were stuffed in the bottom drawer, along with photos of his first boyfriend, who went off to become a successful banker.

Robert drank to mask his pain and overcome his self-contempt. There were times when he would completely wipe himself out and wouldn't remember a thing the next day. Although Robert wouldn't hurt a fly, when it came to himself he was extremely self-destructive. Oh, Mr Morgan, where did you leave that Prada jacket you entered the nightclub wearing? Not to mention the credit cards in the top right-hand pocket. Robert had slowly turned into a wayward soul who needed to claim his pride and dignity from the 'lost and found department'.

Robert went through a period of being booked constantly for drink driving. During his fifth or sixth confrontation with the police, they withdrew his already suspended licence and placed him on probation. He was forbidden to drive and received an ultimatum: 'Dry out and stay sober or go to jail.' That put the 'fear of God' into him and he opted for Alcoholics Anonymous and hailing cabs. With probation officers keeping a close eye on him, he managed to stay clean for eight months. But although he curbed his drinking, he still wrestled with his ego. His mood swings shot up; this wasn't helped by the amount of sugar he consumed. When his blood sugar was down, he got snappy with his clients. He was frustrated with his life as a hairdresser and arrogance replaced his usual humorous nature. In short, Mr Morgan developed a bad attitude.

Something in Robert's life had to change, but what was it going to take? He still needed to face his inner demons. Rather than be constructive and build a substantial life for himself, he squandered his money, lived for the moment and let the reckless part of his nature drive him through life. Our soul will always tell us when we are way off course and encourage us to move back home. If we run ourselves ragged, our soul will ultimately protest and turn us in a completely different direction on 'the game board of life'.

One night after he closed the salon, Robert decided to have dinner with his friend Frank, who lived a few blocks away. Frank picked him up and they drove to a restaurant less than a mile from where they lived. Frank was having a few problems with his girlfriend and was more than a little disturbed. As Robert offered him a sympathetic ear and a few wise words, Frank downed copious shots of tequila. After Frank finally conceded that he had had enough, he stumbled to his car and sat behind the wheel. Mr Morgan was a little perturbed by his friend's drunken state, but they were only a few blocks from home and Frank assured him that he was fine to drive. Famous last words! Five minutes later the police pulled them over and charged Frank with driving under the influence. Robert was arrested for getting into a car with an inebriated driver while on probation. The police came down on Robert like a ton of bricks. The officer told him he deserved to be taught a lesson and hauled Frank and him off to the station.

Frank had his licence suspended and Robert was ordered to appear before the court. Dazed, shocked and confused, Robert immediately called his attorney. Of all the weeks for his case to come to trial, this must have been the worst. There was a campaign being waged by MADD (Mothers Against Drink Driving). Just to add fuel to the fire, the judge on the day was also a grandmother. She took one look at Mr Morgan, dressed impeccably in his navy blue suit and crisp white shirt, and told him she was tired of people making a mockery of the law. She decided to make an example of Robert and prosecuted him to the full extent of the law. He was sentenced to two years in prison. His attorney attempted to appeal and reminded her that Robert hadn't touched a drink in over eight months. She refused to listen. For the second time the words resonated through Robert's ear, 'Let this be a lesson to you.'

It was time for the 'ever glamorous Mr Morgan' to trade his Armani suit for prison clothes. He was challenged to the max. In prison, fresh food and fresh air were a treat, let alone freshly pressed shirts or sheets. There was only one thing left for Robert to do—pray. Every day in his tiny cell, he would talk to God and write in his journal. He would write about his mistakes, his lessons, his sorrows and his dreams. As each day passed, he became more humble and recognised the value of gratitude. His old fantasies were quickly replaced by a deep appreciation for the human spirit. He knew if he had the strength to survive his sentence, he could do almost anything. In the meantime, he learnt to make the most of what he had.

He was promoted from the laundry room into the kitchen. Robert was occasionally offered the special privilege of eating an orange, and if he was very fortunate, a real egg. The rest of the time it was the usual concoction of powdered eggs, fortified with dehydrated milk. Every ounce of food that went into the jail was canned, frozen or dehydrogenated. The only time of the year the rest of the prisoners saw a piece of fruit was on Christmas Day. It isn't any wonder Robert came out of jail looking trim. He traded his ration of cigarettes and chocolate with the inmates for extra TV privileges. They all took turns on deciding what to watch. So Robert would forfeit the bulk of his stash to watch a Barbara Streisand special or an episode of *Melrose Place*. The rest of the time it was back to his trusty journal and having a word with God.

The saddest part of the experience for Robert was that not one of his friends came to visit him for the entire duration of his sentence. Not even Frank, who was the catalyst for his downfall. Robert held no malice, but he was extremely disappointed. One of two things will happen to a person in jail: they will either reshuffle the deck of their priorities and turn over a new leaf or hit the streets looking for vengeance. There are a lot of angry prisoners in jail who feel like rejects and outcasts, but Robert became determined to turn his life around. Being alienated from society amplified Robert's core belief of not belonging. He couldn't relate to his inmates, his family, or even his friends. With his life and persona ripped to shreds, there was only one place left for Robert to search for real evidence of who he was. He needed to look deep within himself. With very few distractions, Robert was faced with an opportunity to commune with his soul.

If Robert was going to survive this ordeal and rise like a phoenix from the ashes, he needed to let go of his self-punishment and transform his outlook from 'being different' to 'being unique'. His current circumstances were a direct reflection of the way he subconsciously viewed himself. Life was showing him, in living colour, how he had chastised and ostracised himself to the degree he'd become a victim of his own behaviour. The miracle was, Robert actually started to review his choices and became remorseful for his actions. He woke up one morning and said the magic words, powerful enough to open any prison door, 'What have I done to myself?' Whenever we are willing to take full responsibility for the quality of our life, we start to claim our personal power.

Robert discovered the key to his liberation while he was locked behind bars. Our soul will take us on some fairly wild detours if we are unwilling to follow the signposts. Betraying our 'real self' will always leave us paying the price. It took Robert losing his job, his apartment, his friends and family—and, more importantly, his pride—or him to finally wake up. The only thing he had left in the world was a key to a small storage cage and a journal full of heartfelt notes. Within those pages lay the seeds of a precious dream. Robert had finally given himself permission to do what he ultimately wanted to do, become an interior designer.

He was no longer concerned about the opinions of others. If he were going to 'have a life', it would be his.

Robert's sentence was reduced and he was released after a year with a newfound sense of humility. He now walked with a sturdy stride and gratitude embedded in his heart. Wanting to leave his past behind, he boarded a plane for California to design a new life. Robert and I met at a time when he was facing a world of uncharted territory. I was writing a book called *Facing the Dawn*. Which is exactly what Robert was in the process of doing. He had already passed through 'the dark night of the soul'; he now needed to retrieve the lost parts of himself. The universe brought us together at a fortuitous junction. We talked about God, self-awareness, architecture and design, and all the while we marvelled at life.

I offered Robert a session, and in exchange he transformed my hair! Viewing the journey of his soul was like watching the threads of a remarkable tapestry weaving together. This remarkable man had left an indelible impression on my mind and heart. After spending only a few weeks together, I felt I had known him a lifetime. I was a little sad to leave Robert when Hayden finally returned. But it was time for me to retreat on my own and go deeper within myself. I thought of Robert often, and pondered on how so many of us take the simple pleasures of life for granted. Little things, like being able to enjoy the seasons. In jail, the scenery, the temperature, the menu and the routine remain exactly the same until you are given the right to walk a straight line longer than the length of a corridor.

After exploring San Diego, Robert eventually decided it was time for him to face his past and return to Michigan. He had come to terms with his choices and had finally forgiven himself. In Robert's world, that was all that mattered. He wanted to go home to familiar turf and pick up the pieces. Within the first month he secured a job as an assistant to one of Detroit's most prestigious interior design- ers. It took a lot of humility for Robert to take a job as an assistant when he was in his forties. But he took on the task with enthusiasm and dedication. He observed very closely and learnt quickly.

When one of Robert's old hairdressing clients heard what he was doing she offered him a contract to decorate her home. This woman was very shrewd: she knew she could hire Robert at a far more affordable rate than his boss and still get 'the look' she wanted. She was thrilled with Robert's work and highly recommended his services to the wealthy women at her bridge and golf clubs and her friends at the synagogue. From then on, Robert never looked back. Robert Morgan Designs was finally born and his dream was now a reality. Within twelve months he had established the foundation of a very lucrative business.

After my first encounter with Robert in San Diego, we stayed in contact. I was always inspired by his progress and was more than curious to see his work first hand. Three years later, Robert and I finally reconnected in person. I was living in La Jolla at the time and he was quoting on a job in Los Angeles. We met for breakfast and he showed me photos from his latest projects. Robert's designs were refreshingly innovative, with a feeling of classical modernism. The colours and textures were rich and sumptuous. I knew he was good, but I hadn't realised he was brilliant.

As an art director, my eye was trained to survey the finest details. When I looked at the photos I was so inspired I offered to assist on the job in LA. This was one of those moments when the artist and the sage within me began to tussle—the prospect of working with a designer like Robert was just too tempting. I showed him my portfolio and a campaign I had worked on for an Australian paint company. He scanned my work meticulously and was impressed. Little did I know I had just planted a seed which would propagate and blossom into an unexpected adventure, and take me on a journey of growth and exploration.

There are times in my life when the 'dial of destiny' has turned promptly, and I end up taking a brief detour to learn a particular lesson. I have learnt to be flexible and go where life calls me. After spending almost a year firmly entrenched in the realm of metaphysics, I started to feel constricted. I was in serious need of a large dose of 'earthly' inspiration. I had been in the cave for far too long, and was scared of going colour blind. Although my spiritual work brought me in touch with many people, I had just been through an extensive run of constantly giving. I felt emotionally spent and physically exhausted. The job in LA fell through for Robert but I still felt a strong desire to work with him for a short period and learn through observation. Although I was a designer in my own right, I knew there was always more to discover and I just wanted to play. Who would have thought I would end up in Detroit to refresh my palette?

I was also curious to see how far Robert had progressed on his journey of self-discovery and witness first hand how much his life had transformed. The next chapter of my life led me straight into the heart of the world of Robert. I entered the playground of 'the artisan', a realm of beauty and sublime creativity. Mr Morgan wouldn't even buy a can opener unless it was both ergonomically designed and visually appealing. I packed my bags and boarded a flight to the vast and cold Midwest. When I arrived in Michigan, I took up residence at my extremely humble abode—which, thank God, was only temporary. Living in a no frills, pre-fab, late seventies motel-style apartment is not my idea of luxury. Complete with tan carpet, brass fixtures and pastel tapestry upholstery, this 'executive' accommodation was five minutes from Mr Morgan's office and centrally located behind Gino's pizzeria.

After settling in, the only signs of good design were my laptop computer and one token Akari light on loan from the style master himself. In extreme contrast to my domestic environment, entering the world of Robert Morgan Designs opened the way to a fresh new vista of colour and creative expression. As I walked through his workspace, Robert showed me the visual presentation he had just prepared for his most recent clients. I was immediately inspired by the delicate combination of pale lavender and chocolate brown which he had chosen for their master bedroom. The samples and swatches on his concept boards boasted a rich composition of velvet, leather and suede, with a wisp of sheer buttermilk voile. What a refreshing change it was to be back in the world of design.

Mr Morgan spiced up his hometown by being slightly eccentric and not stereo-typically gay. We would often drive to an early morning meeting and he would pull up to the Dunkin' Donut window in his black Jaguar to pick up his morning treat—no fat-free muffins or frothy cappuccinos for Mr Morgan. He would order a large black coffee and a fresh cream-filled donut. He was a small town boy at heart. Robert had mastered the art of steering the Jag with his knees while he delicately balanced his cup in one hand and his breakfast in the other. This was a manoeuvre that needed to been seen to be believed.

The first time I walked into a house designed by Robert, I immediately felt a sense of peace and was inspired by its beauty. The clean, uncomplicated lines and harmonious combination of soft, earthy colours actually altered my emotional state. The house featured floor to ceiling windows with an expansive forest view. Every element of the room was meticulously chosen and displayed sheer elegance. I felt as though I had stepped into a page from *Architectural Digest*. Robert had finally manifested his dream; he had placed his unique signature on a creation that was awe-inspiring.

As we sat with his clients, Mrs Steinberg shared her experience of how much joy and serenity the adjustments to her home had brought her and her husband. Her eyes began to moisten and she sighed deeply. It appeared Robert had risen in stature to the exalted position of spiritual healer. He had made a profound contribution to the Steinbergs' life.

I had created beautiful interiors for many years as an art director when I dressed a location for a shoot. But I had never realised just how much impact crafting an environment for 'real people' had on their lives.

As Robert and I were escorted through the grand entrance foyer to the front door, I reflected on just how far he had come. Just a few years ago, Robert sat silently in prayer, gazing at the grey walls of his jail cell. He had not only become my design mentor; he was quickly becoming a metaphysics teacher as well. There is always so much we can learn from one another if we are willing to go beyond our egos.

I had come to America with the intention of making a contribution spiritually, and it was becoming apparent to me that I had no idea what that really meant. Yet here I was, inspired by a man who changes people's lives by teaching them the value of beauty. Was the universe telling me something? I had worked as a designer for many years, and yet I thought that wasn't enough. My mind would tell me that I needed to do something more substantial and meaningful with my life. I completely dismissed the fact that I loved what I did. Had I fallen prey to the belief that artistic people aren't taken seriously? Taking something from mediocrity to magnificence commands respect no matter what field you work in.

Whether we are arranging a vase of flowers or designing a city, if the action is done with care and thoughtful attention, we have the potential to inspire the entire planet. I ignored my father as a teenager when he told me to 'get a real job'. In this moment I am thankful that the rebellious part of my nature, along with my gypsy spirit, was strong enough to take a stand for freedom of choice, otherwise I would probably have died of misery, locked in a prison of mediocrity and compromise. Life would be very bland if we lived in a world without music and the arts. We can all be grateful for people like Robert who take a vanilla world and add that touch of chocolate and raspberry. Or at times brighten the day by playing Rosemary Clooney singing 'Come on to my house, my house, I'm gonna give you candy'.

Yet there is no sugar coating with Mr Morgan. He can be tough to reckon with if you don't like his choice of floor coverings. He will respond to your disapproval by telling you your taste is undeveloped or your attitude is bad. At times he would fall into the category of the Nazi decorator. I prefer to see him as a member of the style police. Robert is simply committed to excellence and is willing to take a stand for the integrity of his work. He is a pioneer in the creative frontier. I watched Robert, first hand, overcome adversity and touch upon greatness. He finally found his place in the world and, in doing so, aligned with his soul's purpose.

Robert claimed his freedom by giving himself permission to do what he really loved to do and be who he authentically wanted to be. Because Mr Morgan never did anything in half measures, he went to extremes to find his way back home to his real self. It took literally being imprisoned for him to finally see that the key to his salvation lay in his own hands. I am thankful for the time I spent with him. He reminded me of the true meaning of courage and the importance of gratitude. Robert is one man who was brave enough to step out of the shadows into the light.

LOOKING BENEATH THE SURFACE

Robert Morgan had buried many of his aspirations beneath a layer of shame. To compensate for his lack of worth, he created a glossy facade. His identity was neither satisfying nor substantial, so his frustration grew to self-contempt. Rather than share his real self with others, he attempted to put on a show. Although he was entertaining, his actions slowly stripped away his pride and dignity. With a fractured sense of belonging, he lost sight of the value of his contribution. Robert was reluctant to talk about his aspirations for fear of being mocked. Those very private, hidden dreams deserved to be acknowledged and brought to life. But if Robert wasn't willing to believe in himself, his dreams would never flourish.

Spending time in prison allowed Robert to reflect on his past, consider the most significant people in his life and determine the impact they had had on his experiences. Robert began to see precisely where he sold out and gave his power away. In his time of greatest need, who was there to help him gather his strength? No one. Why had he given so much credence to the opinions of others when he was the person who counted the most? He knew being selfish wasn't going to work; that was something he had already tried and it simply pushed people away. He kept hearing this voice in the back of his mind whisper, 'Be true to yourself.' After twelve months of quiet reflection the murmur became a declaration. Robert was tired of pretending; he wanted to be himself.

Whenever he felt sad or lonely, he would write in his journal. With every heartfelt page he wrote his disappointments and unfulfilled expectations came to the surface. Robert made notes about all the things he wanted to experience when he was finally liberated from the confines of his cell. He longed to express himself fully in the world and dance through life, rather than hide in the shadows. As he wrote about his aspirations, Robert's imagination became a refuge. Although he was still in prison, his inner strength gathered momentum, and sparked a vision of hope. Robert finally became humble enough to see that his life could be completely different.

We all need to be aware of how distressing it is to give up a personal dream in order to please others, or to avoid loneliness. If we are not willing to be true to ourselves, we turn our back on our soul and disregard our true potential. That is a high price to pay to hold onto our anonymity. Robert finally forgave himself and the people who had supposedly held him back. Then Robert reclaimed his right to choose. Just like Mr Morgan, we all need to muster the courage to come out of the closet and be acknowledged for our uniqueness.

Imagination and passion are often dampened by conformity or doubt. When Robert was young he wanted to share his aspirations with his family, but their response discouraged him. When we receive feedback that our aspirations aren't important, we can misinterpret it as, 'I am not important', which is precisely what happened with Robert. He toned down his ambition to curb his disappointment, and denied his creative powers.

If we are unwilling to endorse our intrinsic worth and foster our dreams, we cannot expect our lives to ever change. There is power in our ability to take a stand for what we believe in. And if we believe in our dreams, we believe in ourselves. Robert realised his dreams were important because when he was in prison, they were all he had left. Without hope, he would have shut down completely. And genuine hope only ever exists if we sanctify our dreams. To transform his world, Robert needed to hold high expectations of being fulfilled, and allow his life to unfold gracefully and with patience.

Each of us is an attractive magnet that draws our experiences through our desires, imagination and expectations. The only thing that gets in our way is an undermining attitude, which is based on our restrictive beliefs. Robert's 'attitude problem' was dowsed by humility. Unfortunately, he learnt to master his ego the hard way.

When Robert was released from prison, he had no idea how he was going to manifest what he wanted. He had very little cash, but a lot of courage. With his dream in his heart, he let his desire fuel his journey. He took one small step at a time and was grateful for every opportunity. Eventually he gathered momentum and, as a pioneer, he discovered new ground. The more his platform for self-expression grew, the more he was inspired and nourished. He was never attached to how the abundance showed up, he just remained receptive and was willing to participate. After keeping a journal in prison, he was clear on what he wanted to experience and he was open to allowing the universe to provide.

We write the script and choose our destiny; the universe simply provides the materials and fills in the blank spaces.

It is our responsibility to hold the vision and simultaneously cherish our dreams. Robert spent the first half of his life drowning his unfulfilled expectations in booze. When he was finally willing to give up his self-pity, he saw he was good enough to receive the bounty of his dreams. How? He prayed and prayed and became humble enough to give up his resistance to being loved. One drop of self-love can heal the scars of many years of abuse and soothe a wounded soul. Robert was finally willing to stop fighting the world. The Michigan maverick was put to rest, and in his place an artisan and mapmaker emerged.

THE PIONEER
RELEASING THE PAST AND CHARTING A FUTURE COURSE

The labels we give to ourselves, which are based on our past experiences, will shape our expectations in the future. Robert ostracised himself because he felt 'different'. He couldn't conform to the conventional ways of his middle class family, nor relate to the jocks at high school. Robert felt a deep sense of shame and subconsciously believed he was a 'reject'. It was clear to Robert, from a young age, that if he was going to fulfil his dreams, rather than surrender to mediocrity, he had to face the world on his own.

Robert didn't feel comfortable being 'one of many'; he wanted to stand out. Running a hairdressing salon allowed him to feel powerful and have a certain amount of control. Because of his inherent talent as a designer, though, being a hairdresser was a compromise; it was nothing more than a means to a 'dead end'.

Many of us are seeking a deeper sense of purpose in our lives, looking to find our 'rightful' place. Recognising our uniqueness, while maintaining a sense of belonging, can be a challenge. Robert struggled with his identity most of his life, until he was willing to look beyond his persona and acknowledge the value of his spirit and soul. He managed to create the highest vision of what was possible for him and was happy to simply be himself. Our soul never demands we do anything; we are free to choose a life we love. We all know in our heart of hearts what we genuinely want, but are we willing to respond?

Just like Robert, we are not always willing to see the truth, because we are afraid of being disappointed. We may even believe we are not good enough to have what we want. It took courage for Robert to return to Detroit after San Diego and face his past with a new attitude. He knew he had one thing at stake his peace of mind. In facing the challenge, he healed his shame and reclaimed his pride and dignity. Whenever we see life and ourselves through fresh eyes, opportunities,which have eluded us until now become visible.

If we reflect on the qualities we liked about ourselves as children, as well as the things we naturally loved to do, we are in touch with our 'real self'. If our passion or interest is sparked in any one area, this will serve as a definite clue. Robert loved to be artistic and had a distinct talent for 'showmanship'. He had a wonderful sense of humour and enjoyed lifting people's spirits. He admired beauty in all forms. Starting his own design business allowed him to use his intrinsic talents and develop many of the skills he had as a child. When we come into this world, we all have the individual attributes we need to be completely self-expressive and fulfill our soul's purpose. We need to be careful not to let other people's opinions deter us from our true course.

It's never too late to acknowledge our talents and develop our skills and creativity. If the contribution we make to the world is based solely on being admired, we are simply aiming to prove our worth. Mr Morgan was caught in that trap, when he became a 'celebrity hairdresser'. He aimed for popularity rather than freedom of expression. If we are ambitious because we love what we do and relish the creative process, we will enjoy the full benefits life has to offer.

When Robert's spirits were defeated and he landed in jail, he was unsure of what he wanted, other than his freedom. Over the course of time, as he slowly mended his heart, his dreams started to surface. He asked himself a series of important questions in the process: 'If I loved myself completely in this moment, how different would my life be? What would I finally let myself do and have and who would I choose to be?' Robert then had the good sense to write down the answers. On those pages, the components of his dream and the qualities of his 'real self' started to emerge. He knew full well that he had to give up his old ways and change his behaviour to make his dreams a reality. Robert was willing to give up his past, as a reference for what was possible, and design a new life.

When we lose sight of our full potential we are likely to compromise our choices. Our career can be an outlet for our creative self-expression or our prison. That is why it is essential that we foster our talents and continue to develop our skills in areas that inspire us to grow. We can use the power of our will to drive us forward but, if we overlook the call of our heart, it will be an empty endeavour. Working with women in the salon, Robert thought he was taking the easy way out and yet he ended up following a very arduous path. His ventures were financially profitable, but there were no emotional rewards and he was uninspired by his projects. Rather than esteem-building, his identity started to weigh him down in the process.

To create anything out of sheer effort and determination, without inspiration, will leave us feeling drained and dissatisfied. If we find ourselves stuck in a 'dead end' job, we need to look deeper within ourselves to find the true calling of our soul. If we don't alter the course of our destiny, we will end up suffering the consequences. When we stubbornly hold onto what no longer serves us, we are simply deceiving ourselves. How did Robert finally get off the treadmill and change his course? He declared his intention to become an interior designer and then turned his attention towards achieving his goals. Using the principles of 'intention' and 'attention' is enough to shift our experience.

Whenever we are committed and consistent in our lives, we create positive results. Therefore we need to be very clear on what we choose to devote our energy to. Robert had lots of time on his hands in prison to reflect on the course of his actions. How often do the rest of us, who are free to choose the way we 'spend' our time, ponder the quality of our choices? If we love ourselves enough, we will give ourselves permission to direct our energy into something that satisfies our soul. We are free to choose, and if we are willing to recognise our true worth, we will focus on the things in this world that bring us joy.

Anything that is born with love brings the greatest rewards.

We have to take a stand within ourselves to break free from the confinement of our limited beliefs. If we declare our intentions and are receptive to being acknowledged and supported, miraculous opportunities can manifest. As soon as Robert became humble and was willing to co-operate with others, assistance came from everywhere. The people in his world became a link in the chain of his success, rather than a thorn in his side. Robert maintained his independence, and for the first time he started to feel a real sense of belonging. For someone who was labelled an ex-con, that was an incredible feat. When he left prison he relied solely on his internal resources to provide him with everything he needed to create a life he loved.

Selecting a path that challenges our skills is an essential component in making a valuable choice. Our soul is calling us to grow, so we are able to acknowledge more of our real selves. Whenever we take on anything new in the world, we learn more about ourselves. Robert was willing to fully explore his untapped potential, and eventually it began to flourish. We can all benefit by doing exactly the same thing. If we are open to taking on new endeavours, we will discover more of ourselves in the process. No matter how small our steps are, eventually we will reap the benefits.

We may think we know ourselves, but do we really? How far are we willing to dive into the relationship we have with our self? If we are wise, we will move way beyond our identity and plunge into the heart of our soul. If we wait until life challenges our integrity, we will be in for a rough ride. Personally, I have learnt how to search deep within myself for the answers, and I relish my moments alone in retreat.

In his early years, Robert placed far too many conditions on giving and receiving love. When people approached him to offer their affection he was reluctant to respond. Robert equated love with being used and hurt, and consequently closed down. He was afraid that if he dropped his defences, he might be abandoned, betrayed or humiliated. When he was inebriated, and let down his guard, that was precisely what happened. As he began building his new life from the bottom up, with his newfound humility, he started letting people in. His relationships took on a far greater depth, because he was finally willing to share more of himself.

On some level we are all afraid of judgment and criticism. Therefore at times we are self-conscious and refuse to express ourselves authentically. Like Robert, we hide the parts of our characters we dislike and put on a pretence. He didn't understand that he had the right to be completely supported and loved. He was too concerned about his shortcomings and primarily focused on what was 'missing'. Many of us have gone through life longing for someone to really value our ideas and support us on our quest. If we believed as a child that no one really fostered our aspirations or acknowledged our contribution, then we often feel a fractured sense of belonging. Therefore, as an adult, creating a partnership where we feel a strong allegiance, may ultimately present a challenge.

The only way we will ever feel complete is when we acknowledge the value of our soul. When we know we are enough, whether we stand alone or in a relationship, even if we are stripped of our identity, we will finally know our true worth.

If that sounds like a tall order, consider what Robert went through and who he is today. He is now a man with pride, dignity and a passion for life. Robert is living out his dream and knows he is loved. He still prays and writes in his journal. Making time to give thanks and commune with his soul is one of his priorities, no matter how busy he gets. Serving his term in jail, Robert learnt first hand about the power of the human spirit and the importance of human dignity.

Without crossing the threshold of our imagination to discover our true potential, we are left partially in the dark, trapped in a prison of forgetfulness, unable to see the brilliance and majesty of our soul.

KEY QUESTIONS TO ASK YOURSELF

This is a checklist to see how on track you are with being *The Pioneer* in your life:

1. Do you strive for excellence or become complacent and settle for mediocrity?
2. Do you take the easy road or take risks to stretch your boundaries?
3. Are you humble and receptive as you approach life or have you become resigned and cynical?
4. Are you committed to fostering your talents and sharpening your skills?
5. Do you cherish your dreams and believe in your self?
6. Are you clear on your soul's purpose and life's lessons?
7. Do you compromise with your choices or align your actions with fulfilling your dreams?

CHAPTER NINE

SHARE AND SHARE ALIKE

Freedom of expression is based on confidence. When we feel as though there is something missing in our world, we need to open up to sharing more of ourselves.

I woke one Saturday morning to another beautiful summer day in Sydney. It was the perfect opportunity to visit my friend Jane, who lived in a stunning house on the edge of the beach. Life can be tough when the biggest decision you have to make for the weekend is which bikini to wear, and whether to swim in the pool or the ocean. Jane's lifestyle was steeped in glamour and spending time at her home was like visiting a fabulous day spa. Our days together would normally start with a brief workout in the downstairs gym, a dip in the pool, and a stroll along the beach, followed by a gourmet lunch on the terrace overlooking the ocean. At the time, both Jane and I were more committed to forwarding our careers than to playing in the social circuit. We both worked long hours in advertising, and spent most of our time getting a 'studio tan' rather than basking in the sun.

Although we had talked on the phone occasionally, it had been more than three months since Jane and I had last seen each other. As a producer, she was always extremely busy, and having a young toddler and a husband didn't leave her much time for socialising with the girls. Jane had also started a new exercise program, and I was anxious to see the results. After the birth of her daughter Courtney, she found it difficult to lose the weight she had gained during pregnancy. She'd shot up three dress sizes. Her snug-fitting feminine dresses were shunted to the back of the closet and replaced by loose-fitting shirts and 'cover-up' clothes.

Although she was only in her late twenties, the girlish skip in her step and her playful personality had been replaced by a formal and reserved demeanour. While it would have been easy to equate her personality shift with becoming a mother, or the increasing pressure of her escalating career, I felt there was a far deeper reason for her changes. During the past few years, I had noticed an increasing amount of tension between Jane and her husband Ken. He was also a film executive, who was highly ambitious and quite ruthless. Ken had the reputation of being arrogant, cocky and insensitive in business and in his personal affairs. He was a big and boisterous man, whose energy would often leave observers feeling awed or affronted.

Jane, by contrast, was gentle, thoughtful and quietly confident. The first time we met, I watched her walk into a film studio wearing a tiny mini skirt and a pair of four-inch heels. Her long, wavy, blonde hair fell softly over her shoulders as she clutched a clipboard tightly to her chest. The male crew members stopped in their tracks to admire her. I initially thought she was one of the models. As it turned out she was a young PA, with her sights set on becoming a producer. She was bright, and eager to learn.

From a very young age, Jane had entertained visions of living a full and adventurous life. She grew up in a small town surrounded by cane fields in northern Queensland. From the age of eight Jane would often climb to the top of the hill on her way home from school and sit and look out across the green fields stretching to the ocean. While the faint smell of burning sugar wafted through the air, she would dream of visiting far-away places and creating a life of her own. She longed to break away from her simple surroundings and the tension between her parents. Her mother would often ignore her father for days She would grow cold and silent as she waited for him to arrive home from work after a few rounds at the pub with his mates. When he had finally quenched his thirst after a hard day at the sugar mills, he would stagger home to face a reheated dinner and a stony-faced wife.

Jane resented her father's behaviour and believed her mother deserved to be treated better. From an early age, Jane vowed she would have a man in her life who would give her everything. After finishing high school, she withdrew her savings from her part-time job, packed her guidebook and said goodbye to her golden labrador. She moved to Sydney, intent on creating an abundant life. She found it easy to make new friends, and in no time found her niche in the big smoke. She landed a job welcoming clients behind the front desk of a high-profile advertising agency. Her youth and attractiveness gave her an added advantage. The advertising boys were more than happy to be greeted by her alluring smile each morning.

It was here that Jane met Ken. He took one look at this impressionable ingénue and decided to take her under his wing. A man with 'wandering hands' and a healthy appetite for young women, Ken strutted his stuff and Jane followed his lead. Although he was still quite young himself, Ken had chalked up some very impressive jobs and prestigious clients. So much so that the agency offered him a position in its San Francisco office. After dating for just six months, Jane traded her steno pad for a passport and moved with Ken to San Francisco. She had no idea her childhood dreams would start to unfold so quickly.

During their three years in San Francisco, Jane lived as a lady of leisure. Each day she worked out at the gym, shopped, went sightseeing and accompanied Ken to a host of social functions. When he travelled, she travelled. When he dined, she dined, and when they were out together, he would show her off. Despite the glamour, Jane grew tired of her endless vacation and became homesick. Ken was also ready for a change. They headed back to Sydney with a sizeable bank balance and a container-load of personal effects.

Now it was time for Jane to spread her wings. Her ambition was mounting and she was anxious to take her own place in the workforce. She had learnt a great deal by observing Ken's strategies and talking to many of America's best advertising people.

Ken sensed Jane's restlessness and allayed his fears of losing her by proposing marriage. Their elegant wedding was staged on the magnificent foreshores of Sydney Harbour, with two hundred and fifty guests at the reception. Ken made sure the who's who of the advertising world were invited. He managed to do a little networking between the obligatory 'cutting of the cake' and the bridal waltz.

Jane found her niche working on television commercials and through her inge-nuity, dedication and drive, rose quickly through the ranks. In four short years she went from production assistant to television producer. Meanwhile, Ken's competitive nature and insecurity kicked in. He became more demanding, bossy and condescending. He finally insisted they work together, and they opened a large office working under the same banner.

Ken insisted on telling people in the industry that he'd taught Jane everything she knew. He was also known for his lecherous advances to models on the job and to female co-workers.

The first time I met Ken on a shoot, I was appalled by his sleazy comments about my tight-fighting jeans and his infuriating habit of patting me on the behind. I was astounded that Jane was turning a blind eye and dismissing his actions as being harmless. Those supposedly innocent pranks got progressively more out of hand. I remember Ken called me late one evening when Jane was out of town on business. Under the pretext of asking me for advice on what to buy her for her birthday, he offered to bring over a bottle of French champagne and discuss the options. It was 10 pm and he knew I lived alone.

'What the hell are you thinking, Ken?' I asked.

'Well c'mon honey, you're a single woman, you probably haven't had a toss in the sack for a while. I'd be doing you a favour if I came round and gave you a good servicing.'

Was he kidding? With his distended beer belly and crass behaviour, did he really see himself as a Don Juan?

'You've got to be joking,' I said. 'Ken, I'm going to have a shower now and I suggest you do the same and turn the tap to icy cold. Good night!'

Over the course of the next twelve months, I became more aware of Ken's wom-anising. I also noticed that immediately after he and Jane had joined offices she'd started to gain weight. As Ken became more bombastic and self-righteous, Jane's waistline expanded. She also became more ambitious and competitive. Unfortunately, her growing success came at a price; the soft feminine side of her nature was gradually replaced by a protective, resilient shell. Jane and Ken discussed business far more often than the state of their marital affairs. Then a spanner was thrown in the works. Jane fell pregnant. When she called to tell me the news, she sounded apprehensive. She was concerned about the logistics of having a baby and maintaining her busy work schedule. Jane and Ken had just purchased their ultimate dream home and the mortgage was enough to make even the most prosperous business owner nervous.

Jane was afraid having a baby would cost her her business and her prominent profile. Personally, I sensed that Jane's soul was calling her to reclaim her femininity and solidify her marriage. Although Jane was a powerful negotiator when it came to striking business deals, she rarely communicated her emotional concerns or aspirations to Ken. He took the news of becoming a father with great enthusiasm. Ken had visions of himself with a new playmate, someone he could ultimately mentor.

The pregnancy was scheduled on the production board and shoot dates were organised around it. Jane also started to interview full-time nannies. She was keen to find someone gentle and nurturing, who also had a strong academic background. She found a lovely, articulate woman who was a retired schoolteacher, with a grown-up family of her own. She was the perfect surrogate grandmother.

During her pregnancy Jane attempted to keep up her hectic work pace. Ken offered little emotional support. Jane went into labour at the end of a twelve-hour shoot day. Ken took her to hospital and left her lying on a stretcher in the waiting room while he ran off to make a business call. Jane was given an epidural, which made her drowsy and numb from the waist down. While left waiting alone to go into the delivery room, she rolled off the trolley and landed face down on the cold hospital floor. When Ken finally came back he charged around the ward, shouting loudly and threatening to sue the hospital staff for negligence.

In the few days following Courtney's birth, Jane's hospital room became a temporary production office. Jane was determined to keep her clients happy, and so with the help of her assistant, she finished shooting a TV commercial and met all her other work deadlines. After leaving hospital, she developed a severe case of painful mastitis and a dangerously high fever. I believe it was Jane's reluctance to surrender to her 'motherly instincts' which manifested in the form of a breast infection. The masculine and feminine parts of her, or her head and her heart, were at odds. The infection forced Jane to stay in bed, which gave her an opportunity to reflect on her priorities. Her mother flew down to offer her support. After a good dose of nurturing from mum, Jane finally began to heal and gracefully readjust to her life as a working parent.

For Ken it was business as usual. He jumped straight back into his independent world and remained emotionally detached. He would often stay back late at the office with his assistant Suzie, and would work on projects over the weekend. When Jane finally returned to the office, with baby and nanny in tow, Suzie became territorial and defensive. Jane also noticed that Suzie was overly protective of Ken's agenda and was unwilling to update Jane on his schedule.

The more Jane denied what was going on under her nose, the more the evidence surfaced that her marriage was in trouble. Most of her friends were well aware of Ken's extracurricular activities and wondered why she put up with him. I told Jane I thought she deserved better. She simply made excuses for Ken's behaviour and changed the subject. What became apparent to me was that Jane's weight gain was a symptom of her denial. Rather than express her emotions, she stuffed them down onto her hips, thighs and buttocks. Her sensuality and sexuality were hidden behind a layer of protective padding. Taking on her new role as a mother, even served as a justifiable excuse to downplay that valuable side of her nature.

What happened to that vivacious and playful young woman who once turned heads? Jane's openness and confidence had been replaced by fear and distrust. Ken was too self-obsessed to acknowledge Jane's feelings.

I remember one Saturday afternoon Ken came to my apartment to drop off some photographs for a job. I wanted to keep his visit brief so I could get on with my day. When we finished discussing the project, he told me he needed to talk about something else. I knew this wasn't a business matter because he became slightly awkward. He told me he didn't approve of Jane's escalating weight and asked me, as her friend, to talk to her about going on a diet. He then went on to announce his dissatisfaction with their almost non-existent sex life.

He accused Jane of not considering his needs because she refused to give him a blowjob. I had to bite my tongue. I cut him off mid sentence and told him I wasn't willing to listen to his sexual fantasies.

'Don't you think that's a little like the pot calling the kettle black?' I said.

Had he looked in the mirror lately? He was overweight, unshaven and dishevelled. He told me he had always given his wife everything she had ever wanted and was confused by her lack of affection.

I suggested he speak to his wife personally. Jane needed his support rather than his criticism. If he weren't willing to listen attentively and rebuild the trust in their partnership, Jane would remain shut down and avoid dealing with the issues. I sensed Ken wasn't really open to advice: he was more interested in having his opinion validated. After this little incident I kept my distance from Ken. I wondered how long it would take for Jane to release herself from the pretence of her marriage.

I was often aware of Jane's sadness and her efforts to attain more of her emotional independence. Between operating her demanding business, and attending to her daughter's needs, there was very little time left to satisfy Ken's whims. He became resentful of Jane's lack of interest in sex, which in his mind justified him satisfying his appetite elsewhere. Jane turned a blind eye and Ken thought that what she didn't know wouldn't hurt her.

As I drove towards Jane's house, I looked forward to enjoying a long, leisurely Saturday with her. I felt a sense of relief in knowing that Ken was out of town. When I arrived at the house, I buzzed the intercom and Jane released the lock on the high metal security gate. When she stepped out to greet me, I was almost bowled over. She was wearing a skimpy pair of gym shorts and a tight little sports bra. 'Oh my God, Jane,' I said. 'You look absolutely amazing.'

She told me she had joined the gym and was exercising with a trainer. I knew there was something more. After a little cajoling and a lot of reassurance, she finally confessed that she was having an affair. She'd met a young film executive called Paul. He'd helped reawaken her playful, sensual nature and made her realise she deserved to have a full and pleasurable life.

Altering her diet slightly, she started to get in touch with her body again through exercise. She dropped three dress sizes. Her passion for Paul reignited her passion for her own life. She started speaking out. Rather than continuing to ignore Ken's disrespectful behaviour she told him to either shape up or ship out. Not surprisingly, Ken reacted by running off to one of his female 'friends' to complain that his wife didn't understand him.

The more time Jane spent in Paul's company, the more she realised how much she missed having a companion she could really talk to. Paul was a man with a passion for music and a keen interest in the arts. He also had a wonderful sense of humour. In his company Jane rekindled many of her childhood dreams and aspirations. She set her intentions to take back her power and care for herself again. It was wonderful to see Jane finally break free of Ken's hold and regain her vitality. As a result, she looked five years younger.

Jane gave Ken a little rope, and he eventually hung himself. The final blow came one day when a very angry man rang to tell Jane he was furious about Ken propositioning his fiancée. Jane thanked him for the information and sent Ken packing. The cheering squad on the sidelines could barely contain itself. During the divorce settlement Jane was generous and gracious, putting her daughter's needs first. After their separation, she started seeing Paul on a regular basis.

In the early days of their relationship, Paul treated Jane with the care and attention she truly deserved. In exchange, she offered Paul love, support and inspiration. Jane and Paul moved in together. Jane's happiness not only enriched her personal life, it injected a new wave of energy into her business. She opened to new opportunities and became receptive to being acknowledged in her power as a woman.

However, the old pattern began to re-emerge. As Jane's confidence escalated, and her company grew, Paul started to feel threatened. He was concerned that she would leave him lingering in the shadows.

He began competing with Jane for status. He started involving Jane in his business interests and dissuading her from her own. Paul's sensitive artistic side developed an arrogant edge. At times he would rage through the office like a bull in a china shop. Jane would calm him down and pander to his needs. Once again she started to neglect her own needs and interests. Rather than rock the boat, Jane turned her attention towards satisfying Paul's needs. Sound like a familiar story?

The more pressure Jane took on, the more she began to override her emotions. Her attention was focused on everything in her life other than herself. The warning bells finally went off when she started to gain weight. Her 'fat clothes' were retrieved from the back of the closet and her little black dresses were pushed to the side.

What happened to the budding goddess who took charge of her life and said goodbye to oppression? She took a detour down the road of co-dependence and ended up at dysfunction junction. When Paul started flirting with some of Jane's co-workers, she finally put her foot on the brake. She wasn't about to go down the same track again. She sat him down and told him how she was feeling and how things had to change.

Fortunately, Paul genuinely loved Jane, and for him this was a wake-up call. He realised that over the course of their first year together, he had tailored his life to suit Jane. He moved into her house, embraced her daughter and adjusted to her hectic work schedule. Although Jane gave Paul ample love and attention, he started to feel powerless in comparison with the dynamic superwoman he was living with. There was only one solution for their relationship—they needed to establish equal footing and build a brand new life. They talked about their personal dreams, discussed their options, and created a mutual vision. In the process, Jane and Paul reconnected emotionally and the intimacy in the relationship was reinstated. They promised to stay in communication with one another and honestly express their fears and aspirations.

As soon as Jane felt close to Paul again, she released her pent-up tension and shed the excess weight. She recaptured her vitality and passion, and her sensuality and sex drive increased. She was back on track, fostering her relationship with herself and her partnership with Paul.

Jane and Paul decided to opt for a fresh start and reinvent their relationship on neutral ground. Combining their entrepreneurial skills, they moved to New York. Jane was keen to expose Courtney to a rich cultural life and Ken had no objection to his daughter living on the other side of the globe. He was now living with his new girlfriend, who, conveniently, put him on a pedestal. He was so preoccupied with his own projects that he had little time for parenting. Jane and Paul were free to follow their hearts and explore a brand new world, with little Courtney in tow.

The dreams that Jane had entertained as young child, as she climbed to the top of the hill, continued to unfold. After the 'glitch' in her relationship with Paul, she learnt to stay clear on her intentions and pay attention to her feelings.

She also became quite skilled at learning to negotiate with Paul, rather than surrendering to his demands or denying her own feelings. Their new life in New York prospered, along with their relationship. They set up a new business that left them ample time to travel and explore their common interests.

Now when Jane sits at the top of a hill and surveys the uncharted territory before her, she has a wonderful companion to weave her dreams with. Jane has moved a long way from the seclusion of the cane fields, but she still carries her innocent, childlike qualities close to her heart.

LOOKING BENEATH THE SURFACE

Jane's story offers a powerful lesson on the value of setting our intentions, and getting clear on where our attention goes. She is also a great ambassadress for authentic self-expression. Although she grew up in modest surroundings with little encouragement from her parents, Jane was willing to break free and follow her dreams.

If Jane had sat on the country fence complaining, or seen herself as nothing more than a small town girl, she would have aligned her attention with her shortcomings, and would probably still be living in a simple house on the edge of the cane fields. Instead, she was open to receiving life's bounty, and now lives in an exclusive residence in New York and owns a portfolio of valuable assets.

Although Jane took on many mentors and allowed people to guide her, she independently created her own fortune. However, when it came to affairs of the heart, Jane had a difficult time declaring her rights and setting her boundaries. One of her primary lessons was learning to negotiate with her lovers.

To respond to others authentically, we need to express what we honestly feel and share our aspirations. We often resist telling the truth because we fear the other person will criticise or reject us. It wasn't surprising that Jane put on weight; she buried the soft, sensual part of her under a layer of protection. With the aim of putting a wall between her and the source of her pain, she grew larger to keep him at a distance. It wasn't until Jane started acknowledging herself that things began to alter; this is always the key to changing the quality of our relationships.

We have to be willing to take a risk and communicate our grievances in order to remain true to ourselves. As long as we do not criticise or attack another person, we are within our rights to voice our objections. Jane refused to argue with Ken. In turn, he was driven by fear and unwilling to yield to the power of love. If someone reacts negatively when we express our preferences, it is simply because they are afraid of being dominated. Jane was doing precisely what her mother did with her father: suffering in silence. She was mirroring the paradigm of romantic relationships she'd witnessed as a child.

It pays to get to the bottom of our feelings if we want to be authentically self-expressive. If we are willing to drop beneath our surface emotions, such as anger, and access what we are experiencing at a core level, our communication will be far more powerful. When we uncover what is hidden beneath our anger, our disappointment and our hurt, we will normally reach our bottom line, which is fear. Jane was afraid of losing Ken because she didn't want to be alone. Ken was afraid of losing Jane but refused to express it for fear of appearing weak.

Anger can be a great mask to hide insecurity and helplessness; it creates a buffer to intimacy. Whether we choose to vent our aggression like Ken, or suppress our hurt like Jane, withholding our grievances builds a huge wall that destroys the trust in our relationships.

Of course, what Jane and Ken ideally wanted was to feel empowered and loved. To reach that state in their marriage, they had to be willing to give up anything else standing in the way. For Ken that meant giving up his desire to be in control, and for Jane it meant expressing herself.

Ken fought for control right up to the day of the divorce settlement. He then went off to find a new partner who was happy to be submissive and allow the king to rule.

Fortunately, Jane recognised the same pattern emerging in her relationship with Paul. Jane gently took a stand for her feelings, expressed her genuine concerns and Paul responded gracefully.

We all need to pay attention to our feelings and gain a deeper understanding of why we feel the way we do before we blame another person. This will increase the intimacy in the relationship with have with ourselves, which then influences the way we express ourselves to others.

It is unreasonable to expect other people to change the way we feel; that is our responsibility. We can, however, expect people to consider our feelings, but only if we are willing to communicate them. We can't expect people to pick up our thoughts telepathically. It negates our power to choose. Control and manipulation don't work; authentic communication does. It frees our spirit and creates an opportunity for us to move forward gracefully.

Until Jane mustered the courage to communicate her genuine feelings with her partners, she remained partially invisible. If a relationship isn't based on a fair and mutual exchange, we are compromising our best interests. If we don't communicate because we honestly believe the other person doesn't care about us, we need to reconsider our reasons for being there. This is precisely what Jane did when she decided to leave Ken, and by taking that positive step, she changed the course of her life.

When Jane finally rekindled her dreams and started to acknowledge her worth, she built a solid platform for her self-expression. By staying clear on her intentions and by paying attention to the things she knew made her happy, she walked a steady path towards creating an abundant, joyful life. Love became her priority. Both Jane and Paul chose to confront the issues that surfaced in their partnership and modified their behavior to establish harmony. Instead of stubbornly holding on to their old ways they chose to grow together rather than grow apart.

THE NEGOTIATOR
GIVING VOICE TO OUR HEART

It can be easy to fall into the trap of looking to others to overcome our inadequacies. When we enter into a relationship to compensate for our own personal dissatisfaction, we often view our partner, rather than the relationship, as a source of security or pleasure. In reality, our partnerships merely support our own internal experience, and serve as a platform for our self-expression. Jane and Ken were attached to one another, rather than committed to building an intimate loving relationship. They both felt unfilled because they were guarded in their communication, and competed for power in the relationship. Although we all have an impact on one another, we ultimately choose what we experience.

At times people definitely come into our world as a catalyst. Both Ken and Paul were powerful initiators for Jane. They ignited the spark of her passion and it was up to her to keep that flame alive. If we go into a relationship feeling whole and complete, we won't be tempted to surrender our power or compromise our choices. If we live in fear of losing our partner in the same way Ken and Jane did, we will often withhold our true feelings, and tolerate negative behavior. It is important that we take a good look at what we are honestly willing to put up with in a relationship and consider the ramifications. Our choices stem from who we believe we are, and what we receive in life is based on our level of self-worth. The relationship we have with ourselves is the most important relationship we will ever have.

If we go into denial, or skirt the truth, we will eventually experience a breakdown. This became very clear in Jane's relationships, when she turned a blind eye to her partners' negative behaviour to supposedly uphold the peace. She ended up feeling frustrated, disappointed and distressed. If we refuse to communicate authentically, we not only destroy our relationships, we end up hurting ourselves. Love and fear can't exist in the same space; therefore we have to be clear where our commitment lies. We choose the game, then write the rules and invite our partners to play. When Jane was still living with Ken, she stated her preferences, and was willing to negotiate with her husband to save their marriage. Ken was unwilling to set up new agreements and refused to change. Once his decision was locked in, he no longer became a suitable partner for Jane and she went on to fulfil her aspirations with Paul.

If a relationship is based on fulfilling superficial requirements, we will be left feeling dissatisfied. That was the game that Ken continued to play and it cost him his first marriage. Jane was no longer willing to hide behind the pretense because she realised that if she settled for a shallow relationship, she would curtail her chances of sharing deeper intimacy. We all need to ask ourselves how much love we are willing to experience and how much of ourselves we are prepared to share. It is important we stop looking at our past to gauge what is possible in our relationships. There is nothing honest, authentic or satisfying about superficial relationships and yet many people insist on having them; they refuse to move out of their comfort zone.

If we are fortunate enough to have a partner who we have a deep emotional connection with, we still have to maintain our level of communication consistently to further intimacy. When we have unfulfilled expectations and unexpressed grievances, we often choose to withdraw from our partner emotionally. Jane knew something was bothering Paul when he became indifferent about sex. He suppressed his internal conflict and pulled away from her because he felt inadequate. When we withhold from our partner on an emotional level, the sexual side of the relationship will suffer. During these times it is easy for us to lose our self-worth and feel as though we are not being acknowledged.

If we spend too much time in our 'heads' we will deny ourselves the physical pleasure and emotional support available in any loving relationship. Most sexual breakdowns in a relationship are based on the desire to avoid intimacy, which stems from a fear of being vulnerable. If a breakdown does occur, it usually has nothing to do with sex. It is more about how much love we are willing to give and receive, and how much pleasure we are willing to experience. When Jane's sex life diminished her weight shot up; when she embraced her sensuality, her body slimmed down.

Opening up to greater intimacy often leaves us feeling exposed and vulnerable. That is where the test in a relationship begins. It will reveal how committed both partners are to experiencing more love.

Laying a foundation for trust in a relationship gives us the strength to overcome our fears. Because Ken was secretive about his sexual escapades, he destroyed his connection with Jane. For the sexual side of the partnership to blossom, both parties need to feel safe and secure. For Jane, the trust was broken. Ken had little sensitivity when it came to approaching women, because he refused to acknowledge the feminine side of his own nature. Generosity on all levels is the key to allowing relationships to grow. Ken made the mistake of believing that his material assets made up for his negligence.

The day Jane ended her eight-year marriage she felt liberated. If we find ourselves in a quagmire, and know that our partner is not willing to alter their behaviour, it is time to move on. If we are unwilling to let go, we end up hurting ourselves. Self-inflicted scars are the hardest to heal. We cast the first blow when we doubt our own virtue and lose sight of what we honestly deserve. It wasn't until Jane expanded her self-image that she finally saw how valuable she really was. She gained the confidence to say 'no' to what she didn't want and 'yes' to what she did. Now Jane is a wise and self-assured negotiator, not only in her business dealings, but when it comes to affairs of the heart.

We cannot blame the other person for our distress. If we ignore the voice of our heart, the wound cuts deep.

KEY QUESTIONS TO ASK YOURSELF

This is a checklist to see how on track you are with being *The Negotiator* in your life:

1. Are you willing to talk to someone about their negative behavior when their actions have a detrimental impact on your relationship?
2. Are you willing to discuss your needs and state your preferences?
3. Do you communicate your grievances or repress your emotions to avoid conflict?
4. How much love are you willing to experience, and how much of yourself are you prepared to share?
5. Are you willing to be vulnerable in your relationships and make an effort to deepen the level of intimacy?
6. Are you afraid to walk away from someone you know doesn't consider your feelings because you don't want to be lonely?
7. Are you fully self-expressed or do you make excuses or blame others for your misfortune?

CHAPTER TEN

MOVING ONWARDS AND UPWARDS

Being loved has nothing to do with our appearance or performance.
It rests on our level of self-worth and how much we are willing to receive.

It was 7 am on a cold Friday morning. After pouring myself a second cup of tea, I switched on my laptop and settled in for a few hours of writing. The rain fell softly outside the window of my apartment onto the street below. The trees in the distance formed a delicate border against Sydney's dramatic city skyline. As I looked out to the misty sky, I reflected on the chapter I was working on, an exposé on how to heal a broken heart.

This was both a theoretical and practical experience for me. I had recently returned from America, where I'd left behind a trail of broken dreams and a reluctant ex-fiancé. With a box of tissues and a bottle of Bach Flower remedies by my side, the words poured forth from the depths of my soul. I'd learned from studying Edgar Cayce's work in the late seventies, that in order to heal permanently, a person needs to raise their level of consciousness by changing their attitude and altering their fundamental beliefs. I was twenty years old when I first read those words and they inspired me to investigate metaphysics and the power of the subconscious mind.

Writing this manuscript would prove to be a valuable experience for me in more ways than one. By closely studying the issues of the people I sat with in sessions, I could simultaneously review my own behaviour, and weigh up my current circumstances. I needed to contemplate life from a higher vantage point before I set off to search for 'Mr Wonderful' again. The working title of the book kept running through my mind like the lyrics of a song, 'Looking for love in all the wrong places'. It seemed to be a parody of my life and a comment on modern society.

I've met very few people who haven't at some stage nursed a broken heart. Over the next few months, I made it my objective to comprehend the mystery of why cupid shoots his arrow and then puts his bow to rest.

Later in the day I had a session scheduled with a young man called Jason who was in need of inspiration. He had been battling with depression, and one of his friends suggested he sit with me to raise his spirits. Although I wasn't exactly filled with joie de vivre, I knew that as soon as I entered 'the zone' in Jason's company, I would step into an altered state of absolute peace. As soon as I detached from my ego sufficiently to commence a session, I felt an overwhelming sense of calm. Learning to meditate has served me well in finding peace in an often turbulent world.

The amount of love that is present when we step beyond the threshold of our rational minds into that receptive space is unfathomable. The question I often ask myself is, how do we maintain that exalted state when we are dealing with people in the world? The secret is to learn to master our ego, with its constant negative commentary and judgment. Our ego creates far too much separation when we secretly crave love and union.

Jason turned out to be yet another casualty of the escalating divorce rate. Still suffering from the aftershocks of a turbulent marriage, he was finding it difficult to fathom the purpose of life. The meaning went out of his world the day his wife walked out. At the ripe age of twenty-nine, Jason felt his life was over. Although still a young man, he had already made a fortune, lost a fortune, married and divorced. This junior empire builder had difficulty holding on to his winnings. Although he was a fan of motivational speaker Anthony Robbins, and had proven the power of his mind by doing a 'fire walk', when it came to love, Jason had been raked over the coals. What would it take to soothe his pain? On an emotional level, he was hanging on by a thread.

Jason was dressed immaculately in a dark navy suit, a pale blue shirt and a crisp lemon tie. He was tall, with short dark hair, a soft, round face and perfectly manicured hands. I told Jason to relax and give me a few minutes to meditate, so I could gather the information I needed to comprehend his soul's journey. As I started to read Jason's energetic profile, I saw first hand just how much pressure he had put himself under in order to succeed. He was so attached to seeking the approval of others that he had lost sight of his real self. Jason was emotionally and physically drained and his spirits were defeated.

With very little energy, Jason was no longer interested in enjoying the active, sporty lifestyle he had once valued. He was carrying a hefty amount of excess weight, which had depleted his self-esteem. Pining and dining went hand in hand for Jason. He had chosen food as a substitute for love and sex. For the better part of his marriage, his wife had been interested in neither sex nor intimacy; expressing affection was as foreign to her as speaking Latin. The honeymoon was over almost as quickly as it began. Jason was married for four years in total and for three of those years he lived in emotional hell. His wife had a cruel tongue and a wicked temper. Her sarcastic comments and spiteful remarks crushed his self-esteem and pulverised his heart.

When I intuitively reviewed Jason's experiences, images came to me of a wounded man on a battlefield. He hobbled lamely on crutches, with his legs and forehead wrapped in blood-soaked bandages. Exposed and vulnerable, he pushed on valiantly in search of safety and shelter. Jason's life was like a house of cards. He would build his world strategically and eventually it would all come toppling down. Whether his goals were centred on his personal development, romantic relationships, or his career aspirations, he would win, only to be faced with betrayal and deceit. Jason's pattern was pervasive. He succeeded in almost every new venture he undertook, but when it came time to enjoy the fruits of his labour, his creation would cave in.

In his teens Jason was a triumphant sportsman who aspired to turning pro. His father ridiculed his ideas and dismissed them as nonsense, though. He suggested Jason use his brains rather than his brawn, and refused to offer his assistance. His father would place hurdle after intellectual hurdle in front of Jason and expect him to jump. Jason would diligently rise to the occasion, but was given neither praise nor acknowledgment. His father was a cold man, highly judgmental and extremely critical. Even when Jason was a very young child, his father rarely offered him encouragement or emotional support. He was more like a taskmaster than a guardian, not only with Jason, but also with his mother, who protected herself by retreating into her shell.

As an innocent child, Jason was eager to please and reluctant to hurt others. Under his father's influence, he was encouraged to set his sights high and approach his life like a good little soldier. Although he was a strong team player, he always felt like an outsider. Whenever Jason shared his conquests, his father would tell him to keep one eye on his back and not rest on his laurels. His father's favourite motto was 'Trust no one.' If Jason showed weakness he was severely scolded. Both his mother and father came down on him like a ton of bricks, locking Jason in an emotional prison.

By the time Jason left home he was longing for some love and affection. He had spent his entire life jumping hurdles in order to prove he was good enough to win someone's love. Jason thought that if he had a great body he'd have more chance of attracting a playmate. He was inspired by an article in a woman's magazine on 'what women want', which suggested that if he could fully satisfy a woman, financially and sexually, she would be inspired to love him in return. It was only after beefing up his muscles and bank balance to substantial proportions that he felt prepared to snag his match.

When Louise came into Jason's world, she entered with her head held high, like a girl on a mission. She took one look at the curvature of Jason's chest and the size of his bank account and knew she had struck gold. Her energetic, vivacious personality quickly caught Jason's attention and the courtship was off and running. Louise was attracted to Jason's strength and virility and the financial security he offered. Jason longed for tenderness and closeness, so he embraced Louise as his chosen partner and showered her with love and affection. They laughed, dreamed and played together. The first year of their relationship was blissful, but then their emotional ties began to fray and things became unstable and twisted. Once Louise's ego pulled the magnifying glass out, Jason was on the firing line.

Maintaining his own welfare and supporting the demands of his wife was wearing Jason thin. He would often come home with fried brains, boulder shoulders and dragging feet, and then cook dinner for the both of them. By the time he got to bed he was exhausted, and just wanted to sleep. Louise was far from impressed with Jason's lack of enthusiasm in bed and told him so. When it came to getting her way, Louise was more like a drill sergeant than a temptress. She would instruct Jason on his duties and expect him to jump when she said jump. With his flagging spirits and physical fatigue, all he wanted to do was rest for a moment. In Louise's world weariness was equated with laziness, and Jason was given a good, swift kick up the butt.

Louise was an ex-athlete like Jason, and was committed to her fitness. She rarely wore makeup and dressed fairly simply. She was an attractive woman with shoulder-length brown hair and a well-toned body. She went to great lengths to make an impression on people. Behind that socially polite facade, her covert hostility and controlling nature clouded her sense of reasoning. Jason's sensitivity to Louise's niggling comments and constant complaints started to get him down. Although Louise thought she was helping Jason by 'coaching' him, her pep talks were counterproductive. Instead of motivating his passion, Jason began to shut down.

The more introspective he became, the more she attempted to pry him open. The emotional tug of war in their relationship sparked a series of sparring matches. Jason was confronted by her aggression. To defend himself he withdrew, rather than counterattack.

As his confidence dwindled, Jason started putting on weight. He stuffed his anger down and started repressing his feelings. Because he was unfulfilled in his marriage his moods also dramatically affected the quality of his work. As he attempted to gain control over his finances and win his wife's approval, he fought hard to compete in the corporate world. He was working on mental overdrive and his weight problem escalated. His gym membership was suspended and his healthy lifestyle took a nosedive. Louise was appalled by Jason's rapidly growing waistline. The one thing she was unwilling to tolerate was an undisciplined man. This was Louise's cue to start calling Jason weak and pathetic; eventually she labelled him a loser.

She grew impatient with Jason's inability to please her and started an affair. Eventually Jason got wind of her clandestine activities and Louise was forced to confess. When Jason threatened her with divorce, she promised to end the affair and recommit to their marriage. Did Louise realise it was her responsibility to rebuild the trust in their relationship? No way. In Louise's mind this 'close call' should have prompted Jason to lose weight and satisfy her desires. Rather than make an effort, Louise quickly settled back into her routine of treating Jason with contempt. But this time, she went way over the line, and compared Jason unfavourably with her ex-lover. What was this woman thinking? Did she realise her vulnerable husband had a heart and her words slashed at the very fabric of his soul?

Jason started crumbling under the pressure and his destructive side kicked in. Rather than lash out at Louise, he turned his hostility inward. His attempts to moderate his eating were undermined by regular trips to McDonalds. Jason would sit behind the wheel of his black Mercedes convertible and down a couple of cheeseburgers, a tub of French fries and a nice big creamy thickshake. After he stuffed himself with junk food he'd become overwhelmed with guilt. He'd then return home to face the broken record of Louise's loud disapproval. Jason would cringe in shame and gain even more weight. She would snort and call him Porky, and accuse him of eating like a pig. Louise refused to have sex with him and said she was embarrassed to be seen with him. Jason piled on twenty-eight kilograms, covering his once sculptured body with a cushiony layer of fat.

The protective wall Jason built around himself did little to soften life's blows. Even though the writing was on the wall, Jason still 'loved' Louise and refused to give up his marriage. The battle finally ended when Jason went home one evening to find a 'Dear John' letter sitting on his empty living room floor. Louise had hired a removal truck and cleared out the apartment. Apart from Jason's clothing, his once plush home was completely bare. Louise had moved in with her new lover. After Jason read the letter, he sat down on the floor and cried. He had repressed those tears for the better part of four years and they needed to come out. No one was there to comfort Jason in his greatest hour of need. On one level, he was relieved that he could finally vent his pent-up emotion. This time, there was no one standing on the sidelines to kick him while he was down. He spent the night alone, sleeping on the floor with a rolled up sweater under his head.

I suppose Jason could thank God for small mercies. Although he felt the excruciating pain of his loneliness, not a single soul was there to torment him. Not his strict father, his emotionally cold mother, or his critical wife. Although he didn't know it yet, Jason was actually free.

Sometimes, during our darkest hour we can be so close to the dawn that there is nothing more to do than surrender to God and allow ourselves to receive the promise of a brand new day.

There was nowhere for Jason to turn but straight into the arms of his authentic self. If he weren't willing to be true to himself after suffering a destructive marriage, what more would it take? Louise went in for the final kill when she demanded a large financial settlement and half of his assets. When Jason first met Louise, he'd had over a million dollars cash in reserve. By the time she finished with him, he was left with very little. As his self-esteem plummeted, so did his net worth. Jason was too tired to fight back, so he surrendered to Louise's tyranny.

Jason passed through the dark night of the soul. His marriage had failed, he was burdened by his work, and his weight had escalated to a point where he was disgusted with himself. Although he was left feeling ravaged, Jason managed to res-urrect himself from the onslaught and commit to his personal growth. Expecting his partner to validate his worth had cost him his pride and his dignity. By the time the divorce was complete, Jason was happy to see the back of Louise and put his losses behind him. He was now ready to go deeper and find out who he really was.

Jason landed on my doorstep six months after his final separation with Louise. He had just started to get back on his feet. After pinpointing Jason's issues in his session, I was clear that he needed a little extra support, so I suggested he join one of my encounter groups—a small group of people with issues around their body image. Jason jumped at the chance.

Every Saturday morning we met to discuss the ins and outs of body transfor-mation. Every now and again the group would take a break for the smokers. I was less than amused when a few would pull out a bar of chocolate to tide them over until lunch. By the time they finished the course, they had overcome a plethora of addictions, from Mars bars to marijuana. They dumped their dead-end jobs, unsupportive boyfriends and bad habits in the reject bin. Each participant emerged with a new sense of worth.

Six weeks into the series, Jason phoned me, in the middle of a mini meltdown. In a state of panic, he called to tell me he had been retrenched and was about to lose his job. I congratulated him on powerfully opening the way to change. He was a little bemused by my comeback. I simply asked him a few key questions. 'Didn't you emphatically declare that you were bored with your job?' 'Didn't you express your desire to head a company rather than follow someone's lead?' 'Didn't you tell me it was time for you to grow?' Jason answered yes to all three questions. I reminded him to hold a strong vision of his optimum future self and suggested he stay open to new opportunities. As an important part of the transformation process, Jason needed to give up what no longer served his best interests. He couldn't possibly create a new job if he was still clinging to the old one.

Three days later Jason called me again, but this time he was elated. A friend had contacted him who knew of a job on offer as CEO for an American start-up company. A large US corporation was about to set up a branch in Australia. They needed someone with Jason's credentials to head their operations and lead the team. He jumped on a flight to Melbourne, and after several interviews and some shrewd negotiation, came back to Sydney with a contract in his pocket. He'd struck a deal for triple his old salary, a prestige company car, an expense account and stock options in the company.

Jason's self-esteem grew by the day because he learnt to develop a much more satisfying relationship with himself. His cravings for junk food diminished and he started riding his bike and exercising regularly at the gym. Now that his energy had increased, it was time for Jason to take a giant leap of trust and start opening up to women. He figured he would ease his way back into the pool gracefully, so he decided to recruit the services of a lovely young 'escort'.

Jodie was in her early twenties and her services came highly recommended. The first day they met, Jason was overcome by her beauty and tenderness. She seemed like an angel sent to heal his scars and he felt at ease in her company. Even though Jodie was paid for her services, after their business was complete, they would often just sit and talk. Jodie was inspired by Jason's sensitivity and philosophical nature. She opened up to him in ways she had never done before. Jodie's thoughtful care and loving attention brought a new dimension to Jason's relationships with women.

After seeing one another regularly for a few weeks they slipped into a friendship. Jason and Jodie talked about life as they strolled along the foreshores of Sydney Harbour. Jason opened Jodie up to a whole new world of possibility. He would often invite her over and cook her a fabulous dinner. Jason loved to cook and would spend hours in the kitchen preparing a feast for his lovely lady friend while listening to his favourite music. Every now and again he would stop to take a sip of wine and admire the view of the harbour and the boats out for a twilight sail. He lit candles, dimmed the lights and made sure the ambience was just right for his guest. Jason took great delight in spoiling Jodie and she responded by treating Jason like a prince.

When she knew she was spending an evening with her prince charming, Jodie would put on a slinky, low-cut dress and show off her figure. She went to great lengths to style her fabulous long red hair and apply her makeup impeccably. The most appealing aspect of Jodie was definitely her gentle heart. Jason was eager to encourage Jodie to explore her full potential. Underneath her sex kitten persona was a vulnerable female who was afraid of life and saw herself as an outcast. Jason and Jodie had a lot in common. On a deeper level, both believed they were unlovable and lived with a fractured sense of belonging. Jason had his addictions and Jodie had hers. She was heavily dependent on drugs and used them to escape from a world where she felt powerless.

Jason taught her to look at alternative options and review her capabilities. He encouraged Jodie to see herself through new eyes, and because of his support she started believing in herself. Through their mutual support and acknowledgment they both developed more confidence. Although they became close, they knew they needed to pursue their independent goals and not become too attached. The more they shared, the more they healed emotionally. Jason overcame his sexual inhibitions, and for the first time, felt completely self-expressed in the company of a woman. Jodie mustered the courage to give up 'the game' and conquered her drug problem. After spending a few months in Jason's company, she decided to find a job working with children. With her new sense of worth in place, she secured a job as a live-in nanny and started to heal her fractured sense of belonging.

By the time Jason completed the eight weeks of group sessions, he was passionate about his dream and felt ready to find a life partner. He was about to embark on his new career as a CEO and wanted to find a companion to share his journey. Jason felt like a new man. During the course of the program, he dropped twelve kilograms and went on to lose another twelve over the following few months. Jason felt confident enough to enter another committed, long-term relationship. I cautioned him to be discerning and hold his best interests at heart. After Louise, he was well aware of his patterns and was concerned about the possibility of a re-run. To keep potential predators from his door, Jason needed to learn how to protect himself by making wise choices, based on knowing his worth. Jason was clear on what was important to him and needed to find a woman who had similar priorities. He wanted to be with a partner who was compassionate, supportive and generous.

After developing his friendship with Jodie, Jason knew exactly what a supportive romantic relationship felt like. The level of their connection would serve as his first yardstick. Strangely enough, the first woman who attracted Jason's attention was someone he already knew. Now that he was emotionally available, his friend Nicole expressed her interest. She was a few years younger than Jason and had often approached him for advice. Nicole was highly creative and wanted to be a makeup artist in the film industry.

While studying her craft, she often assisted on large productions. A voluptuous blonde with alabaster skin, Nicole was physically striking. Often known to play the femme fatale, her womanly charms captured many a man's attention. Jason was exactly the sort of man Nicole was searching for. Now he had healed his broken heart, and with his executive lifestyle nicely in place, it was time for her to make her move. Two months later, Nicole packed her cosmetic cases and moved into Jason's apartment.

Not long after they began living together, Jason noticed Nicole becoming more demanding. Her list of needs was long and her expectations were enormous. The more Jason gave, the more Nicole wanted. Nicole's intense mood swings started to worry him. One minute she was sweet and affectionate and the next, she would sulk and withdraw. When Nicole started to moan about Jason's rigorous work schedule, he became nervous. She would sometimes say she was sick just to get his attention. And when all else failed and she felt she was losing her hold on him, her claws would come out. How did he handle Nicole's emotionally volatility? He became her therapist, guardian and gallant rescuer.

Unlike Jodie, Nicole was unwilling to take responsibility for resolving her own issues. She expected others to carry her emotional baggage until they were exhausted and had no more to give. When she felt powerless she became defensive, and attacked others to strengthen her own position. To Jason's dismay, he realised he had walked blindly into repeating his old mistakes. Rather than build a new relationship on solid ground, he had compromised his integrity by choosing a partner who was unwilling to offer her acknowledgment and support. For a man with Jason's character, whose main priority was to explore his full potential, he was heading up the wrong path. But as Jason had done time and time again, he allowed himself to be deceived by a woman wearing the mask of 'niceness'.

As with his marriage, he did everything in his power to make their relationship work. But Nicole became judgmental and then downright vicious. Jason's confidence plummeted. He started to withdraw emotionally and experienced fits of depression. Rather than express his anger he repressed his feelings and reopened the old wound in his aching heart. Consequently, his energy started leaking; he was like a man filled with bullet holes.

Despite all these signs, Jason continued to support Nicole like a puppy waiting in vain for a bone. But it got worse. Nicole called Jason weak and pathetic and accused him of being half a man. She developed the nasty habit of literally kicking Jason out of bed if he couldn't perform sexually. She would then accuse Jason of having a problem and suggest he seek professional help. Perhaps he should have called his lovely friend Jodie, whom Nicole categorically forbade Jason from seeing. It wasn't until his spirits were completely depleted and he had nothing more to give that he finally told Nicole to leave. Jason allowed her criticism and cruelty to destroy the foundation of his esteem and consequently he sabotaged his job.

His employer decided to send a US representative to take over Jason's position in the company to build a stronger alliance between the two countries. Jason was ruthlessly dismissed. After eighteen months of steadily increasing the assets of the multinational corporation he worked for and tripling the original target proposed by his seniors, Jason was made redundant. Jason felt crushed between two unsympathetic parties: Nicole and the US corporate giants. At long last, Jason was finally willing to take a stand for his worth. He called his attorney and started proceedings to sue the company for wrongful dismissal, and from that day forward, Nicole was on her own.

I was in America when the wolves devoured Jason. By the time I got back to Sydney, his world had come toppling down. He came to see me just after my return, in need of spiritual guidance and clarification. I took Jason through a process that allowed him to come face to face with his distorted internal self-image and dysfunctional beliefs. It was time for Jason to have a reality check. His life's story was starting to resemble the tale of the *Three Little Pigs*. His means of protection was as flimsy as straw. He had been 'blown away' by Louise's howling criticism and was eaten alive in the process. Jason knew after that catastrophe that he needed to safeguard his assets by building a stronger self-image. After rebuilding his self-esteem, he started to develop a greater sense of worth. Jason's decision to find a life partner was slightly premature. Although he was warned, rather than be discerning and use careful deliberation, he shacked up with Nicole. Jason's 'house of sticks' tumbled fairly quickly when he allowed himself to be ruthlessly intimidated yet again.

By changing his attitude and increasing his expectations, Jason is currently in the process of building a sturdy platform for his future. He now irrefutably knows not to sell himself short when it comes to business or romance. Jason is well on the way to increasing his financial status after securing a position with a rapidly growing company. In the past four months, through commissions alone, he has almost doubled his previous salary. Working with a generous group of individuals who acknowledge his efforts has made an enormous difference. He has become far more discerning with his choices.

Because Jason is still in the process of restructuring his internal self-image, he consistently holds a vision in the back of his mind of the man he ultimately wants to be. Until he meets a potential partner who has similar priorities, he prefers to stay detached. Jason learnt well from his harrowing experiences. How has he changed? He is happy to create an abundant life for the joy that it brings, rather than to attract a partner or substantiate his worth.

Like the third little pig, Jason is now building a house of bricks with thorough, careful consideration. By overcoming his own self-doubt, he now feels far more secure within himself. Now that his partnership with Nicole has ended, he has restored his connection with Jodie. Because Jason is much more comfortable being himself, their friendship has changed. The last time Jason and Jodie met for dinner, he made her a grilled cheese sandwich and they sat on the couch together and watched *The Simpsons* on TV and laughed like a couple of kids. They have both come a long way since those days of 'wine and roses'. Their friendship offers them a haven of mutual support and serves as a reminder of the importance of building trust in a relationship. To safeguard their innocence, they are also there to remind one another of one important point. When someone takes time to consider their most beneficial options and is wise enough to protect their best interests, they can overcome the forceful tactics of hungry prowling wolves.

Looking Beneath the Surface

It is fairly clear that Jason's big downfall was selling himself short. He put himself beneath his partners rather than standing solidly on equal ground. The only reason he allowed his loved ones to call him weak and pathetic is because on a deeper level he believed them. His relationship with his parents left him feeling like an outsider who had to prove he was good enough to find his place in the world. Although he managed to jump the hurdle to a certain degree in business, loving relationships were his Achilles heel. His parents were emotionally unavailable and rarely offered support when he faltered. In his father's household, there was no room for mistakes. No matter how much Jason attempted to win their love, it didn't seem to work. In search of resolution, he carried the identical pattern into his relationships with women.

If we get into the habit of giving to others generously in order to prove we are worthy of love, we quickly set ourselves up for disappointment. No matter how much Jason gave, or what he did, it was never enough. He approached others with the subconscious belief that he was 'empty', and therefore his contribution was seen as insignificant. With both Louise and Nicole, he felt his efforts were futile. Attempting to satisfy their needs was like pouring water into a bowl covered with a lid. The women in Jason's life, including his mother, were incredibly guarded and resisted intimacy. If we give to someone wholeheartedly and they are unreceptive, it is simply because they are not willing to be loved. Louise and Nicole were closed down because they inwardly disapproved of themselves. When we foster a relationship with a partner who has low self-worth, we will often be confronted by the value of our love. Jason's love didn't land on fertile ground and, as a result, there was no growth in his relationships.

Jodie, on the other hand, trusted Jason and was open to his affection. She allowed his contribution to inspire and nourish her to the degree that it altered the course of her life. With Jodie, Jason stood in his power and conquered his self-doubt.

The way we create what we want in this world is by loving and appreciating ourselves. It has nothing to do with the way we look, the capacity of our brain, or the level of our performance. It has everything to do with our level of self-worth and how much we are willing to receive. When we seek outside validation we give our power away. Jason believed he was weak and empty and therefore wasn't worthy of being loved. Even Louise's criticism regarding his weight fed into his belief that he was powerless. Those negative labels we attach to ourselves separate us from what we ultimately want to experience.

We cannot force another human being to demonstrate their love or affection. It is always their choice, and it is based on the value they place on their own contribution. If we attempt to push people or control them, they will only become defensive or shut down. When Jason criticised Louise or Nicole for being insensitive, it only created further separation. They would then highlight his inadequacies to justify their own positions in order to feel better about themselves. The power struggle would continue until Jason had nothing left to give. Rather than their union being based on love, it was perpetuated by fear and driven by ego. The way we free ourselves from an emotional tug-of-war is to recognise the potency of our love and acknowledge our worth.

At times we become oblivious to the negative conversations we have with ourselves. The internal critic can be very subtle. Those little comments about our limitations need to be detected and challenged immediately. It was Jason's self-criticism that drove his appetite for junk food and his obsession to build the 'perfect' profile. When he finally decided to take positive steps for his own benefit, rather than prove he was acceptable, he created balance in his life. Most of us have a range of guidelines we place on being valuable or lovable. We have to constantly upgrade the quality of our thoughts to successfully alter our beliefs. When Jason stopped placing unreasonable demands on himself, he relaxed and things started to flow gracefully. He dropped his excess weight and increased his finances by changing his attitude and modifying his lifestyle, rather than pushing himself to achieve results.

We need to stop and tell ourselves that we deserve to be loved in each and every moment exactly as we are. We can then turn our focus towards what we want to experience and open up to receiving the bounty of life. Self-doubt casts a shadow over our self-worth. Our beliefs are a product of our past and have little to do with our true potential. Jason was trapped in time by re-running his parents' conversations in his mind. Until he was willing to give up those limited concepts, he felt powerless.

When we have a negative attitude, we need to stop and ask ourselves, 'How am I viewing myself right now?', and then, 'Is this who I really am?' Whenever Jason hit the wall with his overeating, he asked himself those two important questions, which gave him the strength to alter his behaviour. He would then focus on who he ultimately wanted to be, rather than surrender to the voice of doubt. It is important that we continue to change our point of reference until we no longer follow a negative train of thought. That is the only way any of us can instigate permanent change.

When we become familiar or comfortable with something over a long period of time, it is often difficult to give it up. Normally the difficulty comes from the fact that we don't know what we are about to face on the next part of our journey. At times Jason felt powerless in the face of change, and so did Jodie. They finally mustered the courage to change by altering their impression of who they thought they could be. Just like buying a new pair of shoes, they looked at what was available, and then made a choice based on their needs and preferences. Changing our shoes at different times to suit our circumstances is customary. We can do the same thing when it comes to facilitating life changes, if we are willing to trust our internal resources and become flexible enough to dance with the rhythm of life.

THE BUILDER
CREATING A FIRM FOUNDATION FOR SECURITY

After Jason started working with me on a regular basis, he became well aware that he was responsible for his own transformation. We all either consciously create our reality, or subconsciously allow events to take place in our lives. If we believe otherwise, we forfeit our personal power and are susceptible to becoming a victim of our circumstances.

Jason's most destructive beliefs were that women couldn't be trusted and that loving relationships lead to being used. When Jason was a child, he took his father's counsel very seriously. In fact, most the fallacies we hold are carried over from childhood.

For any of us to change our lives, we need to expand our existing beliefs. The way we instruct our subconscious is by visualising what we want to experience and simultaneously intensifying our feelings. When Jason decided to change the shape of his body, he took the time to literally see himself as a person who was lean and fit. He then sensed the vitality that his new body would bring, which accelerated his progress. This little exercise allowed Jason to feel better about himself in the moment, which helped him build his commitment and make healthier choices. He didn't force himself to diet or exercise. For Jason, altering his lifestyle became the next natural step. By imagining his new body and elevating his confidence, he was inspired to take positive action. His desire to be slim and energetic outweighed his need to overeat. If we don't consistently hold the vision of the person we aspire to be, we lose our motivation.

Inspiration and motivation go hand in hand. They are the fuel that sparks our drive.

Jason is now in the process of using the same technique to create an intimate loving partnership. He's examining the existing files his subconscious has compiled about romantic union. If we wish to change anything in our world permanently, it is important to uncover our basic beliefs. We need to get clear on our patterns and clarify the scripts we are living out in the world. The easiest way to do this is to review our profile, like a character in a play, and simply ask, 'What would a person have to believe about themselves and the world, to create this experience.' Jason played the wounded victim in his relationships and attracted woman to perform the role of tormenter. They helped keep his beliefs alive. To change his story, he had to see himself as a different character and use his imagination to create an alternative ending. The rubber meets the road when we make our choices and decisions. If we compromise, we repeat our old experiences the same way Jason did.

Reviewing our past is a helpful way to pinpoint the negative conclusions we have made about ourselves. After his relationship with Nicole ended he finally 'got' that he was reliving his childhood experiences to seek resolution for his internal unrest. In uncovering his underlying reasons for staying in a destructive relationship, he was able to learn something from his negative experiences. It is important that we extract the valuable lessons from our past and then let go of our disappointment so we can move on. We have the potential to allow the love that is present in each moment to soothe any pain we've incurred.

We don't need to eliminate our old beliefs; we simply need to build a new framework to go beyond them. Jason needed to make peace with his past by forgiving himself for his shortcomings, and then acknowledge the fact that he was willing to change. Then finally, he could become humble enough to embrace more of his potential. We form the beliefs that are the impetus of our creation. Therefore we have the power to alter them in a way that carries us forward. Struggling against our past doesn't work. Distinguishing our beliefs and choosing something different is the way we transcend our limitations.

For Jason to heal his situation permanently, he needs to abstain from self-criticism and continue to be a loving caretaker in his relationship with himself. Jason's greatest form of protection, to prevent him from experiencing further hurt, is to make wise and thoughtful choices. Through his entire dilemma with Nicole, he never once turned to food for comfort or stopped his exercise program. Jason now has an extremely positive relationship with his body, based on caring for and about himself. He has turned that level of deliberate attention towards attracting a partner who recognises his needs, and acknowledges his contribution. When Jason, as we all do, fully realises that he deserves to be loved, he will experience a rich and rewarding life.

All internal conflict is born from denying our personal power and our right to be fulfilled. If we feel insecure and our mind does not offer a solution to our unrest, the conflict begins. Constantly maintaining a positive attitude has been a challenge that has plagued Jason most of his life. His negative beliefs and self-doubt were initially promoted by his father's relentless criticism. Those harsh words impacted on Jason's emotions to the degree that he became defensive, and shut down to being loved. How we see ourselves is everything in this world. That is why we need to assess where we are coming from whenever we make a decision. If Jason had held a higher opinion of himself, he may have overlooked Louise as a potential life partner and nipped things in the bud very quickly with Nicole. If we allow ourselves to be criticised and take people's negative opinions to heart, we will continue to believe, on some level, that we are never good enough. We have to be very clear on where a person is coming from, before we take their words as the gospel truth.

There is always more for us to experience and create. We are whole and complete; we are simply in the process of discovering more of our potential as we expand our vision of who we are. Whenever we compromise our choices because we lose sight of our full potential, we sell ourselves short.

We cannot hold others responsible for the way we feel about ourselves. We are the ones who ultimately decide who we are and what we are worthy of experiencing.

As the mother swine said to the three little pigs as they set out to make their fortune, 'The way you get along in this world is to do things as well as you can.' They were wise words from a mother who knew the importance of commitment, consistency and care. If we remember the importance of the three Cs, no matter what project we undertake, we will strengthen our resources and protect ourselves from harm. And just like the third little pig, which heeded his mother's counsel, we can create both security and comfort in our world by considering our best interests and laying a solid foundation for success.

KEY QUESTIONS TO ASK YOURSELF

This is a checklist to see how on track you are with being *The Builder* in your life:

1. Do your beliefs support a solid foundation for your future?
2. How often do you acknowledge and commend yourself?
3. How much love do you honestly believe you are open to receiving right now, before you change a thing?
4. Do you repeat your old negative behaviour patterns or learn from your mistakes and make progress?
5. Have you made peace with your past, or are you dragging it into the future?
6. Do you make positive, intentional choices and take affirmative action to attain your goals?
7. (Take a little time to answer this one.) If you loved yourself completely in this moment, how would your life change?

CHAPTER ELEVEN

CROSSING THE BRIDGE FROM DREAMS TO REALITY

If we stay focused on what inspires us, rather than what defeats our spirit, we will keep moving forward. It is therefore important to develop a vision of our optimum future self, as a reference point for our dreams and aspirations.

It was Christmas in La Jolla and the streets were dressed with thousands of tiny fairy lights. I had been invited to join one of my friends for a drink, even though I was tempted to decline his offer, my intuition told me to accept. It turned out to be a memorable evening. I had the pleasure of meeting a lovely young woman named Katie; later I became instrumental in influencing the course of her destiny.

As Katie and I first struck up a conversation, I noticed her continuous sneezing. She excused herself politely and expressed her concern about her incessant allergies. Her pale, delicate skin was flushed and her large blue eyes were slightly watery. Katie was an extremely beautiful young woman, with poise and confidence. Tall and slim, with blonde shoulder-length hair, she had a soft and feminine charm which captured the attention of quite a few male onlookers. They were free to observe and dream, but this fair maiden was already married.

Her husband, Carl, was an astute young Englishman. He was lean and athletic, with sharp, striking features. Both being foreigners, we started talking about cultural contrasts and the merits of living in the United States. Katie was curious to know more about what I did. I am usually reluctant to talk to people socially about my spiritual convictions, but for some reason, with Katie I was completely candid. She was fascinated, and asked me question after question about the nature of my work. Carl became slightly hot under the collar and excused himself politely.

Katie's sneezing increased as she apologised for Carl's scepticism. He was a practical realist who had very little time for philosophical discussions or sentimentality, she said. By contrast, Katie was extremely sensitive, a dreamer at heart.

Katie had come to the crossroads in her life after recently renouncing a lucrative corporate career. She was earnestly searching for direction, which is precisely why the universe brought us together. For some reason, I felt compelled to support Katie and in the spirit of Christmas goodwill I offered her a free session.

Strangely enough, it turned out that Katie and I lived in the same street. The morning of her session, we sat and enjoyed tea in the garden. After a few sips of Earl Grey, I closed my eyes for a few moments and 'tuned in' to Katie's energy. Although the prominent issue at hand was finding a new career path, the first wave of information I received pointed to her marriage.

Katie was only in her late twenties, and after a year of marriage, she felt her life was a complete compromise. After graduating from college with a marketing degree, she worked hard to build her financial status and reputation in the business world. When she first met Carl, she was on a mission to prove she was powerful and smart. Because of his highly developed intellect and slightly lofty nature, Carl sparked Katie's competitive side. With a strong desire to win his approval and affection, Katie developed the attributes she knew would arouse his attention. Her charms were very difficult to resist and Carl became enamoured of Katie's strong and sexy persona. She was attractive and upwardly mobile, which made her his perfect match.

For the first three years of their relationship, they lived independent and busy lives and at the end of the working week they shared romantic, playful weekends. Together they developed a mutual vision of the wonderful life they wished to create. Carl loved being with a partner who was both dynamic and emotionally self-sufficient. And to complete the picture, Katie enjoyed being with a man who challenged her intellect and kept her on her toes.

When Katie started to feel burnt out by her hectic lifestyle, she turned to her husband for comfort. Carl was perplexed by his wife's change of attitude and was concerned about her diminishing ambition. Katie was so distressed by her demanding workload and lack of inspiration that she became more and more fatigued. Her allergies and lethargy escalated to the point where she was forced to give up work. Her allergies were a symptom of feeling stifled and suppressed. And although she threw in the towel in the corporate arena, she remained unwell.

There were times when Katie felt she couldn't breathe in her marriage because she thought she had to perform. Although Carl was a dependable and loyal husband, Katie felt she couldn't connect with him emotionally. His head ruled him, and he questioned her interest in spirituality and metaphysics. When it came to expressing his heart, Carl was way out of his comfort zone. With a cold, overbearing mother and an emotionally repressed father, he was inclined to restrain his feelings. Although he would often cook wonderful dinners, and arrive home with little gifts, when it came to building emotional rapport, he just wasn't up for the game. As far as he was concerned, there was no problem in their relationship, other than Katie finding a more significant job.

Katie's masculine or assertive side was overruling the feminine side and she had lost sight of her real self as a result. Desperate to reconnect with her soul, she turned towards her spiritual convictions to boost her morale. Unable to share that part of her world with her husband, her actions created an invisible wall between them. The more emotional Katie became, the more Carl disengaged. He didn't want to lose control of his world, so he stayed detached to maintain his strength and composure. In his mind, his once resilient wife was having a 'mini meltdown'.

There were far too many mornings when Katie sat under the shower crying. A barrage of denied emotions rushed to the surface, longing to be released. Katie felt her life was disappearing down the drain hole. She began to question everything in her world, from her career moves to her choice of husband. What had happened to Katie's genuine dreams and aspirations? She had left them somewhere in Texas, along with her abounding creativity. Rather than follow a path like her mother's, she had vowed to use the power of her mind and the strength of her independence to craft her own life.

Katie's mother was a beautiful and creative woman. She was a loving wife and mother, but, sadly, denied her own talents. Her life revolved around her husband, an ambitious, hard-working doctor. Katie watched her fragile mother being overwhelmed by her father's stature. Rather than grow together, they grew apart. Sensing her mother's anguish, Katie vowed to triumph over weakness and be like her father. Although she was incredibly feminine, she dismissed many of her charms in order to overcome her fears. It was only a matter of time before Katie realised what that monumental decision had cost her. In denying her sensitivity, she had sacrificed her genuine dreams and instead developed an impressive facade.

I talked to Katie about recapturing her dreams and giving herself permission to finally follow her heart. Over the course of the following twelve months, she did everything she could to strengthen her connection with Carl. She supported him in launching his own business. They worked alongside one another every day, and Katie's allergies returned with a vengeance—along with blinding headaches. She was mentally, physically and emotionally spent. With an outburst of tears she told Carl she needed to leave and could no longer go on living a lie.

In a final attempt to rescue her marriage, Katie asked Carl if he was willing to meet with me in a couple's session. He agreed, and I sat with both of them for almost two hours to identify their areas of conflict. After clearly defining their issues, Carl still refused to acknowledge responsibility for his behaviour. He just wanted Katie to go back to being the person she was when they first met. It took a lot of courage for Carl to agree to meet with me, but he was still unwilling to initiate positive changes. From that point on, Katie decided she no longer wanted to live with a partner who was emotionally detached. Carl challenged my perception and told me he thought Katie was being unreasonable. He insisted their marriage was fine. I asked Carl to take a good look at his sobbing wife and then tell me there wasn't a problem. Carl looked at Katie's grief-stricken features and was silent. He had become so mentally rigid that he was unable to offer her a consoling embrace.

It was clear to me at that stage that Carl was emotionally numb. It wasn't until Katie literally packed her bags and pulled out of the driveway, that the penny dropped. When her car was no longer visible, he finally broke down and cried. He called Katie on her mobile phone and pleaded with her to come home. But by this stage, it was far too late.

During the next few weeks, Katie and I worked closely exploring all the things she loved to do. As Katie allowed her imagination to expand beyond the boundaries of her rational mind, her heart began to sing. We laid all her options on the table, based on her natural talents and interests. It was fascinating to see how all the little pieces of the picture came together to form a clear view of her future possibilities. A few features were consistently highlighted: her interest in wine, food, travel and culture. Katie longed to enjoy a more cosmopolitan lifestyle and connect with people who were sensitive, creative and refined. She wanted to work with a company committed to quality and excellence. She was also clear that she didn't want to return to the corporate arena.

It was important that she focus more on what she wanted to experience and the person she wanted to become, than specifically on what she wanted to do. Part of Katie's life lesson was to weave her own dream and bring it to fruition. To do that powerfully, she needed to listen to the call of her soul. I encouraged Katie to develop a strong vision of her optimum future self and call upon her as a guide and ally.

Finally, Katie decided to move to San Francisco. It not only felt right intuitively, but from a practical standpoint, the city offered her a vast platform for complete self-expression. Katie wanted to work for a winery. The Napa Valley and Sonoma County were brimming with vineyards that undoubtedly needed dynamic people to market and promote their wines. Although she had no experience in the field, she understood the principles of winemaking and had a keen interest in developing her knowledge. Katie wasn't certain of how everything would come together, but she was willing to embark on her journey one step at a time. She knew that if she set her intentions clearly and focused on what she wished to create, doors would eventually open. With the outline of her dream recorded in her journal, and her creative visualisation tapes packed in her suitcase, she went off to explore uncharted terrain.

When Katie arrived in San Francisco, she made a wonderful circle of new friends. She talked to as many people as she could about her goals and aspirations. In the interim, she took a couple of part-time jobs to pay the bills. After dismissing the sceptics who told her that the wine industry was a closed shop, she eventually secured a prominent position with an exclusive boutique vineyard. Her new boss was a prestigious winemaker with a passion for producing exceptional wines. Katie felt proud to be an ambassadress for his products, and flew from state to state promoting the fruits of his labour. She quickly developed her skills; her employer was more than happy with her efforts and acknowledged her generously.

Eighteen months after leaving La Jolla, with her allergies and lethargy well and truly behind her, Katie had established a wonderful new lifestyle. She settled in a lovely old apartment in the Marina district, where she worked from home two days a week when she wasn't travelling extensively throughout America. Katie was in her element, but there was one thing missing—an intimate, loving relationship. After dating a few contenders, she ended up feeling despondent. Sorting the wheat from the chaff can be tedious and when it comes to creating relationships, we are often tempted to compromise. Fortunately, Katie had already learnt that without challenge there is no growth.

Clear on her patterns, she kept her eyes wide open and watched the play unfold. She attracted either men who were arrogant, successful and self-centred, or who were insecure and lacked strength in their character. Katie observed the pendulum swing from one side to the other. Men either wanted to dominate her, or wanted her to overshadow them. Katie stayed on the ball and wrote in her journal every day. All the while, she strived to develop the qualities of her optimum future self and balance the receptive and assertive sides of her nature. Katie was clear that she wanted to be in an equal relationship with a partner who was both sensitive and strong. Knowing her worth was an important factor, and with her optimum future self as her guide, she was assured of the ultimate role model. She just had to conquer the voice of doubt and refrain from comparing herself with other women.

Every now and then Katie would call me for reassurance, and I would suggest a few simple techniques to lift her spirits. Due to her demanding work schedule, Katie rarely had time to sit and formally meditate. And yet it was important for her to expand her imagination and create a sensual connection with her optimum future self. For Katie to attract her ideal relationship, she needed to intensify her desires and visualise herself as a woman who was acknowledged, loved, and fully embraced. Rather than imagining Mr Wonderful, she needed to sense his presence and focus on the essence of the experience she wanted to create. Those feelings would act as a magnet to draw him into her world. I suggested that Katie make the most of her long drives to the Napa Valley and her time on aeroplanes.

If she were willing to 'daydream' with intention, she would build up her resonance and attract new opportunities.

Patience is a great asset, and so is perseverance. Katie had her fingers burnt a few times, compromising her choices and getting involved with men who were not up to her speed. Those little diversions blurred her vision and drained her confidence. After her marriage with Carl, she was wise to remember the importance of upholding her values. Katie and I had a little standing joke. When she was tempted to compromise, I reminded her to hold the vision of marrying the 'vineyard owner', which was merely a symbol for a man with substance and great sensitivity.

Katie got into the habit of visualising the outcome of her dream regularly. As she set out on her long morning drives through the winding roads of the Napa Valley, she would open up to sensing her optimum future self. She declared her intention to create a life of abundance with a man who inspired her heart. She began to sense his presence, and beautiful images came to her of sharing a life with a man she loved. At times she was so entranced by the images that she would look down at her hand on the steering wheel and see a sapphire and diamond engagement ring. During those wonderfully pleasurable moments, Katie 'sensed' that she was already married.

When Phillipe entered Katie's world she was overwhelmed by his poise, his charm and his soulful nature. Although he was only in his early thirties, he had the intellectual maturity and wisdom of a much older man. Who was this remarkable man Katie had met at a wine expo in New York? He was the son of a winegrower, who owned a reputable vineyard and winery in the South of France.

After the business day concluded, a mutual friend, Peter, invited Katie and Phillipe to a wine-tasting event at a fashionable restaurant in New York. The restaurant was warm and inviting, with rich timber panels and deep, subdued colours. Adam, who completed their party of four, joined them for a drink. As the wine flowed, Adam brought up the topic of whirlwind romances. One of his friends had just announced his engagement and Adam was very cynical. After knowing his girlfriend for only two months, his friend had proposed. Katie rebutted Adam's sarcasm and told him she had recently met a lovely couple who married after knowing each other for just three days and have lived together happily for thirty-five years. The couple knew they were right for each other from day one.

At the end of her poignant story Katie turned to Phillipe, and for the first time, their eyes met in an intimate gaze. Everything around them faded and time stood still. Although they were in a busy restaurant in downtown Manhattan, they were captured by the stillness, and momentarily intoxicated by one another's soul. Phillipe knew from that instant that he had met his future wife. He had an overwhelming sense of his connection with Katie that went far beyond the parameters of the physical world, and his heart was deeply touched. As Katie was swept up in the sweet emotional exchange between them, she realised that Phillipe's energy was identical to that of the man she had sensed in her meditations. As Katie surveyed Phillipe's gentle face both of them became conscious of their undeniable soul connection.

The next morning they were scheduled to leave New York. Phillipe, 'by chance', just happened to have a ticket to San Francisco. He had planned to visit the wine country and take in the sights. Who could possibility be a better guide than his irresistible new acquaintance? Phillipe and Katie made the most of each precious moment they spent together. When he returned to France, they spoke on the phone every day until he faithfully flew back into his lover's arms. Caught up in a childlike sense of wonder and delight, their love blossomed. As they eagerly learnt as much as they could about one another, their priorities and preferences lined up like a checklist from heaven. Phillipe was a deeply spiritual man who was committed to his personal growth. He worked in the family winery, alongside his father. Phillipe's level of integrity and dedication to his profession were matched by his generous, sensitive nature. Katie had finally attracted her ideal partner, a man who was caring, tender and strong.

Six weeks into their romance, Katie flew to Paris to meet Phillipe and spend Christmas with his family. They decided to have a few days in the city alone, and then travel down to the vineyard. The 'honeymoon' couple booked into a charming boutique hotel and Phillipe made reservations for Le Jules Verne restaurant, on the second level of the Eiffel Tower. It was cold on the streets; the two lovers donned their coats and braved the elements to explore the shops on the Champs-Elysées. Although Phillipe was well travelled, he loved being at home. Proud to be French, he wanted to share the culture and beauty his country offered with the woman he cherished. Phillipe felt blessed to have the life he did, and with Katie by his side, his dream was complete.

He had recently bought a five-hundred-year-old farmhouse and had started to think about having a family and settling down. He had been back in France for just over a year after living with his ex-girlfriend in Australia for almost seven. They split amicably after realising they had different values.

That night, after a long leisurely bath, Katie changed into a soft, pale blue blouse which Phillipe had given her that afternoon. She slipped on a long black skirt and a sexy pair of ankle-strap, high-heeled shoes. Katie was transformed into a radiant picture of elegance. Being in love always puts a little extra colour in our cheeks and a definite skip in our step. Phillipe was also glowing. Freshly shaven, with his jet-black hair lightly gelled, he put on a dark blue shirt and was ready to face the concluding chapter of a delightfully romantic day. Katie and Phillipe grabbed their coats once again, and made their way to the Eiffel Tower. Katie took the arm of her handsome escort. Never before had she met a man she felt so at ease with and inspired by. Katie was deeply and absolutely in love.

When they arrived at the restaurant, Phillipe was greeted by name and recognised as the son of his well-respected father. As honorary guests, Phillipe and Katie were given the best table in the house—by the window, with a bird's eye view of Paris. Phillipe ordered a fine bottle of champagne. He then reached across the table and clasped his strong fingers tenderly around Katie's hand. He asked her if she was happy and Katie told him she had never felt more joy than she had in the past few months with him. Phillipe then reached into his pocket and pulled out a sapphire and diamond engagement ring. He carefully slipped the ring onto Katie's finger and asked her to be his wife. Katie cried and looked at her sweet lover's smile and graciously accepted his proposal.

The day Katie drove through the gates of the winery to meet Phillipe's family, she felt like she had finally come home. There was something distinctly 'déjà vu' about the vineyard. Katie may have been a little overwhelmed, but she was very clear on one thing: she was living her dream. She had taken one giant step toward embracing her optimum future self. Although there was much more room in her world for growth, she was well on her way to creating a full and abundant life.

They planned to be married in the spring, with a lavish wedding at the vineyard. Katie and Phillipe would restore the old farmhouse and start a family. With her experience of the wine industry in America, Katie was also more than happy to work with Phillipe in the winery. Exporting to the US was a large part of Phillipe's plan, and Katie's contribution was invaluable.

As all the beautiful pieces of the puzzle fell into place, Katie acclaimed her power to create an extraordinary life. Rising way above mediocrity, she challenged her restrictive lifestyle and opted for freedom. By taking a strong stand for her creative self-expression, and intensifying her desire to create a deep, intimate relationship, she unlocked the secret to manifesting her dreams.

Will and desire are two very powerful ingredients when it comes to creating a formula for success. With the vision of her optimum future self indelibly imprinted in her mind's eye, Katie eventually left San Francisco and boarded a plane to France. With her wedding dress safely stowed in first class, she looked down at the engagement ring on her finger and counted her blessings. Most of her belongings had been packed in a container and shipped across the ocean. But there were a few essential things that Katie lovingly carried close to her side. One was her personal journal and the other was the blossoming dream she held in her heart.

LOOKING BENEATH THE SURFACE

Imagination is the mother of invention. Albert Einstein

Katie experienced first hand the power of her imagination and learnt to use it to her advantage. Our imagination offers us a window into the realm of possibility, a place where dreams are born and inspiration abounds. Who we imagine our-selves to be in this world is who we potentially become. Katie kept expanding her vision of what was possible, and in the process she created a wonderful road map of her future.

After being stuck in a corporate rut and a frustrating marriage for many years, she finally decided to take a risk and step out of the box. Katie was willing to take a stand for her preferences and acknowledge the value of her dreams. It takes both courage and commitment to give up our false sense of security and create a brand new life. With her heart aching and her health failing, Katie knew she had to make that choice. Our choices and decisions always align with who we think we are, and Katie knew she was living a lie.

If we refuse to awaken our passion, we sabotage our dreams and dissuade our success. If we continually compromise and are repressed by fear, we are out of integrity with ourselves. Because of her severe allergies, Katie wanted to break out of her skin and be someone else. The thing that supports us in fulfilling our dreams is the attitude we have about ourselves. And the way we feel about ourselves will be reflected in the attitude we have towards our world.

We are all powerful magnets that attract our experiences. There is nothing in the outside world that is a hurdle other than what we create with our own self-doubt. Katie surmounted those obstacles by learning to remain focused on the person she ultimately wanted to be. Although that took a certain amount of discipline, Katie's desire to live out her dream inspired her efforts.

When she left for San Francisco, she was wise enough to know that she needed to create her new identity from the inside out. This helped her rebuff other people's negativity and scepticism about her quest to break into the wine industry. Katie continued to reflect on her character and slowly developed her inner strength. For the first time in her life she was carefully crafting a life of her own design, rather than building an identity to seek approval. Her identity started to reflect her unique signature as an individual and became the perfect vehicle for her to express her specific talents and distinct creativity. After our extensive time in session, Katie knew wholeheartedly how dangerous it was to compare herself with others.

Her strong desire to be in an intimate, loving relationship drew Phillipe into her world. By using her imagination and feelings, Katie started to connect with the resonance of the person she wanted to be, who was already happily married. She started to experience life in the same way her future self would, which provided her with a new level of self-assurance. Performing this exercise on a regular basis allowed Katie to build a new framework for her reality. She discarded her old self-image and attracted new opportunities.

Katie and Phillipe's paths may never have crossed if she wasn't willing to be fully loved. When Katie was married to Carl, she saw herself on a deeper level as 'invisible, overshadowed and oppressed'. With her new self-image, she began to see herself as 'unique, powerful and loved'. Katie transformed her persona from the inside out and the universe provided her with a platform to celebrate her beauty.

If Katie had been complacent and continued to tell herself that things would never change, she would still be living an uninspired life in La Jolla, suffering from chronic fatigue. Instead, she lives a rewarding life in the south of France with a man she loves deeply. She gave herself permission to have what she really wanted.

Our subconscious is in its most receptive state first thing in the morning. Katie made it a rule to write in her journal and express her thoughts and feelings on a daily basis. She also made notes about the components of her dream and acknowledged herself when she achieved her goals. When Katie first woke up each morning she would sit quietly and connect with her inner self. Even when it was extremely early, she would take a few moments to become still and centred and would briefly write a few heartfelt lines in her journal before she faced the world. Meditation and contemplation are best practised in these early waking moments. We can then set a positive course for the rest of the day. If we take a tip from Katie, we will develop a strong vision of our optimum future self as a reference point for our highest aspirations. In the same way Katie did, if we are challenged by limitations, we can redirect our attention towards what we intend to create, rather than compromise our choices.

Katie had to learn how to say no before she said yes to some of her suitors who didn't share her priorities. Our subconscious will test us to see if we are serious about achieving our aspirations. We have to be willing to stand firm and maintain our focus. Our subconscious is like a very impressionable child that responds to our tuition. We may consciously think we want something in particular, but do we firmly declare our intentions and monitor where our attention goes? If we look at the analogy of a bank account, how many credits are we making to support our dreams and how many debits are we extracting that deplete our resources?

Our subconscious knows no difference between the physical world and the world of our dreams and imagination. Therefore, when Katie continued to visualise her aspirations and feel the resonance of her optimum future self, she harnessed her power to attract new opportunities. For Katie's dreams to finally manifest, she had to know wholeheartedly that she was good enough to receive the bounty of her harvest. It took time and effort for Katie to cultivate her new existence, and in the process she discovered her real self. As Katie enjoys the fruits of her labour, she ponders just how far she has come. On an ongoing basis, she turns her thoughts inward and continues to create an exceptionally wonderful future.

THE VISIONARY
CREATING A VISION OF OUR OPTIMUM FUTURE SELF

We can all learn a valuable lesson from Katie's story, which is to believe in the magic of our dreams. It is imperative that we give ourselves permission to live our lives to the fullest and allow others to support us on our journey. Our future selves already exist in the realm of possibility. Our supreme purpose is to be fully self-expressed and undeniably know the value of our essence.

Love is the most powerful magnetic force that exists in the universe. When Katie successfully established her career in the wine industry and created her wonderful relationship with Phillipe, it all came down to how much she was willing to be acknowledged, admired, valued and supported.

It wasn't enough for Katie to simply visualise her future self; she needed to strengthen her connection by using her internal senses. Katie reached the point where she could feel Phillipe's energy before they met. He even bought her the exact engagement ring she'd seen on her finger when she drove through the Napa Valley. Was this a premonition? Or was it because Katie was powerful enough to manifest her preferences and Phillipe showed up as the bearer of gifts?

When I asked Phillipe why he chose a sapphire, he told me he just couldn't imagine Katie wearing anything else. Subtle messages are transmitted constantly via our subconscious through feelings and pictures. On a soul level we are all connected, and every day, people enter our world as messengers and benefactors. Whether a person is a stepping stone or a stumbling block, we all have something to offer one another.

What we request we ultimately receive, so we need to be very clear what we ask for.

In building a vision of our optimum future self, we need to avoid constructing an idealised image of perfection. Katie focused on the essence of the person she wanted to be and simply allowed her physical appearance to reflect those qualities. After moving to San Francisco, she had far more physical strength and stamina, and at times she looked radiant. Her skin was clear, her allergies disappeared and she became far more charismatic.

Whenever we hold a negative self-image, our feelings will respond. We dim our light and shut down to being acknowledged. If we are disciplined in the practice of holding a vision of our optimum future self, we will be far more inspired to give generously and receive more from the world.

Anything we can imagine is possible. When Katie imagined herself married to a European man who was cultured and romantic, she wasn't just fantasising. When she was married to Carl, although she was steadfastly faithful, she would often feel a strong connection to European men. Katie was often inspired by their depth and sensitivity. By paying particular attention to one possibility, it then becomes a probability. Katie spent a lot of time focusing on the essential qualities of her potential partner, and as a result Phillipe appeared.

When we have established a strong sense of our optimum future-self, we need to simultaneously practise self-acceptance. If we chastise ourselves for not being enough in the moment, we will sabotage our progress. Katie knew she needed to stay open to being loved, no matter what stage of development she was at. Whenever she became blind to her power and beauty, I was there to remind her to change her outlook and see herself through the eyes of love. After Katie's 'training wheels' were taken off, she accepted the responsibility on her own. With every hurdle of doubt she crossed, her life returned bigger rewards.

If we feel stuck or confused, we can always turn to our optimum future self for wise counsel. He or she has already navigated the course and knows the best approach to take. All we need to do is ask ourselves what our optimum future self would do if he or she were in our situation, and the answer that comes is usually a liberating one. Using our imagination is the only way we can connect with it, which is why our imagination is a great source of ingenious ideas and inspiration. We have to learn to think beyond our logical minds.

Katie built a little bridge between her life in La Jolla and her life in France, based on the quality of her choices. With each step, she was willing to embrace more of her potential, and her attitude opened the way to greater prospects. Katie remained both humble and grateful for each opportunity she was given. She was brave enough to declare what she wanted, and was willing to take steps towards achieving her goals. We can chant a positive mantra all day long, but unless that impacts on the way we see ourselves, it will have no effect. Our feelings, and not just our mind, need to be impressed. We have to believe wholeheartedly that we are good enough to receive the bounty of our dreams and then, with patience, they will become a reality.

Our choices act as the bridge between our past and a bright new future. Katie started her journey by taking small steps. Before she left her corporate job in La Jolla, she began to consider more positive options and was willing to take affirmative action. Leaving the security of a well-paid job and a conventional marriage took courage. Without risk there is no reward. If Katie hadn't been willing to move out of her comfort zone, she would probably still be in Texas. We need to continue to give up what no longer serves us and hold the vision of what we wish to experience. If we constantly affirm that we are open to experiencing more, we will start to see results.

Katie was willing to make mistakes, and during her development she made quite a few. It was normally when she compromised her worth, but she wisely learnt from these experiences. Focusing on what inspires us rather than what defeats our spirit will help us move forward. Katie had no formal experience in the wine industry, yet she was eager to learn and willing to play. By having faith in her potential, and practising patience, she slowly learnt to trust her internal resources. Katie not only acclaimed more of her power and beauty; she became a benevolent caretaker towards herself and recognised the potency of her love.

We are all a magnificent refection of our soul, with a heart of immeasurable value. The things we cherish most about ourselves will attract our greatest rewards. Over the course of three years, Katie dramatically changed her opinion of herself. During that time, she discovered more of her strengths and attributes, and developed her level of self-worth. Phillipe is a significant mirror in her world; he reflects the way she feels about herself. For the first time, Katie is now willing to be supported, cherished and loved.

When the decision was made for Katie to move to France, although she was overjoyed, she was concerned that Phillipe would lose respect for her if she didn't have a career. Katie was being challenged to finally complete the pattern she perpetuated with Carl. When Katie expressed her concern to Phillipe about giving up her financial independence, her demeanour completely changed. Her gentle, feminine side was overshadowed by the hard, cold, protective part of her nature. Phillipe took Katie's hand and gently said, 'You don't have to be afraid.' Her defences instantly dissolved and Katie's fear was replaced by a greater desire to surrender to love. Katie did not yield to Phillipe's control, but surrendered to the love that was available in their relationship and remained receptive to the contribution he was more than happy to make.

Phillipe and Katie then sat together and created a mutual vision, based on their personal preferences. They were both clear that they needed to be fully self-expressive. For the first time, Katie knew the meaning of equal partnership. We all contribute to one another in different ways. When two people are committed to making a generous contribution in a relationship, they ultimately create a foundation for greater freedom, as well as a deeper sense of security. Phillipe and Katie were both willing to give emotionally, physically, mentally and spiritually to one another, which allowed them to strengthen their union and connect harmoniously.

The important thing to remember is that our contribution is valuable. If we know that above all else, we will come to know the power of our essence.

KEY QUESTIONS TO ASK YOURSELF

This is a checklist to see how on track you are with being *The Visionary* in your life:

1. Do you have a strong sense of the person you want to become?
2. Do you use your imagination as a powerful resource to grow?

3. Are you a dream weaver or blocked by reason and logic?
4. Do you ever visualise yourself living out your preferences?
5. How strong is your desire and passion?
6. Do you retract your energy and withdraw or participate?
7. Do you draw on the past or on your future as a reference of what is possible?

Chapter Twelve

Waking Up and Staying Awake

Vanity, vanity, all is vanity. If our identity becomes more important than our essence, we will always be subject to outside opinion. It is our responsibility to acknowledge and accept ourselves before we expect others to do the same.

It was a warm Saturday afternoon in La Jolla. Through the open window, I could smell freshly mowed grass and hear children playing and laughing next door. In sharp contrast, I was looking at the face of a woman sobbing deeply. During my sessions, I often deal with people who are in a lot of pain. I have to remain extremely focused so as not to lose my composure. On this occasion, I felt as though I was being tested. I would need to remain very detached, otherwise I would be drowned by the emotional wave that had just entered my space. I looked pensively at the familiar face in front of me and thought it better to let her release her anguish before I gave her a pep talk.

She looked like a woman grieving the loss of a lover, but eventually I saw she was mourning the loss of her own innocence. I gave her my full attention and embraced her compassionately with my thoughts. She was an extraordinary woman, who had been given the nickname 'the Goddess' by her closest friends, due to her unwavering commitment to her spiritual growth.

The trials and tribulations of life can be daunting, but nothing cuts deeper than a broken heart. It took a great deal to break the Goddess's spirit, but in this instance she was completely distraught. She appeared more like a defenseless child than a spiritual avatar.

What had brought the Goddess to this point of despair? She was cut down in her stride by the rejection of her fiancé, who went back on his word and retracted his proposal. With very few outward signs of conflict, her boyfriend Daniel woke up one morning and decided to cancel their wedding. His excuses appeared immature and superficial and the Goddess was in a state of shock.

When Daniel's wife left him for another man, he was devastated. After living with her for eight years, it took more than a minute for him to adjust. He had grown accustomed to having a partner, and he detested being alone. After a few months of grieving, he decided to venture out of his cave and seek a new relationship. He dated a few women, but none of them captured his interest. One of Daniel's friends suggested he spend a little time with the Goddess, to help lift his spirits. Daniel emailed her and they agreed to meet for breakfast the next time she was in town. As they swapped stories and enjoyed freshly brewed coffee and hot bagels, Daniel was inspired by the Goddess's deeply passionate nature. He was soothed by her encouraging remarks and prolific words of wisdom. Knowing he had just ended a painful relationship, she offered him acknowledgment, and in the process became extremely fond of him. There was a hint of chemistry between them and the Goddess was deeply impressed by Daniel's gentleness and sensitivity.

Daniel suggested they have dinner the next evening at her favourite restaurant. She was a little taken aback by his generous offer, but graciously accepted. He reserved a quiet table on a small terrace overlooking the beach. The conversation flowed beautifully and every now and then they would pause to listen to the restful sound of the ocean. As fate would have it, this incredibly romantic background would set the tone for the rest of the evening.

The energy between Daniel and the Goddess was so intense that they bonded very quickly. It had been many years since the Goddess had met a man she was even remotely attracted to, and with Daniel she felt a deep connection. She knew intuitively that this was more than a 'chance' encounter.

It was a refreshing change for her to spend time with a man who was interested in metaphysics and who was also strikingly handsome. Had the Goddess met her match? There was something mysteriously familiar about her charming escort, which she couldn't quite put her finger on. As she looked across the table at his sensitive eyes, she wondered if he was attracted to her physically.

Judging by the way Daniel was transfixed by her smile, she felt the odds were in her favour. He then caressed her hand gently and invited her back to his house for a nightcap. He promised to be a gentleman and the Goddess trusted him implicitly.

After paying the bill, Daniel rested his hand on the curve of her back and led her upstairs to the valet's desk. As they waited for Daniel's car, he slipped off his jacket and swung it loosely over her shoulders to shield her from the chilly night air. Driving through the winding hills of La Jolla in Daniel's Porsche was one of those rare occasions where both the Goddess and Daniel felt as though they were living inside a lucid dream.

When they arrived at the house, Daniel lit a cosy fire in the living room. He lived in a lovely Californian bungalow, with hardwood floors, and French doors overlooking a magnificent garden. Daniel lit a candle and poured her a glass of red wine and they walked out to the edge of the patio. As they leant against the balustrade, the Goddess was overwhelmed by the majesty of this tropical garden, complete with a tiny brook.

Standing in this idyllic setting, the Goddess felt as though the 'angelic scenic department' had orchestrated the backdrops for the entire evening. She felt as though she was being courted not only by Daniel 'the man', but also by the essence of his soul. The Goddess attempted to stand up straight but felt a little weak at the knees. Daniel placed his hand around her tiny waist and leant a little closer. They looked at each other attentively and Daniel kissed her tenderly.

For the Goddess, that first kiss was like coming home; she melted in Daniel's arms. When he finally pulled away, he looked overwhelmed and was noticeably flushed. After a few languid moments on the deck, they went into the living room and nestled in front of the fire. Completely captivated by one another's attention, they talked until 3 am and then Daniel walked the Goddess home. By some strange coincidence, she happened to be staying with a friend who lived in the same street. Which, over the course of the next few weeks, turned out to be very convenient.

After that first incredibly romantic evening, it was very difficult to pry the Goddess and Daniel apart. They played beautifully together, and inside their relationship they blossomed as individuals. He started to heal the scars from his painful marriage and reinstated his confidence. Daniel created a magnificent vision of his future, which inspired him to change the course of his life. The Goddess became his muse and in her company he felt empowered. In the first month of their relationship, he created a business alliance that tripled his company's assets. He expanded his interests, adopted a healthy lifestyle and became far more self-expressed. For the first time in his life, Daniel fell in love with not only the Goddess, but with himself too.

The Goddess finally connected romantically with a man, who supported her spiritual pursuits. Daniel loved to listen to the Goddess's views on life and learnt an enormous amount in her company. He showed his appreciation as a sweet and tender lover, which was a first in the Goddess's experience. As a token of his love, Daniel presented the Goddess with a dozen roses at the end of each week, from the very beginning of their courtship. Daniel and the Goddess connected—spiritually, mentally, emotionally and physically. Their romance was like a beautiful dream, and as they danced together their spirits sang.

The first time the Goddess met Daniel's Jewish grandmother she said, 'I have never seen Daniel so happy.' She was relieved to finally see her grandson with a woman who truly appreciated him. In her way of thinking, their relationship was *bashert*, which in Yiddish means 'fated'. Her conversation simply affirmed what the Goddess already knew in her heart.

Early one morning when she was lying next to Daniel, she remembered a dream she had had when she was twenty-eight years old. She was now in her mid-forties, but the dream had never lost its significance. As she walked down a street in San Francisco, she crossed a roadway and recognised a man who was standing on the corner. The Goddess called out the name 'Daniel' and he turned to acknowledge her presence. He took her hand and escorted her across the street to an old bookstore.

The store was filled with volumes containing ancient wisdom, the secrets about life and the destiny of souls. Daniel pulled out a rolled-up map, and as he stretched the old parchment across a table he said, 'I want to talk to you about the journey of your soul and uncovering your life's lessons.'

The Goddess felt so much affection for Daniel in the dream; she took him to the back of the store and tenderly made love to him. Daniel was completely overwhelmed by the potency and the purity of her offering. He was a fractured man, who had been wounded by a woman in a destructive sexual relationship. Daniel had given until there was nothing left to give and ended up feeling worthless.

During the course of the dream, the Goddess loved Daniel unconditionally. Every time he went to return her affection, or ask her what she wanted, she placed his hands behind his back, and loved him even more. The Goddess simply said, 'It is your turn to receive.'

At the end of the love-making session, Daniel was completely healed. He told the Goddess that he needed to return to his life, and resume his relationship with his current partner. Although she didn't want to let him go, it wasn't her time to be with him.

When the dream ended, the Goddess woke up and sat bolt upright in her bed. Realising that her lover wasn't by her side, she burst into tears.

Strangely enough, four years earlier, the Goddess was vacationing in San Francisco with her girlfriend Jennifer. They were both single at the time and were anxious to meet a suitable partner. During a shopping expedition on Union Street, the Goddess was overwhelmed when she came across the metaphysical bookshop she had seen in her dream.

Intrigued by all things mysterious, Jennifer sighted a book entitled *Goddess Spells*. Although she normally stayed clear of anything even remotely occult, she was attracted by the book's beautiful design and playful version of 'modern magic'. It was a full moon, and just for fun, Jennifer decided to perform a few harmless rituals. As suggested in the book, she purchased an assortment of appropriately coloured candles and a bunch of soft pink roses before setting off back to their hotel.

Although the girls did more giggling than cackling, they set up their 'altar', and Jennifer began to read out the incantation. By the light of the full moon, she recited the rhythmical chant. Jennifer paused mid-sentence and looked at the Goddess despondently.

'Oh no, we need a silver dollar,' she said. This called for a little compromise. The girls decided to use a shiny quarter as a substitute.

After the ritual was complete, the girls reclined on their beds and talked about their dreams and wishes. As they shared their innermost thoughts, the lamp on the console began to independently switch on and off. Jennifer's face turned white and she became frightened. The Goddess simply laughed at Jennifer's reaction and told her to relax.

'Things like this have been happening to me most of my life,' she said. 'It is a sign that our declaration has been acknowledged.'

The girls were both being 'divinely' watched over. With their 'sacred objects' placed lovingly under the moonbeams, they finally drifted off to sleep.

Apparently, the ritual wasn't quite over. Early the next morning, the Goddess woke to find a rare silver dollar positioned perfectly at the end of her bed. She looked over at Jennifer, who was still in a deep sleep. Was this a sign that the girls didn't need to compromise? The Goddess carried that silver dollar with her for almost a year; as mysteriously as it came, it then disappeared.

When she came across the bookstore in San Francisco, the Goddess knew it was more than happenstance. It was even more alarming that Jennifer insisted on doing a 'love spell' and the fact that the silver dollar appeared, is a classic sign of good fortune.

It took a little time for the Goddess to fully acknowledge Daniel as the man in her dream, but as she looked at him lying peacefully asleep beside her, the penny finally dropped. In that moment she also realised that she was completely in love with him. From that moment, the bond between them grew.

Before the Goddess was willing to fully embrace a partnership with Daniel, she had to rise beyond her personal doubts. She was uncomfortable with their age difference. Daniel was ten years younger than her. The Goddess had her fingers burnt once before, with a young architect who'd replaced her with a younger model. After that relationship, she vowed never to get involved with a younger man again. The Goddess lacked confidence in her physical appearance. Most of the men in her past were attracted to models. Although Daniel was extremely attracted to the Goddess, she wondered how long his fascination would last.

Rather than suppress her fears, she spoke to Daniel about her concerns. He was surprised by her comments. 'I have no problem with our age difference,' Daniel said. 'You are the most extraordinary woman I have ever met. I'm not interested in being with someone else; I want to be with you.'

As a final gesture of love, he shared how much she meant to him and offered to support the Goddess in overcoming her areas of self-doubt.

At that moment, the Goddess thought she had finally met her match. Daniel presented himself as a partner who was willing to 'call her on her issues' and even offer her coaching. Daniel even spoke to his mother, Natalie, about her concerns. She called the Goddess and offered her encouragement. Natalie was thrilled by their relationship and wanted to make certain that both Daniel and the Goddess made the most of the opportunity that was in front of them.

After a few glorious weeks with Daniel, the Goddess flew home to attend to her business affairs. Although they lived in different cities, the spirit of their relationship continued to grow. Life sent them a series of clues about the nature of their partnership, and offered them a beautiful window into exploring the realms of spiritual union. The 'life speak' began to unfold the moment the Goddess boarded her flight home. On the way to the airport, a friend suggested she watch the movie *Pay It Forward*, and told her there was a significant message woven into the story. As fate would have it, the very same movie was screening on her flight home. As the Goddess sat comfortably in her seat, she became completely engrossed in the theme of the story. Tears streamed down her face, as her heart was deeply touched. All she could see was her potential life with Daniel, based on the principle of giving selflessly to others.

The Goddess was already committed to making a contribution to others spiritually, but during this tender film, she realised how amazing it would be to share that vision with a partner. The film offered her a beautiful portrayal of the potency of human love, and how the exchange that occurs between two individuals can open the way to miracles. For the first time in her life, she felt she was on the final leg home of her spiritual journey. Although she had experienced a great deal in her life, she was entering a realm of co-creation, not only with her soul, but also with a romantic partner.

The first thing she did when she arrived at her apartment was call Daniel, who was in Florida on business. The Goddess implored him to watch *Pay It Forward* as soon as possible.

Later that evening, Daniel called the Goddess, both stirred and elated. After returning to his hotel room, he turned on the 'pay per view' channel, and just by chance, they were screening *Pay It Forward*. Daniel was moved by the film; it brought him in touch with his deep longing to make an altruistic contribution. He expressed his aspirations to the Goddess and told her he was willing to start 'paying it forward'. Daniel set himself the task of acknowledging and contributing to as many individuals as possible without seeking recognition.

Within a few short weeks, Daniel's world completely turned around, and he was well on his way to fulfilling his soul's purpose. He was completely inspired on a daily basis, as his relationships started to take on new depth and meaning.

At the beginning and end of each day, Daniel would call the Goddess and they would share their experiences. Watching Daniel embrace his spiritual quest inspired the Goddess to share some of her most personal insights. One night, she talked to Daniel about her relationship with her Higher Self. She aptly called her Higher Self 'Rose', based on the miraculous appearance of roses in her world since childhood. Many of her significant teachers and mentors were also linked to the name Rose, and the symbol of the rose marked the heralding of love and new awakenings.

When the Goddess finished telling Daniel about her mystical experiences, things went very quiet on the other end of the phone. For a moment the Goddess was unnerved by Daniel's silence. After a long pause, he told her he was deeply touched. 'I have tangible evidence that we are meant to be together,' Daniel said. 'It appeared the day I was born.'

'What sort of evidence?' the Goddess asked. 'Have you had our astrology charts done?'

Daniel held back with his response, 'I can't tell you right now; you will have to wait.'

The Goddess then told Daniel about the dream she had had when she was twenty-eight. One portion at a time, the pieces of this magical puzzle came together.

After being separated from Daniel for a few weeks, the Goddess boarded a plane to California. After a few deliciously romantic days together in La Jolla, Daniel and the Goddess packed up the Porsche and headed for Sausalito. They decided to drive to San Francisco to take in the sights and spend some time with Natalie. They took two leisurely days to do the drive and enjoy the dramatic coastline. By the time they reached San Francisco, there was very little they didn't know about each other.

When they finally arrived, they checked into an intimate boutique hotel on the water's edge. Daniel then made plans to meet Natalie and her husband Jay, Daniel's stepfather, for dinner. The Goddess was looking forward to meeting Jay, after listening to Natalie lovingly sing his praises.

During dinner, the Goddess and Jay talked incessantly about the arts and metaphysics. Jay had also been an art director, so they shared many similar interests. She bonded deeply with Daniel's family and they decided to spend the following day together.

The next morning, the Goddess, Daniel, Natalie and Jay drove over the Golden Gate Bridge and headed for Union Street. Daniel was eager to find the bookshop the Goddess had seen in her dream. It had been some time since she had explored this part of San Francisco and she wasn't certain where the bookshop was. They started at one end of the street and leisurely wandered through the stores.

At one point, they were attracted to a small gallery that sold precious Chinese artifacts. As they admired the delicate jade bowls inside the glass showcases, Natalie let out a long sigh. She was quite taken by a small, very fine piece, which was pale green and slightly translucent. At that moment, the Goddess was inspired. She pulled Daniel aside and suggested he buy the bowl for Natalie as a token of his gratitude for her loving support. Although the piece was expensive, Daniel sensed this was an opportunity to 'pay it forward'. When Natalie wandered to the back of the store, he discreetly took his credit card to the counter and bought his mother the bowl.

Natalie was deeply touched by Daniel's offering, and was overcome by his generosity. As they left the store, the Goddess looked down on the steps to find a fortune cookie insert lying at her feet. She bent over to pick up the small slip of paper and read it to the others. 'You will make a decision that will have great impact on your future.' Everyone went silent for a moment and then Daniel suggested they keep searching for the bookstore.

Eventually they came across a bookseller across the street. As they browsed through the store, Daniel turned to the Goddess and said, 'Is this the bookstore you saw in your dream?'

'No,' she said, 'I think the store may have closed.' At that moment Daniel dropped on one knee, took the Goddess's hand and slipped an engagement ring on her finger. He looked up at her and said, 'Will you marry me?'

As the Goddess looked down at her hand, she was overwhelmed. The ring was crafted with gold rose petals holding a large one-carat diamond. She was speechless. Daniel was a little unsettled by her silence but eventually she pulled him towards her and accepted his proposal.

Daniel then explained the history of the ring. The day he was born, his grandmother went to a jewellery store and had the rose ring made to celebrate his birth. The ring was left to Natalie, who passed it on to Daniel. Somehow, through his grandmother's legacy, he was left a significant clue. He saw the ring as further evidence that they were destined to be together. After listening to Daniel's heartfelt words, the Goddess was light-headed; she felt as though she was living inside a dream.

Suddenly she turned to the right, and saw a book sitting beside her on the shelf. The title *Pay It Forward* stood out like a beacon. Daniel took his lover's hand and slid the book off the shelf. He wanted to buy the book as a memento. As the woman behind the counter rang up their purchase, Daniel asked her if there was another bookstore on Union Street. She told him there used to be a lovely old new age bookstore across the street, but unfortunately it had recently closed down.

With a copy of *Pay It Forward* in hand and an impressive diamond ring on her finger, the Goddess walked out onto the street with her beloved Daniel securely on the other end of her arm.

Daniel and the Goddess enjoyed the next two weeks together in La Jolla, creating a mutual vision for their future. They were very much in love, and they planned to marry when Daniel's divorce came through in six months. The Goddess then flew home to tie up her loose ends and pack up her personal effects. She then returned to her lover. The Goddess had been something of a loner and gypsy most of her life, and now for the first time, she felt she could finally settle.

The night she officially moved in with Daniel, they both leaned against the balustrade on the deck and looked out over the tranquil garden. As Daniel stood closely behind her and wrapped his arms around her waist, she felt as though her entire life made sense. It was as though every step she had ever taken had led her right into Daniel's arms. The incredible thing was, Daniel felt exactly the same.

Over the next few weeks, the Goddess transformed Daniel's house into a home and sanctuary. The remnants of his painful marriage were replaced by beautifully designed, careful chosen objects which brought a new sense of elegance into Daniel's world.

But after suddenly hearing from his ex-wife, he was plagued by thoughts of her betrayal and became very unsettled. The Goddess offered her support and encouraged Daniel to resolve the issue. As Daniel vented his hurt and anger, she listened with a compassionate ear. And all the while she was nervous.

Weren't they supposed to be making plans to create a bright new future? Instead, Daniel was preoccupied by what he had lost, rather than what he had recently gained. The Goddess was very patient with Daniel—she was not only focused on renovating the house, she was also kept busy restoring Daniel's spirits.

After living with Daniel for just over a month, the Goddess woke up one Saturday morning and noticed her lover standing on the deck. Daniel was deep in thought as he stared into the garden. She sensed that things weren't quite right for him, and left him alone for a while. When Daniel finally came back into the living room, he sat down next to her on the couch.

'What's on your mind, Daniel?' she asked. He looked at her mournfully and simply said, 'I can't go through with this.' Before she jumped to any conclusions, the Goddess asked Daniel to explain: 'I am not too sure what you mean by that.'

Daniel paused for a moment and said, 'I can't go through with this marriage.' The Goddess went into a mild state of shock and was overcome by fear. 'What specifically is bothering you?'

'I am terrified of making a mistake,' he said.

'Where are your doubts coming from?'

His answer was so unexpected she thought she was hallucinating. Daniel blurted out the words, 'I think I want to be with a blonde'.

Overcome by an intense wave of emotional pain, the Goddess wondered if she was having a nightmare.

Although the Goddess struggled to keep her composure, her body started to shake. She collapsed in an uncontrollable flood of tears. All she could say was, 'This isn't happening.' Daniel attempted to console her, but what could he say? His adolescent fantasies had led him right up the garden path, away from his spiritual quest. Over the course of the past few weeks, his penchant for gorgeous blondes had overshadowed his love for the Goddess—a striking brunette. The Goddess knew this wasn't a problem that a bottle of peroxide could fix. It was what being 'blonde' symbolised, rather than a matter of hair colour.

The Goddess walked into the bathroom to centre herself and be alone for a few minutes. She reached for a tissue and looked at her reflection in the mirror. A barrage of tears had washed away her radiant smile. It was difficult for this once-confident woman to look herself squarely in the face. How many years would she continue to see herself as 'imperfect' and how long would it take for her to finally acknowledge the value of her essence?

She looked deeply into her large brown eyes and attempted to reconnect with her soul. As she started to focus on her breathing, she fell into a slightly altered state.

Thoughts drifted through her mind of days gone by, as she mused over the mystical journey she had taken with her once dedicated, and now despondent, lover.

There was a soft knock on the door, and Daniel called out, 'Are you OK?' As if emerging from a deep, yet lucid trance, she turned in his direction and told him she was washing her face. If he only knew that all she wanted to do was run into his arms. But somewhere inside she knew that Daniel had already checked out emotionally, leaving her standing at the crossroads.

It was time to make a crucial decision. Would the Goddess take a stand for her worth and pack her bags and leave? That way she would give Daniel a chance to get his priorities straight. Or would she stay with Daniel in order to try to convince her lover that he had made a mistake and attempt to prove to him that she was 'good enough' to love?

The Goddess overrode her intuition, which was telling her not to remain in a situation where she gave her power away and allowed another human being to determine her worth.

After that fateful Saturday morning when Daniel postponed the wedding, she decided to stay with him for another few months, to see if they could turn things around. During that time, their doubts and insecurities came bubbling to the surface. The Goddess did everything she knew to help him overcome his issues and try to make the relationship work. Daniel did very little.

During this process she learnt an important lesson first hand—if someone isn't willing to be responsible for their own personal growth, there is nothing you can do to help them. It brings to mind that old saying, 'You can take a horse to water but you can't make it drink.' Attempting to satisfy Daniel's thirst, the Goddess became emotionally drained, and by the time she left the relationship, she felt completely empty.

LOOKING BENEATH THE SURFACE

Is it possible for a person to declare their undying love, and then, for no plausible reason, dismiss their partner so readily? Such is the influence of the voice of doubt. Under its spell we not only discredit our own merits, but also diminish the value of others.

Even though she was renowned for her astute perception, the Goddess had been easily hoodwinked when it came to assessing the character of her lovers. Time and time again, she looked beyond her lovers' arrogance and pledged allegiance to their innocence—ignoring her own innocence in the process.

With Daniel, she was drawn forcefully to the sweetness of his soul, which blinded her to the potency of his ego. Her desire to be loved outweighed her ability to be discerning, and although Daniel had a list of appealing qualities, she overlooked his genuine priorities.

At the beginning of a relationship, we all have a tendency to put our best foot forward, which is precisely what Daniel did. Being dedicated enough to maintain that stride is up to us. Rather than raise the bar on his own aspirations and strengthen the depth of his character, he turned to the Goddess to satisfy his expectations and resolve his inner conflict. Daniel may have been inspired by the notion of living an extraordinary life, but when it came to making a consistent effort, he lost his momentum. He was easily seduced by his adolescent fantasies, because his ego had him tied to the end of a leash.

Daniel's sudden change of character made him the ideal partner for the Goddess to play out her old patterns with. She knew wholeheartedly she had attracted yet another man who mirrored her dysfunctional beliefs.

As a rule, she attracted men who were seductive physically, but who had very little conviction when it came to their personal growth. Each one of her lovers, including Daniel, was obsessed with finding 'Miss Perfect'. Until that day came, they were reluctant to open their hearts. Over the years, the Goddess had tried everything in her power to win the guarded affections of emotionally withdrawn men. And slowly but surely, after giving until it hurt, she would come to the end of her tether.

Tripped up by the voice of her ego, she believed she had to be 'perfect' in order to be loved. Spiritually, she undeniably knew her virtues, but when it came to men, she had deemed herself unworthy of love. As a metaphysician she knew that unless she was willing to accept all her human flaws and weakness, she would never know true liberation. Although she had ticked off a long checklist of attributes, when it came to acclaiming her power as 'the temptress', she was left out in the cold. And what kind of woman did Daniel ultimately want to be with? His fantasies led him to a woman who resembled the 'sex goddess on heels'.

Daniel was subconsciously searching for someone to replace his wife. His ex-wife had lived by the old expression, 'treat them mean, keep them keen' but that was one game the Goddess wasn't willing to play. In hindsight, the Goddess came to understand why Daniel refused to let go of his wife, even though she betrayed him. He was still carrying an enormous amount of contempt for himself—on a deeper level, he didn't believe he deserved to be loved.

Although Daniel seemed like an outwardly confident man, inwardly he was searching for a woman to prop up his self-worth. He was longing to be with a woman to make him feel better about himself. Although the Goddess offered Daniel a flood of acknowledgment, her words fell on deaf ears. He fell into the trap of believing his partner could 'make' him happy. After the fairy dust wore off and it came down to building a substantial relationship, he no longer wanted to play. The child part of his nature was crying out for attention—and her love wasn't enough.

For the first few months of their relationship, Daniel believed the Goddess was his 'soul mate'. He then changed his attitude, which prompted a change of heart. Had anything altered in the physical world? The only thing that changed was his point of focus. When we look at anyone under a magnifying glass we are able to amplify his or her faults. Daniel zoned in on the Goddess' Achilles heel and highlighted her two areas of self-doubt.

After suffering from an advanced case of tuberculosis in her mid-twenties, the Goddess had been treated with chemotherapy, which left a small area of her hair quite thin. Considering the severity of the disease, the Goddess was lucky to be alive. However, Daniel became paranoid that his partner was going to go bald. That one spot on her head consumed his gaze and sent him turning in the opposite direction. When Daniel and the Goddess parted, he finally broke down and told her he wanted to be with someone younger. The prophecy was fulfilled. The Goddess's own doubts cast a shadow on the relationship and Daniel simply played out the script.

Daniel closed down his affections because he didn't fully trust that the Goddess was 'the one'. He was paralysed by fear and created a stalemate in the partnership. Daniel disengaged from the relationship emotionally.

We can't force another person to open up, but we can make them aware that their behaviour is having a detrimental effect on the partnership. If nothing is said, we will remain on the treadmill and the relationship will never progress. We all create our own reality and our actions either contribute to a relationship or create separation.

Even though she was tempted to see Daniel's behaviour as superficial, the Goddess knew she had no right to criticise him. He was simply mirroring her own superficiality; otherwise, she wouldn't have taken his comments to heart. On a deeper level, the Goddess made her appearance far more valuable than the contribution of her love, which is why Daniel began scrutinising her physical imperfections. Because his attention was focused on what was 'missing', he disregarded the substantial contribution she made to his life.

When they first met, Daniel thought he had found a woman with the checklist from heaven, but when his ego came in, he assessed her in 'worldly terms' as not being good enough. Daniel was a great teacher in her world, because he showed her exactly where she had betrayed herself.

Why would someone who has the spiritual convictions of the Goddess fall prey to such shallow principles? Learning to value her essence above all else had been her most significant life's lesson. Having an insecure and vain mother who believed 'men were only interested in one thing' and a father who told her that 'love doesn't exist', she had a fair amount of conditioning to alter. Her father claimed, 'Lust is the only thing that motivates people in relationships' and therefore he was the perfect partner for her mother. Having an older sister who bought into their philosophy early in life simply added fuel to fire. From a very young age her sister had used her sexuality as a drawcard—the Goddess watched her go through a tremendous amount of pain.

Even when we are small children, our soul will set the stage for our development and orchestrate events that activate our life's lessons. When the Goddess was seven, she and her mother and sister visited a family member in another city. Her father stayed behind. During the stay, she and her five-year-old cousin were invited to take a drive in the country with a distant relative. He was an older man, in his mid-sixties and related to her aunt.

That afternoon, they drove out of the city to a remote dairy farm. When her cousin walked off to go to the toilet behind the cowshed, the old man jumped into the back seat and sexually molested the Goddess. The old man told her not to tell anyone. In a mild state of shock and paralysed by fear she remained mute until she returned to her aunt's house.

When the Goddess and her cousin were safely inside the house, the Goddess ran to her sister and told her what had happened. The Goddess's sister immediately told her mother what had happened and she went completely crazy. After wailing dramatically and praying out loud to the Virgin Mary, her mother ran into the kitchen and screamed like a banshee at the old man for several minutes without stopping. All the while, the old man's wife stood by, seething. The Goddess and her sister stood quietly in the corner while her small cousin was quickly ushered out of the room. The old man was rendered speechless.

His wife then turned to the Goddess with an icy grin, pointed her finger directly at her face and said, 'You did this, you temptress!' Although she was only seven, the Goddess knew exactly what the woman meant. Her mother then grabbed her and took her into the next room. Still caught up in her personal anxiety, she instructed the Goddess never to tell her father. She shouted senselessly and claimed that the Goddess's father would kill both of them, as well as her assailant, if she ever uttered a word. The Goddess was then promptly told to put the incident behind her.

The shame the Goddess experienced around that incident took many years to heal. It wasn't so much the sexual molestation that was difficult to come to terms with; it was the reaction of the women around her. Rather than enquiring about her emotional welfare, or offering a single word of consolation, the issue was quickly dismissed. Her mother's comments about her father served to intensify her thoughts that she had done something gravely wrong. As an outward manifestation of her inner humiliation, two days following the event, her mother discovered that the Goddess had head lice. Her mother was still angry, after dealing with her overwhelming guilt, and so she accused the Goddess of being dirty. To make matters worse, her mother stayed away from her for the next few days for fear of catching lice.

When the Goddess arrived back in her hometown, her long dark hair was cropped very short. As those precious locks hit the floor, she forfeited a large chunk of her femininity. She felt it was no longer safe to be seen as a desirable female, and deep down somewhere in her gut, she feared her mother's assumptions about men were right. After all, she had been telling her about the offensive side of men's sexual appetites since she was five years old. In her mother's painful world, her own husband saw her as nothing more than a sex object, and so that's how she viewed herself. They lived together for thirty-six agonising years, in a marriage where their only form of expression was through sex or emotional torment. Their actions supported their destructive beliefs—'Love doesn't exist; lust is the only thing that motivates people in relationships.'

At the age of fourteen, the Goddess left home in search of solace and freedom. She declared her independence and promptly found a job at a fashionable women's clothing store. As she got older, she rejected her family's values and vowed to become a person of substance. In the process, she subconsciously denied her sexuality and refused to be seen as a 'temptress'. Although there were times she dressed like one, there was no conviction behind the facade. The Goddess spent most of her life attempting to prove to her family that they were wrong and show the world she was nothing like them. On a soul level, she chose her parents as her greatest teachers, because they played out the darkest parts of her shadow. Denying those parts of her nature would never bring resolution; she had to learn to fully accept them and choose to be different.

At the age of thirty, she met an intriguing man called Simon, who was a profound catalyst in awakening her sexuality and overcoming her inhibitions. But as time progressed, it became very clear that his attitude towards their relationship simply supported her parents' beliefs. Taking the Goddess as his lover was acceptable, but when it came to considering her as a wife, she didn't measure up to his standards. To quote Simon, 'How could I possibly be serious about someone who doesn't have a university degree and has a dubious ethnic background?' He was looking for a partner who was physically beautiful, well bred and academic. Although they had an extraordinary list of common interests and were extremely sexually compatible, Simon was more concerned about pleasing his arrogant father. Proclaiming to be an elitist, he literally told the Goddess she wasn't good enough to be with him. Simon ended the relationship with the Goddess to marry his 'perfect' partner. And yet for many years he was reluctant to let go of their involvement.

It took her quite a few years to recover from that relationship. Simon amplified her belief she had to be perfect in order to be loved. Her harrowing childhood was still haunting her, and on a deeper level she felt flawed and defective. She worked diligently on her core issues for many years and spent long periods in retreat and meditation. She focused her attention on developing her pride and dignity and eradicating the remnants of her shame.

Unfortunately, when she met Daniel a few components of the pattern were still in place. When they first met, not only was the sexual side of their relationship incredible; their spiritual and emotional connection was also strong. The depth of intimacy she experienced with Daniel was unique. For the first time in her life, she felt she was truly loved.

She thought the spell had finally been broken, but his actions once again aligned with her childhood beliefs and the relationship disintegrated.

To feel secure in a relationship, we need to know that our partner cares enough to make the effort it takes to overcome obstacles. Both partners need to be willing to drop their defences and risk being vulnerable. It is impossible to create a healthy relationship with a partner who is not willing to participate. All we can do is send someone an invitation; it is up to them whether they choose to respond. Repeating her old patterns, the Goddess gave and gave until she had nothing left to give, while Daniel remained uncommitted. Rather than be fully responsible for maintaining her own happiness, she allowed his behaviour to add to her grief.

In the beginning, Daniel vowed he would always be there to throw the Goddess a 'rope' whenever she lost her footing. They agreed to rise above adversity together and be there to support one another in the process. Daniel's wedding ring was even crafted with a twisted rope of gold across the centre as a symbol of his commitment. When it came to throwing someone a 'lifeline', the Goddess was a veteran. The more rope she gave him the more he took, until she was left hanging precariously under the pressure.

By continuing to stay with a partner who wasn't willing to respond to love, she was simply denying her own worth. When we catch ourselves repeating a pattern, we need to respond to life differently in order to break the spell of our old conditioning. Rather than continue to sit on the fence with Daniel and coax him to move forward, the Goddess would have saved herself a lot of pain if she'd jumped off and moved on. If Daniel were serious about the relationship, he would have made the effort to follow. If we are not willing to protect the things we love, we eventually lose them.

Did she ignore the signs? In the beginning the signs were all positive and she embraced them wholeheartedly. When Daniel's ego came into play, and the 'writing was on the wall', she turned the other cheek and looked away. She gave far more than she received, and with her history, that was the biggest red flag of all. She jumped right back on the treadmill again, and perpetuated the same routine.

We all need to change our course of action to create different results. And unless we are willing to see ourselves differently in the process, nothing will ever change. If Daniel had been capable of seeing himself as a man of substance with powerful convictions, and if the Goddess had been open to seeing herself as a desirable, lovable female, they would probably still be together. In the early stages of the partnership, the love in the relationship allowed them to blossom. They played out those roles beautifully, but then they were put to the test. As soon as Daniel started critiquing her 'feminine attributes' she lost her footing and he in turn was blinded by his own self-doubt.

No matter how far we travel, or how often we change relationships, the voice of doubt will continue to accompany us until we learn to practise self-acceptance. If the Goddess wasn't willing to honestly embrace her uniqueness and see herself as 'desirable', then why should Daniel? If we refuse to be responsible for loving ourselves in the first place, we will always be left searching for love in all the wrong places. We will continue to conjure up thoughts of who we are supposed to be in order to be loved. The Goddess had betrayed herself, in order to satisfy the needs and desires of her lovers. After Daniel, that pattern was put to rest. She finally learnt that being lovable has nothing to do with 'the package'.

How could she be so certain? After she left Daniel, he went searching for 'Miss Perfect'. Within a few months, he came across his 'perfect' partner. She had all the vital statistics. Julia was a tall, gorgeous, blonde, an ex-model, a former cheer-leader and beauty queen. Daniel's adolescent fantasy had finally manifested. Julia quickly took a prominent place on Daniel's arm; she enjoyed being the centre of attention. In the first few weeks, Daniel was happy to accommodate all of Julia's wishes until, of course, her requests turned to demands. Once she knew Daniel was hooked, she started to push for control. In a short period of time, he realised Julia was very similar to his ex-wife. After a confronting six-week relationship, he walked away.

Daniel learnt one valuable thing in his relationship with the Goddess—if he wasn't being acknowledged and appreciated in a relationship, he needed to move on. Unfortunately, Daniel continues to move on and on; he is still searching for the perfect package.

The dream the Goddess had when she was twenty-eight turned out to be an interesting premonition. Daniel rolled out the map in the dream and talked to the Goddess about her soul's journey and life's lessons. Because of their relationship, she was forced to tackle her issues head on. Not only on the play-ing field with him, but also by going even deeper in her spiritual quest over the following twelve months. At that point, she severed her ties with Daniel and reclaimed her power. She refused to support him as a 'friend', therapist and spiritual mentor, while he searched for his 'perfect' life partner. She was break-ing her own heart in the process, but she finally learnt that she wasn't willing to betray herself in order to win someone else's approval. She had done that in the relationship she had had with Simon. She stood on the sidelines and offered him her love and support for almost five years after their break-up. She watched Simon go on to get married, have a child, get divorced, and then find his 'soul mate'. And all the while she was still in love with him—and single. She wasn't about to repeat that pattern again.

The second part of her dream was also predictive. Daniel was overwhelmed by the amount of love the Goddess was willing to give to him. Her offering helped him to recover from his painful marriage and reinstate the course of his life. A healing did occur for Daniel, and as a result he not only mended his broken heart, he also augmented his business. Their relationship ended in the same way the dream did. Daniel had to leave to resume his old way of life, and the Goddess woke up with a jolt, alone, with no lover by her side.

By attracting Daniel into her world, the Goddess created a deep connection with a man she had a remarkable soul contract with. Because we all have free will, the final outcome always depends on how much we are willing to have, and what we choose for ourselves.

How do I know this? Because I am the woman in this story and her pain is my pain.

We all experience the same pain. Whether we are a Hollywood celebrity, an eccentric designer, a wealthy empire builder or a spiritual teacher—on a core level we are all one. Our feelings are the common denominator and the only things that really matter. If we recall the Hollywood celebrity in the first chapter, who outwardly appeared to have everything, she still wasn't peacefully satisfied. Our real power lies in how we feel about ourselves, not in how others see us.

WAKING UP AND STAYING AWAKE

THE CO-CREATOR
KNOWING OUR WORTH

On one level we are all perfect, whole and complete. After my painful split from Daniel, I finally learnt how important it was that I refrain from being so hard on myself. We all need to give up our self-criticism and treat ourselves with compassion and thoughtful attention. It wasn't until I finally acknowledged the value of my feelings that I took those principles to heart. After putting myself through an unnecessary amount of pain with Daniel, I offered my soul a sincere apology. From that point on, I felt liberated; a huge weight was lifted from my heart.

Where does forgiveness live in the relationship we have with ourselves? If we haven't forgiven ourselves for all our mistakes or shortcomings, we will block ourselves from being loved. After Daniel, I reflected on what my self-doubt had cost me. Because I didn't fully believe I was 'good enough' to satisfy him or my previous boyfriends, I started to condemn myself. Rather than forgive and accept myself, I chose to punish myself by isolating myself from love.

Perhaps Daniel chose to do the same thing because he didn't believe he could satisfy his ex-wife? If we are not willing to forgive ourselves in totality we will continue to pay penance. God never punishes us; we punish ourselves. Daniel and I were both responsible for creating the outcome in our relationship, based on our internal self-images.

With an open heart, life takes on greater depth and meaning, which is why Daniel's world opened up at the beginning of our relationship. He then closed his heart when he was overcome by doubt. Fear and love can never exist in the same space. I had that message driven home loud and clear after my relationship with Daniel. I now choose to honour my soul and value my essence above all else. The 'blonde conversation' I used to run in my own mind has now subsided. I am quick to remind myself that when I compare myself with others, I slap my soul in the face. It is 'who' we choose to be that really counts. I now choose to be a woman of integrity who stands by her word. I have always had little difficulty upholding that position with others. Now I take that same point of view in the relationship I have with myself.

It is possible to evolve to a place where we see the outside world as nothing more than an illusion. Then we are free to enjoy our life as if it were a wonderful dream we consciously create. I have always made my relationships with men so 'real' that my lovers have become gods in the process. I waited for them to cast the decree on whether I was worthy of being loved.

Becoming detached from men's opinions has put the onus on me for my own happiness and the freedom to be myself. Now I focus on what is real—my feelings—rather than obsessing about the level of my performance and appearance. I still take pride in the way I present myself in the world, and I am committed to being both creative and productive. The difference is, I now do these things for myself, rather than to be accepted.

When I moved in with Daniel, I gave up a great deal. I moved cities and turned my back on a successful career to be with him. The one thing I wasn't willing to forfeit was my dedication to my spiritual growth. In hindsight, my time with him was invaluable; I emerged from the relationship with the reward of embracing more of myself, even though I lost a man I loved.

To know our true worth, we need to stop buying into the ego's conversation and start listening to the voice of our soul. Our soul is perfect and pure in its essence and springs from the heart of creation. Every human being is therefore worthy of unconditional love. If we place ourselves outside that equation, we will simply continue to see ourselves as flawed or defective in some way. Although I have had a profound relationship with my Higher Self and my soul for many years, when it came to romantic partnerships, my ego lulled me to sleep. Whenever I would chant that old mantra of 'not being good enough', I would dim my light and turn my back on being loved.

During my times in retreat and meditation I have travelled way beyond the confines of my physical body to experience sublimely exalted states. The true test of one's character lies in maintaining that state of awareness in intimate loving relationships. They potentially offer us our greatest rewards and our greatest challenges.

We are all free spirits who define our own boundaries. If we cherish our feelings and are sensitive to others, we will never be led astray. Our soul will protect us through the love we have for ourselves, and will inspire us in the process. If we work in co-creative partnership with our Higher Self and soul, we will attract opportunities to advance steadily and gracefully. The only way we can do this successfully is to follow our intuition and keep our best interests at heart. Any choice that aligns us with love and expansion will take us in the right direction.

The issue in my relationship with Daniel had nothing to do with whether we were 'right for each other' or even 'meant to be' together. It all came down to both of us knowing we were worthy of being loved, and how much we were willing to receive. We decide the amount of love we want to experience; it is always there for the offering. Our arrogance and ignorance are the two things that stand in our way. Daniel and I lost sight of our full potential, which altered our view of what was possible in the relationship. Initially, we were inspired by love and followed our souls' calling, but then the ego rose up like a demon from the shadows and sabotaged our journey with its subtle trickery.

There is nothing more precious than our soul, and yet how often do we stop our rambling thoughts and make time to sense its presence? Although the rewards from an encounter with our soul are immeasurable, we still prefer to court the company of our ego.

The road we take home to our soul is ultimately one we have to walk alone.

To be at peace, we need to get into the habit of aligning with the higher aspects of our consciousness. This is the only way we will ever learn to master our ego. Over the course of many years, people have asked me how to make that connection. The stronger our desire becomes to merge with our soul, the more apparent our opportunities become. Daniel set his intention to embrace his soul's calling. He then remained receptive to the messages his soul sent him through 'life-speak'. When he was open, and remained humble, the messages and gifts appeared.

The cycle was broken when he started to focus on his past and his issues with his wife began to surface. He then had a choice—the old way or the new. Overwhelmed by anger, he sought resolution for his internal unrest externally, rather than turn within himself. At that point, he realigned with his ego. Once he steered off that track, it was difficult for him to find his way home. When he closed his heart to being loved, he also blocked the inspiration. The vision of his optimum future self was replaced by doubt and uncertainty, which left him feeling estranged.

Once we have started on our spiritual quest, our soul will provide the knowledge we need to go to the next level of awakening. If we are receptive, our soul will present us with tiny pieces of the puzzle until we are able to gain the 'bigger picture'. All the incredible signs that appeared when I first met Daniel led me down the path of discovering more of myself. Although the road became treacherous, it was one of the most beneficial learning experiences of my life, and ultimately led me to the gates of liberation. My soul was calling me to move towards union, and to open up to being loved. At times we will meet mentors on the path who offer us information or point us in a certain direction. We are all here to learn from one another. What we choose to do with those offerings is always left to our discretion.

During the most turbulent period I went through with Daniel, I would often sit and meditate and ask my Higher Self what to do. Rose would always say, 'Simply let him be.' Not 'walk away', not 'defend yourself' and not even 'declare your rights'. She waited patiently for me to stop reacting to Daniel's arrogance with a desire to prove my worth. The lesson for me to gain from facing my nemesis was, 'know your worth'. The day I knew wholeheartedly that I deserved more was the day I severed the ties. I am now at peace with my experience and every man in my past. The way I protect myself from further pain is to make choices born from knowing my worth.

The key to our freedom lies within all of us. If we are able to give up our misconceptions about who we really are, we will discover that the source of all love resides in our core. If we allow ourselves to be nourished and inspired by this divine aspect of our nature, we will automatically become a powerful magnet that attracts the greatest gift of all—a life that inspires us to love and be loved. After my experience with Daniel, I could easily have shut down my heart and become bitter and cynical. I know that I created that experience, and every other event that followed. I have overcome my desire to force my will or prove my worth. Rather than continue to search for love externally, I have learnt to surrender to the love of my soul.

We all need to take a stand to be loved for who we are in the moment; otherwise we continue to be misled. When we weave a dream for ourselves, inspired by self-love, we will finally be satisfied to the depths of our soul. We will then stand as a unique being who truly knows the value of their dreams and cherishes the essence of life itself. Not just as a philosophy, but as a practical way of life.

If we are willing to give up our arrogance and remain humble, we will awaken our sleeping beauty, and finally discover the magnitude of our true potential.

KEY QUESTIONS TO ASK YOURSELF

This is a checklist to see how on track you are with being *The Co-creator* in your life:

1. Do you take time to sit quietly and commune with your soul?
2. Do you take time to contemplate and search for deeper meaning in your world?
3. Do you listen to life's whispers and follow the call of your soul?
4. Have you considered the importance of making a spiritual contribution, and do you know your soul's purpose?
5. Do you know wholeheartedly that you are worthy of being loved, no matter what you do, or whom you face in the world?
6. Do you value your innocence or believe you are flawed?
7. Do you acknowledge yourself as a source of infinite wisdom and unconditional love?

After reviewing the true stories of the people portrayed in this book, we know it is possible to rise above adversity and manifest our dreams. The key is to move beyond self-doubt and break the ego's spell. We always have two choices: to align with our real self or listen to the negative conversations in our minds.

When I finally healed my broken heart and severed all ties with Daniel, I felt free to create a new life. After learning as much as I did about the importance of personal integrity, I wasn't willing to compromise. This time, I would face the journey ahead, working from the inside out. My allies on the path were the twelve virtues, or noble truths, one of which is highlighted at the end of each chapter.

Although there is no 'fairytale' ending to this chapter, it's a potent lesson that it isn't enough to just wake up to the value of our full potential: we need to stay awake!

The first essential attribute, when it comes to self-development, is personal responsibility. It isn't enough to manifest the dream; we have to be willing to maintain it. As our dreams expand, we need to grow as well, or we will experience a breakdown. How do we do that? If we are willing to implement the twelve virtues we can attain a state of power and balance. If one of the twelve qualities escapes our attention, we will ultimately feel incomplete. Together, they stand powerfully as noble truths and provide a strong foundation to help us acknowledge our true worth.

THE TWELVE VIRTUES

1. THE CARETAKER accepts responsibility for fostering happiness.
2. THE OBSERVER is perceptive enough to remain clear and mindful.
3. THE PEACEMAKER moves beyond judgment and criticism.
4. THE EXPLORER discovers and develops internal resources.
5. THE DREAMER inspires, imagines and creates possibilities.
6. THE HEALER resolves the past and restores esteem and vitality.
7. THE NURTURER administers care and loving attention.
8. THE PIONEER uses initiative and implements change.
9. THE NEGOTIATOR communicates and upholds fairness.
10. THE BUILDER chooses wisely and establishes security.
11. THE VISIONARY holds the vision of the optimum future.
12. THE CO-CREATOR works in partnership with the Higher Self and soul.

ABOUT THE AUTHOR

Tricia Brennan is an internationally acclaimed intuitive counsellor, author, teacher and life-coach. Prior to devoting herself full-time to assisting others, Tricia had a highly successful fifteen-year career as an art director in the advertising and film industries.

As an intuitive counsellor, she has guided thousands of people on journeys of self-discovery and acknowledging their true potential. Her wisdom and insight enable her to pinpoint a person's core issues and life's lessons with great ease and accuracy. Tricia's childhood gifts of clairaudience, clairvoyance and clairsentience allow her to swiftly uncover a person's behavioral patterns, character traits, strengths and challenges.

Her heightened perceptive abilities allow her to retrieve valuable information from the subconscious of an individual and decipher messages from their counsellors in the Higher Realms. She helps them gain a deeper understanding of their life's purpose and create a vision of their optimum future self.

As a part of her ongoing commitment to personal growth, she has discovered profound insights through her lifelong study of metaphysics and through countless hours in retreat and meditation. She has learnt to go beyond the threshold, and is able to transcend time and space.

Her findings have been published in two books—*Facing the Dawn* and *Vision and Heart*. To augment her work, an accompanying audio meditation series—*Facing The Dawn*, *The Stress First Aid Kit* and *Body Transformation From the Inside Out* have been released. For more information, log on to www.triciabrennan.com.